Post Rosa
Letters Against Barbarism

Hjalmar Jorge Joffre-Eichhorn (ed.)

**ROSA
LUXEMBURG
STIFTUNG**
NEW YORK OFFICE

KICKASS
BOOKS

Published by Rosa Luxemburg Stiftung – New York Office, with funds from the German Federal Foreign Office (AA).

Edited by Hjalmar Jorge Joffre-Eichhorn
Language editing by Patrick Anderson
Cover and layout design by Johann Salazar
Cover Image by Gerhard Augst

ISBN: 978-0-578-99616-5

"Long live the revolution! Keep your spirits up and be joyful, or I'll be seriously cross with you!"

"Write as often as you can, it brings me such solace."

—   Rosa Luxemburg

Contents

Introduction: Tidalecting Left Loneliness – Luxemburg, Letter-Writing and Us

> What we can say is that Rosa was always alone […] She is still alone.
>
> Ana Muiña[1]

> Rosa Luxemburg – a woman whose existence was expressed in the tension between *solitaire* and *solidaire* (solitariness and solidarity).
>
> Walter Jens[2]

> Hänschen, good day to you, here I am back again. I feel so lonely today and I need to refresh myself a little by chatting with you.
>
> Rosa Luxemburg[3]

Ditto, Rosa. So let's start chatting. The starting point for this book was an intense and still ongoing bout of Left Depression, Left Loneliness and a (re-)encounter with Rosa Luxemburg, "[the] lone voice in the wilderness,"[4] just a few weeks before her 150th anniversary on March 5 this year. More precisely, the meeting was one between my increasingly disintegrating self and Luxemburg's *Letters* – from inside prison and the prison inside her – with the surprising outcome being a sense of (temporarily?) resurrected vitality and desire to move, once more, against my inner and our outer chains. The next thing I know, I am frantically reaching out to Luxemburgians from across the globe, trying to cajole them away from their busy schedules and enthuse them about contributing to a slightly unorthodox, deeply personal Luxemburg publication in the midst of a barbarous(ly handled) pandemic. The responses were overwhelmingly positive, and the decidedly non-commercial product of these overall life-affirming collaborations is the book you are about to read, *Post Rosa: Letters against Barbarism*.

But let's "tarry with the negative"[5] a little longer. I have been battling with mental health issues for close to six years now and, frankly, things have not begun to look up at all, no matter what I try. I find it quite amazing how many shades of powerlessness, hopelessness, paralysis, disillusion, demoralisation and despair one can experience, though I get the feeling I haven't yet seen the whole rainbow. And what to say about how all this affects, in the most subversive ways, what once seemed like your own, reasonably vigorous body? Sometimes it's an uprising of headaches striking you "with the hammer-blow of [counter]revolution,"[6] the next moment it might be your insides setting up burning barricades for hours on end, only to be (temporarily) purged a few minutes later by General Secretary Heart aching and breaking you

---

1 Muiña 2019 (Min. 39:25; Translation: Patrick Anderson).
2 Jens in von Soden 1995: 12.
3 Luxemburg 2013: 418.
4 Brie & Schütrumpf 2021: 231.
5 See Hegel's *Phenomenology of Spirit*.
6 See Luxemburg 1900.

1

until you "drip from head to foot, from every pore, with [the] blood and dirt"[7] of your mutilated dreams and shattered self-image, condemned to carry on, "living with what is."[8] Anyway, no self-pity here, just a thoroughly debilitating process of self-destructive, primitive accumulation born-in-struggle that I didn't really see coming and, frankly, did not need. Gotta learn how to love those downward spirals without an emergency break. O Walter [Benjamin], where art thou?

In other words, it really isn't much fun to live with a Left-Wing Zombie festering inside of you. Then again, I am even more afraid to imagine who I would be without him, as he is at least a version of the former me that I have been so desperately trying to become again for the past 1500+ days. Pathetic, isn't it? What's also slightly pathetic – and I am trying to say this with love and respect – is to bear witness not only to our own self-implosion, but also to the utter helplessness, wilful ignorance and oftentimes straight-out abuse we receive from our family, friends and comrades in response to our alleged 'whining.' Of course, we know that Rosa L. herself often adopted a carrot and stick approach when dealing with people, including being pretty impatient, not to say harsh, with comrades she perceived to be indulging too much in their personal pain,[9] but really, we must do a better job of taking care of each other, to genuinely have each other's backs. A Molotov of oblivious advice, presumptuous minimising, self-lefteous sulking and plain old Left *Schadenfreude* is not good enough.

"The first time the community failed you, what did you tell yourself to get up the next morning?"[10]

"Oh how I dread meeting people. I wish I lived among animals."[11]

"Solidarity means fuck all when you're alone."[12]

I don't know if any of this resonates, but I sense there are quite a few of us who have been feeling pretty fucked up for a long time – starting way before the pandemic – and although I get the impression that Left Depression is never in fashion, I am putting it out there anyway, with what's Left of my (com)passion, because, who knows, in one of our next self-help sessions, we may eventually develop some antidotes together, i.e. refreshen and at long last put a human face back on ourselves. I could do with a new one ASAP. Can I borrow one of your fancy hats, Rosa? Besides, from what I understand introductions are meant to give context and rationale to what is about to come next, which in our case is a book of letters in conversation with Rosa Luxemburg, conceived in a state of dwindling life force, intense loneliness and a corresponding drop in energy that has made limping along what our Comrades Rosa and Karl [Liebknecht] – happy anniversary to you, too, KL – called the "Golgotha-path"[13] towards socialism a very rough endeavour indeed. After all, "it's not words, but lives – and in the first place our own – that we are committing,"[14] as our brother

---

7 Marx 1887: 538.
8 Luxemburg in Ettinger 1981: 157.
9 See Michaelis 2011.
10 Hadikwa Mwaluko 2019: 109.
11 Luxemburg 1982: 85 (Translation mine).
12 Mullaney 2019: 105.
13 See, for example, Luxemburg 2004: 321 & 357.
14 See Serge 1938a.

Victor Serge, himself no stranger to the ontologising power of defeat, once wrote. Serge also wrote, on the occasion of the death of Trotzky's son Leon Sedov:

> It was obvious that his physical strength was exhausted. His spirits were good, the indestructible spirits of a young revolutionary for whom socialist activity is not an optional extra but his very reason for living, and who has committed himself in an age of defeat and demoralisation, without illusions and like a man. Such epochs alternate, in our century, with other periods, of revival and strength, which they prepare the way for – which it is the job of all of us to prepare the way for.[15]

Patriarchal language aside (sorry), and acknowledging and admiring all the amazing people and movements out there fighting the good fight "despite all," as Rosa might say, I think there is a good case to be made that Serge's 1938 age of defeat – yes, he was referring to the murderous developments in the USSR, but no doubt it was an age of barbarism(s) all over – is still ongoing, arguably starting even earlier, say in 1919 with the murder of L & L, and that one of our main tasks today continues to be that of preparing the way for revival and victory, based on a recognition of the "illusion that it is possible to start over from the top, from zero, or simply go on in an unbroken line,"[16] as Queer Communist Bini Adamzcak so leftfully pointed out. In other words, this age of defeat was in no small part brought upon us by our own capacity for Left barbarism and there is hence no innocent position for us to return to, Rosa Luxemburg included, and from which to reconstruct a new socialist-communist horizon.

Other than that, this labour of preparation and creation will preferably include tasting some of its juicy fruits in the here and now – no *haricots verts*,[17] please – because tomorrow may be too late for some of us too exhausted to keep committing our lives to what so often seems like an impossible 'romantic utopia,' that anathema of Left-wing sensibilities, considering the violent morons that rule and sustain our world of actually existing capitalism, colonialism and (hetero-)patriarchy. Gramsci was spot on: now is the time of monsters, and sometimes they look like you and me. Mirror, mirror on the wall… "As for the Jadzios [the Warskis], they found me 'enchanting' in my black dress and new hat. All of that has to do with my outer appearance. My inner appearance is somewhat less 'enchanting,' though it is equally black, for which the depressing dimensions of Berlin are to blame."[18]

Well, Brand Berlin is still pretty depressing in 2021, but the idea for this book did originate there. Mid-January. Heavy snow. 102 years since their murder. The letters of Rosa Luxemburg, Volume 1-6, German Edition. Read every single letter. Bingeing on Rosa. Sometimes bored, sometimes elated. Always ready (not!).[19] Brie and Schütrumpf are correct, some of her language is outdated, "[b]ut getting past this language allows one to unlock the lived reality behind it and discover the enduring reason for her radiance over an entire century: her empathetically sensitive

---

15 See Serge 1938b.
16 See Adamczak 2021.
17 Luxemburg 2013: 400.
18 Luxemburg 2013: 40.
19 'Always ready!' was one of the key slogans in the Young Pioneers, the Youth organisation of school children in the former GDR and CCCP.

relationship to the world."[20] Rosa, the Sensitive. Rosa, the Radiant. For sure. But what (re-)connects me to her in those lonely Berlin days is precisely that, her Loneliness, her Left Loneliness, her emphatically dialectical relationship with it, sometimes being devoured, at other times yearning for it and making it productive. Not always palpably present, but never totally absent. Sounds familiar? Here is a sample of Red Rosa's expressions of solitude and loneliness, put together from multiple letters in what I wouldn't dare to call a poem. A joyful elegy, perhaps? Check it out:

Lonely Lux

Alone, alone
I lie there quietly, alone
Wrapped in these many-layered black
veils of darkness, boredom, lack of
freedom
All day long
Up in my room, as usual
The stage remains empty
Finally alone

I don't go anywhere, don't see anyone
I am lazy like a corpse
Mimi is happy
All alone
It will always be that way
Completely alone
Terribly alone
Everything else is bilge

Sitting in my little 'den' at around
midnight
I do things like an automaton
Cold and calm
As though something in me has died
The prison yard is empty
Boarding myself up
Now and then
A stranger to everything around me

All by myself
A kind of deadly apathy
Do you not see how beautiful the world
is?
Do you not have a heart like I do to
rejoice in it all?
It seems as though we're in a tomb

Very, very happy
Insane and abnormal

I break into cascades of laughter the
way you know I do
How lovely it is to be alive in the
springtime
Bad dreams, trembling hands
One day of solitude is all I need to find
myself again
Awake, the light goes out
Lying on a stone-hard mattress
I'm terribly exhausted both physically
and spiritually
The sand crunches hopelessly
Mimi is merry

I laugh at myself
But that's certainly the way things are at
times, when there's loneliness
The deep darkness of night is so
beautiful and as soft as velvet
God forgive me for this prose poem of
wretched quality
My heart constricts
Patching up my inner self

In spite of the snow and frost and the
loneliness
I am beginning without wanting to, to
hatch plans and nourish hopes
So alone, so free with my reveries
Invisible
Smiling at life
A twinge of despair
Solitude and work
A storm is brewing

---

20 Brie & Schütrumpf 2021: 4.

I am standing here as though enchanted
There's a glaring flash of lightning from
time to time
The coming of spring
I feel quite ill
Let's not drag out the matter unbearably
The Revolution is magnificent!
A cheerful youngster, a boisterous child
A flowering meadow in radiant
sunshine
A caricature that I fear more than
loneliness

It's simply Life
And if out of impatience I don't live
through it

Remember:
The revolution can never be victorious
in St. Petersburg alone
A storm is brewing
Let's shake up the masses
Let's trust in the masses
Auf, Auf zum Kampf
WE were, WE are, WE shall be!!!

PS:
Have a good day on Sunday
The deadliest of days for prisoners and
solitaries
I will spend tomorrow as usual, all day
long, alone
Dancing (on) the Golgotha-path...

Ok, I admit I added the dancing part. Couldn't resist. Did Emma Goldman and Rosa Luxemburg ever meet? I can certainly imagine the two of them hardtalking, almost at each other's throats, only to eventually start sipping away at a bottle of champagne, "extra dry,"[21] and soon after taking off their shoes and beginning to move to the rhythm of *Die Internationale*. But I am getting side-tracked here. Clearly, dancing and revolution go together, but so do Left activism and mental health problems, as well struggling against barbarism and (seemingly never-ending) periods of profound loneliness. Rosa knew this and seems to have found a dialectical – or rather tidalectical[22] – response to it, understanding and embracing the ebbs and flows of revolution and the people who make it, that is, Us. A long quote is due here, from the (in)famous February 16, 1917 letter to Mathilde Wurm:

> You argue against my slogan, 'Here I stand – I can do no other!' Your argument comes down to the following: that is all well and good, but human beings are too cowardly and weak for such heroism, ergo one must adapt one's tactics to their weakness and to the principle *che va piano, va sano*. What narrowness of historical outlook, my little lamb! There is nothing more changeable than human psychology. That's especially because the psyche of the masses, like Thalatta, the eternal sea, always bears within it every latent possibility: deathly stillness and raging storm, the basest cowardice and the wildest heroism. The masses are always what they must be according to the circumstances of the times, and they are always on the verge of becoming something totally different from what they seem to be. It would be a fine sea captain who would steer a course based only on the momentary appearance of the ocean's surface and did not understand how to draw conclusions from signs in the sky and in the ocean's depths.[23]

21 Luxemburg 2013: 405.
22 With thanks and respect to Caribbean poet and scholar Kamau Brathwaite (1930-2020), whose genius for words gave birth to the expression 'tidalectics,' though I am giving it a different use in the context of this book.
23 Ibid: 374.

Well, I have never aimed for the captaincy of anything, but I confess that I am struggling mightily not to drown in the "raging storm" that is living in this absolutely unacceptable world anno 2021. But Luxemburg is right – that is, left – when she scoldingly laughs at her (former) lover Kostya Zetkin, upon hearing about his plans to leave the German Social Democratic Party (SPD) after their treacherous support for the *Kaiser*'s war effort: "You big baby, do you want to 'opt out' of being human too?"[24] Ouch. Again, Left Depression and Left Loneliness are *not* forms of Left self-pity, though admittedly the (party) line may sometimes be thin, but it's true, why leave the struggle or the world when we "are always on the verge of becoming something totally different from what [we] seem to be." *La lucha* does *continúa*, with or without us, so we might as well hang on, even if battered and bruised. Gotta keep on keeping on.[25] Somehow, somewhere, with somewhom.

In the case of this book, with you, dear readers, as well as all those who helped to make it happen[26] – especially Pat, Jo and Daria, THANK YOU – and, of course, the amazing author-comrades, all 18 of them, hailing from at least 17 countries, who agreed to join this spontaneous, unfunded, experimental, letter-writing *Samizdat*[27] initiative at very short notice and during a global pandemic that has once more exposed and confirmed that capitalism, colonialism and (hetero-)patriarchy are but the intersectionally connected expression of the same barbarism that's been relentlessly violating bodies and minds, so-called 'nature' included, since at least 1492. The invitation extended to the authors was 'simple': Pair up and write from the heart, in loving solidarity with Rosa Luxemburg, the letter-writer, in the year of her 150th anniversary. That is to say, let's engage in an exchange with a 'pen-comrade,' in most cases from another part of the world, in a writing style of your choice, with references to and reflections about Rosa L. and the times we live in, as understood through our own bodies and geopolitical locations and always informed by an epistemology of both the head and the heart, or *sentipensar* as we say in Spanish, i.e. to feel think. My hope for these exchanges was for them to be(come) a source of affective-intellectual inspiration, encouragement and enheartening for everyone involved – authors, editors and, I trust, for you, reader-comrades – with the final aim of joining (once more) the rank and file of those of us committing our words and lives, *solitaire* and *solidaire*, to the struggle *against* barbarism and *for* socialism. Letters against Barbarism. "Not a wo/man and not a penny to this system!"[28]

"The revolution is marvellous, everything else is bilge!"[29]

See you on the barricades,

Hjalmar

August 13, 2021
Tallinn, Estonia

24 Luxemburg 1987: 7 (Translation: Patrick Anderson).
25 R.I.P., Curtis Mayfield.
26 See acknowledgment section at the end of this book.
27 Russian for 'self-publishing.'
28 Luxemburg 1925: 120.
29 There are many English versions of the original German *"Die Revolution ist großartig, alles andere ist Quark,"* for example, Luxemburg 2004: 12.

References

Adamczak, Bini (2021), *Yesterday's Tomorrow: On the Loneliness of Communist Specters and the Reconstruction of the Future*. Cambridge: MIT Press.

Brie, Michael & Schütrumpf, Jörn (2021), *Rosa Luxemburg: A Revolutionary Marxist at the Limits of Marxism*. Cham: Palgrave Macmillan.

Ettinger, Elzbieta (1981), *Rosa Luxemburg's Letters to Leo Jogiches*. London: Pluto Press.

Hadikwa Mwaluko, Nick (2019), "A Love Letter to Andre Lancaster," in *The Graveside Orations of Carl Einstein*. Eds. Dale Holmes and Sharon Kivland. London: MA BIBLIOTHÈQUE.

Jens, Walter (1995), "Rosa Luxemburg – Weder Poetin noch Petroleuse," in *Rosa Luxemburg*. Ed. Kristine von Soden. Berlin: Elefanten Press.

Luxemburg, Rosa (1900), Reform or Revolution (Ch.4). *Marxist Internet Archives*. Accessed on 28.08.21, at https://www.marxists.org/archive/luxemburg/1900/reform-revolution/ch04.htm.

Luxemburg, Rosa (1925), *Letters to Karl and Luise Kautsky from 1896 to 1918*. Ed. Luise Kautsky. New York: Robert M. McBride & Company.

Luxemburg, Rosa (1982), *Gesammelte Briefe. Band 3*. Institut für Marxismus-Leninismus beim ZK der SED. Berlin: Dietz Verlag.

Luxemburg, Rosa (1987), *Gesammelte Briefe. Band 5*. Institut für Marxismus-Leninismus beim ZK der SED. Berlin: Dietz Verlag.

Luxemburg, Rosa (2004), *The Rosa Luxemburg Reader*. Eds. Peter Hudis and Kevin B. Anderson. New York: Monthly Review Press.

Luxemburg, Rosa (2013), *The Letters of Rosa Luxemburg*. Eds. Georg Adler, Peter Hudis, and Annelies Laschitza. London and New York: Verso Books.

Marx, Karl (1887), Capital: A Critique of Political Economy Vol.1. *Marxist Internet Archive*. Accessed on 14.08.2021 at https://www.marxists.org/archive/marx/works/download/pdf/Capital-Volume-I.pdf.

Michaelis, Loralea (2011), "Rosa Luxemburg on disappointment and the politics of commitment," *European Journal of Political Theory*, 10(2), 202-224.

Muiña, Ana (2019), Presentation of the book *Rosa Luxemburg, en la tormenta*. Accessed on 14.08.2021, at https://soundcloud.com/traficantesdesue-os/rosa-luxemburg-en-la-tormenta-de-ana-muina.

Mullaney, Martina (2019), "Orating this Oration," in *The Graveside Orations of Carl Einstein*. Eds. Dale Holmes and Sharon Kivland. London: MA BIBLIOTHÈQUE.

Serge, Victor (1938a), "Farewell to Andres Nin," *Marxist Internet Archive*. Accessed on 13.08.2021, at https://www.marxists.org/archive/serge/1937/08/25.htm.

Serge, Victor (1938b), "Obituary: Leon Sedov," *Marxist Internet Archive*. Accessed on 13.08.2021, at https://www.marxists.org/archive/serge/1938/02/sedov.htm.

1. Paul Le Blanc
&
Helen C. Scott

Dear Helen,

One reason I look forward to corresponding with you in this project involves the friendship and close working relationship we have forged over the years. That has been animated by the kinds of qualities we have both responded to in Rosa Luxemburg, as we each have helped edit, share, and engage with her writings, which are inseparable from the person she was.

Luxemburg continues to be vibrant: in a sense she remains alive. Even though the world is so dramatically different now than it was a hundred years ago, the oppressive social and economic dynamics of her time remain with us, generating new crises and new waves of resistance (which frustratingly are still not strong enough). Her passionate responses, her insightful analyses, the struggles for a better world to which she hoped to give strength – they all feel deeply relevant to our own time. She has become a mentor and a genuine friend for us both, and – actually – the three of us are involved in this conversation.

I am hoping that my writing here will be true to the person that she was. It seems to me that life (and truth) involves a continual flow of evolving, contradictory, interacting elements. This first email to you will be in two 'installments' – early in April and again early in May – in hopes that this will do honor to such truth.

…

In our telephone conversation yesterday, I found myself expressing frustration about how to cope with the terrible aspects of the present moment. The Covid pandemic has killed more than two million people around the world, among whom are people I have known and loved – such as Pittsburgh's wonderful and wondrous, radical labour singer-songwriter Anne Feeney, whose farewell celebration was attended on Zoom by more than 600 of us earlier today. There are too many more unsung victims brought down by this terrible plague – and even our ability to celebrate Anne doesn't wipe away the hurt of losing her.

Yet I cannot believe she is gone. I am reminded of Luxemburg's words after the loss of a beloved friend who perished in the horrific plague of imperialist war: "Actually I am living in a dream world in which he is not dead. For me he lives on, and I often smile at him when I think about him."[1] Anne's many songs continue to resonate, making us smile, radiating with the same spirit that draws us to Rosa Luxemburg:

> Have you been to jail for justice? I want to shake your hand
> Cause sitting in and lyin' down are ways to take a stand
> Have you sung a song for freedom? or marched that picket line?
> Have you been to jail for justice? Then you're a friend of mine

---

1 Luxemburg 2013: 451.

You law abiding citizens, come listen to this song
Laws were made by people, and people can be wrong
Once unions were against the law, but slavery was fine
Women were denied the vote and children worked the mine
The more you study history the less you can deny it
A rotten law stays on the books til folks like us defy it

The song's jaunty tune (so typical of her creations) matches the lyrical celebration of all who have gathered in the picket-lines, protest marches, mass confrontations and arrests to bring meaningful change. Anne was a trained lawyer, so her advice to us (defy rotten laws) carries weight – though I know she would also agree with Rosa that the problem of rotten laws goes deeper than simply the people who are "law-makers" sometimes being wrong. Her songs indicate that there has been a pattern of rotten laws and rotten policies – the problem is systemic.

The pandemic is only one of an accumulating number of disasters related to the intertwined realities of globalization and climate change driven forward by something Luxemburg analyzed in her great book on economics. This is the relentless process of capital accumulation, a voracious pursuit of corporate profits on a global scale, at the expense of vast numbers of people, damaging the environment on which our lives depend. Many of us in the United States are at last benefitting from anti-covid vaccinations, yet we are warned that this plague may take away increasing numbers in a fourth surge that threatens to sweep our planet. Beyond this, it is predicted that more climate-related catastrophes will afflict us as the twenty-first century unfolds, undermining the capacity of more and more people to survive. The durability of civilization and humanity over the next hundred years seems open to question.

The strains of the present 'moment' reflect what seem bewildering contradictions. The early months of 2020 saw amazing explosions of protest (reminiscent of the "mass strikes" that Rosa talked about) against the racist brutality permeating police forces in our society. This mass upsurge seemed to dovetail with a radicalization causing millions of people to vote for open socialists running on the Democratic ballot-line of one of the country's two capitalist political parties – to the horror of that party's corporate-liberal leadership, which employed powerful manipulations to ward off the radical challenge. On the other hand, the Republican Party was intimately aligned with the right-wing of the corporate elite – projecting a phony 'populism,' pretending to be Godly while pandering to bigotry and gun lobbies, cutting social programs while promoting massive tax-breaks for the wealthy, a party led by a rich, dangerously irresponsible, trash-talking Huckster.

While President, the Huckster nurtured a mass base that tended toward authoritarian attitudes and violent fantasies. To defeat him, the radicalized elements in the Democratic Party base (socialists and all) subordinated themselves to the corporate liberals who dominated the party. In a narrow victory, Democrats defeated the Huckster and secured a tenuous hold on Congress. There is much more that must be said about the current political realities – for example, issues of foreign policy, militarism, and imperialism that were so central to Luxemburg's revolutionary orientation. But I want to focus here on three realities that highlight the frustration I feel.

First, the corporate-liberal leadership of the Democratic Party does not have an orientation that can go far enough or deep enough to overcome the profound crises threatening to overwhelm us.

Second, an inability to overcome the profound crises can demoralize the radicalized elements in the Democratic mass base, while giving sustenance to the authoritarian, bigoted, violence-prone elements within the Republican mass base. The frequent inability of 'progressive leaders' to address such crises with clarity and courage, and to show the way forward, is similar to what Luxemburg perceived in the bureaucratic-reformism that was infecting and corrupting much of the trade union and socialist leadership in her own time. Now as then, an absence of revolutionary vision and practice gives nurture to the forces of barbarism on the Right.

Third – in stark contrast to the realities of Rosa Luxemburg's time – there is no mass, organized, independent socialist movement of the working class capable of providing a serious pathway out of the crises that afflict us. Despite the dramatic growth of socialist consciousness in the United States, the organized socialist movement is relatively small, relatively inexperienced, fragmented, weak. Luxemburg was part of a serious organization – what she referred to as a "socialist vanguard" – that she believed could play a role in doing what needed to be done. We don't have such an organization, and we don't have all the time in the world.

What should we do?

Early May

A month has passed, and we each have been immersed in our end-of-the-semester workloads. The semester is coming to a close and will soon be behind us, allowing us to turn our attention, once again, to completing the editing of the fifth volume of Rosa Luxemburg's *Complete Works*. It has been a joy to engage with this wonderful friend – her humor, her passion, her brilliance as she shares more and more facets of her understanding and insights, her advice and urgent appeals, her further explanations to us of what she's getting at. The thought that our labour of love will bring what she had to say to many hundreds and thousands more has been exhilarating.

In the cracks and crevices of such labours I have continued to find time – as I imagine is the case with you – to wrestle with the kinds of things raised in my previous comments, in realms both of thought and action.

Even as the covid death toll rises horrifically on portions of the earth, in the United States things are beginning to ease, at least for now. Vaccinations proliferate, the Center for Disease Control has signaled the setting aside of some safety restrictions, and we begin to breathe easier. The more benign image of Biden has replaced that of Trump as the leader of our land. Seeming success in pushing back covid is matched by new proposals that reflect some of last year's deepened radicalization. There are not only promises but also the stirrings around new policies to push back against aspects of the economic and environmental hardships afflicting so much of the working class, and also against aspects of the systemic racism and sexual bigotry impacting on broad sectors of our people. (At the same time, Biden has signaled that

12

he is willing to compromise on some things – though which things, and how far the compromises would go, remain unspecified as of early May.)

What would Comrade Rosa have made of all this? I suspect she would not have assumed that the person she was and the perceptions she held, from youth to middle age, should be set aside to facilitate an adaptation to 'the new reality.' Her insights and passion would cut through to an understanding that:

a) it has been a toxic corporate-liberalism (animated by imperial visions of 'globalization') that facilitated Democrats no less than Republicans refusing to put people above profits, that helped generate the neo-liberal right-turn afflicting our planet, in more than one way poisoning its economic, social, political and ecological atmosphere;

b) it has been the collapse of an independent working-class Left that facilitated the adaptation to what proved to be the disastrous trajectory of corporate-liberalism, contributing to the misery of many millions to such an extent that some scared and suffering layers were prepared to respond to the fake 'populist' appeals and bigotry of demagogues funded by corporate-reactionaries, Trump being one among many in a variety of countries;

c) it has been the semi-spontaneous mass action and insurgent "mass strikes" – particularly those associated with the Occupy movement and the Black Lives Matter movement – spearheaded by young working-class activists (although many are not particularly conscious of themselves as being working class) that tilted the political scene to the Left, opening up new possibilities to which corporate-liberals such as Biden have felt compelled to adapt. Welcome as such a leftward adaptation feels, it continues to prioritize the needs of corporate capitalism over the needs of the working-class majority, and still seems unlikely to me to provide genuine solutions to the grave problems we face – suggesting that future crises loom, and also the danger of a future desperate swing toward destructive reaction. Just as progressive pressures 'from below' have brought us some temporary relief, so genuine solutions for humanity will need to come from the bottom up.

There is an additional thought that would surely have haunted Luxemburg. Noam Chomsky (in a preface to *The Green New Deal and Beyond*) says we face an "existential crisis" in the form of environmental catastrophe: "Those alive today will decide the fate of humanity – and the fate of the other species we are now destroying at a rate not seen for 65 million years, when a huge asteroid hit Earth […]"[2] Some say we have little more than thirty years before impact.

According to my friend Jonathan Neale, in his book *Fight the Fire: Green New Deals and Global Climate Jobs*, "there is no way to build the renewable energy and smart grids we need except with public ownership and government money,"[3] adding that the push to create climate jobs associated with a genuine Green New Deal "is a method for getting the necessary work done, but it is also a method for building a

2 Chomsky in Cox 2020: xvii.
3 Neale 2021: 82.

mass movement."[4] I especially like Neale's injunction that the most radical people are not the ones who enunciate the most extreme predictions or conclusions, but rather the "the people who are looking for ways to organize mass movements for rapid and radical action."

I believe Luxemburg would have been drawn to such lines of thought. I know that I am.

In my yearning for the related terrain of revolutionary action, I feel a deepening impatience with the 'leftism' of self-indulgent commentary and side-line criticism. There is a natural tendency among people to find a sense of self-worth (or superiority over others) through their ability to demonstrate (to themselves and others) their Political Correctness, often through an unyielding adherence to theoretical abstractions and denunciation of others who do not measure up. I believe very deeply that we need to do better than that.

Among my proudest moments in this century have been those devoted to struggles and victories of Pittsburghers for Public Transit. Ideas are important, and we were united by a Transit Bill of Rights: 1. safe, reliable, environmentally-sustainable, and affordable transit that is accessible to all; 2. living wages, benefits, safe working conditions, and union rights for transit workers; 3. dedicated and sustainable funding for public transit; 4. equitable distribution of public transit costs with corporations paying their fair share; 5. transit that meets the needs of each community with no communities left out. We built effective coalitions and mass actions to push back on attempts to cut funding for mass transit. We fought successfully for the restoration of services where cuts had been carried out. We always linked struggles for the well-being of transit workers and transit riders. We have not been satisfied with what we have done – there is so much that must be done! – but we have done good work.

I am hoping that the Green New Deal will be similar in going beyond words – translated into organizing, struggle, and ultimate victory. To paraphrase Rosa, it is through actual struggles capable of winning victories today (reforms) that we provide the pathways to social revolution.

As I cut deeper into my 70s, with a keen sense of past wrecked hopes, I am afraid there may not be enough time. I should explain what I mean by this.

There is, of course, the wreckage of specific organizations to which I belonged, and in which significant energies and hopes were invested – from Students for a Democratic Society, to the Socialist Workers Party and Young Socialist Alliance, to Labor Party Advocates, to Solidarity, to the International Socialist Organization. There is also the larger and more complex wreckage of the labor and socialist movements, and of their aspirations and promise (at least as I perceived them in earlier years). Such things must be rebuilt in order to accomplish the goals which we have embraced in common with our friend and comrade Rosa Luxemburg.

But then there is the question of time. It will take time to rebuild the Left, and time to build the mass movement and mass struggles required to win a Green New Deal.

---

4 Ibid: 142.

Personally, I am running out of time. I cannot expect to be part of such struggles beyond a decade or two, at best. And the necessary victories must be realized, it now seems to me, within about three decades. Scientists tell us that preventing global warming from a disastrous rise above 1.5 degrees Celsius will require a reduction to near zero by 2050.

An engagement with the natural world, of which we are all organic elements, has become more important to me than ever, and the walks that my beloved friend Nancy and I have been taking with increasing frequency have impacted on the way I see such things. I want to share with you four photographs that give a sense of what I mean. Even when my own ability to struggle comes to an end, life and struggle will continue – see image #1 and #2. And even from a damaged base, amazing things can arise – see images #3 and #4.

You and I have found strength from the qualities of Rosa Luxemburg – the vibrant qualities touched on throughout this communication. The fact that you and I are working to help share those qualities with rising generations strikes me as truly good work, and that is a source of immense satisfaction.

Warm regards,

Paul

The eternal sea always bears within it every latent possibility: deathly stillness and raging storm, the basest cowardice and the wildest heroism. The masses ... are always on the verge of becoming something totally different from what they seem to be.[5]

5 "The eternal sea always bears within it every latent possibility: deathly stillness and raging storm, the basest cowardice and the wildest heroism. The masses [...] are always on the verge of becoming something totally different what they seem to be." (Luxemburg 2013: 374)

Dear Paul,

Our friendship was in fact forged by Rosa Luxemburg. I remember cold-calling you some time in 2007 to ask for feedback on an essay I was writing about her life and works. You took the time to read and respond in some detail, giving me helpful suggestions and encouragement, and urging me to trust my own voice, as a corrective to a tendency to defer to "the experts." This had a lasting impact on me. We also discovered our mutual delight in Luxemburg's approach to writing, in particular the 1898 letter quoted in Paul Frölich's biography, where she criticizes the standard party articles – "so conventional, so wooden, so cut-and-dry" and commits to an alternative approach: "I believe that every time, every day, in every article you must live through the thing again, you must feel your way through it, and then fresh words – coming from the heart and going to the heart – would occur…"[6]

This marked the beginning of what has been a series of collaborations on books, panels, and events all with the goal, as you put it, of sharing Luxemburg's legacy with rising generations. I too am delighted that we have this opportunity to correspond about the many ways she "remains alive" more than a century after her murder.

I was saddened to hear of the death of Anne Feeney. Thanks for sharing your thoughts about her, and that wonderful song. It is a testimony to the tradition of socialism from below that is embodied by Luxemburg. "The more you study history the less you can deny it/A rotten law stays on the books till folks like us defy it." This would make an apt epigraph for our correspondence!

As I write, my heart and mind are with Palestine. On this Nakba Day the Israeli state is several days into a full-scale military assault on Gaza which has already killed over a hundred Palestinians, injured hundreds, and displaced thousands more. On top of the immediate devastation, the assault will compound the economic and social crises resulting from the ongoing blockade and wreak havoc on efforts to contain the pandemic (the occupied territories are lagging far behind Israel in Covid-19 vaccination levels). The latest development comes after weeks of escalating Israeli offensives, including evictions of Palestinian families in Sheikh Jarrah, and the storming of Jerusalem's al-Aqsa mosque by Israeli police during Ramadan. It is devastating to witness the full force of the Israeli state unleashed on a people who have endured over 70 years of dispossession, settler-colonialism, military occupation, and apartheid.

But it is at the same time inspiring to witness Palestinians' continued resistance, in the occupied territories, in Israel, and in the diaspora. This time around we are also seeing a new and stirring demonstration of global solidarity. I have had texts from friends and family in the UK describing mass Palestine solidarity rallies in Bristol and London. Here in Burlington we had a solidarity rally of several hundred people which was overwhelmingly young and multiracial; I hear that more than fifty other such 'Rise up for Palestine' events have taken place across the USA.

---

6 Frölich 2010: 45.

Luxemburg is very much alive in all this: her internationalism, principled opposition to imperialism and colonialism, passionate advocacy for mass struggle against all forms of oppression. These values and aspirations animated the Burlington rally today, where the politics of global solidarity countered both rightwing racism and Islamophobia, and liberal evasions and distortions. Amid the catastrophic forces unleashed by Zionism and US empire – threatening "the durability of civilization and humanity" as you put it – this fresh global uprising is another manifestation of the radicalization animating the mass Black Lives Matter movements of last summer.

These events connect also to those "bewildering contradictions" of the past year and to the particular "three realities" that have frustrated you. The new radicalized elements are participating in the global solidarity campaign, and elected figures such as Ilhan Omar and Rashida Tlaib – who delivered a powerful and moving address to Congress – have spoken out against Israel's apartheid regime and advocated for Palestinian liberation. But President Biden, in keeping with the party establishment, unsurprisingly continues his role as stalwart supporter of the Israeli state, reiterating "Israel's right to defend itself" – and approving a $735 million weapons sale – while discounting the right of Palestinians to resist ethnic cleansing. This underscores the incompatibility of the Democratic Party and emancipatory aspirations.

The party's problems go beyond "corporate-liberal leadership" to its fundamental character as a capitalist formation. Not only does it answer to its corporate funders, but it also co-opts and disorients progressive movements, earning it the title of "quicksand of the left." The various mass movements that animated the downfall of Trump's regime have become largely quiescent since Biden/Harris have come to office and there is overwhelming pressure against protesting their administration within liberal-left circles, always with the threat of the greater evil of the Republicans – and their "dangerously irresponsible, trash-talking Huckster" leader – waiting in the wings. But as the current upsurge of protests around Palestine indicate, levels of struggle ebb and flow, and the movements provide the momentum for change.

I agree that elements of Luxemburg's critique remain relevant, even though the context is so different. *Reform or Revolution* describes political and legal systems as the products of previous class struggle: "revolution is the act of political creation, while legislation is the political expression of the life of a society that has already come into being."[7] This means that certain fundamentals of capitalism – class exploitation, economic crises, imperialism – cannot be legislated away. Meaningful reforms within the system can be won, but class struggle is the primary motor for this, not parliamentary or congressional activity. As Howard Zinn put it almost a century later in a very Luxemburgian formulation, "What matters most is not who is sitting in the White House, but 'who is sitting in' – and who is marching outside the White House, pushing for change."[8]

This of course brings us back to the looming problem that you identify: the lack of an organized mass independent socialist movement of the working class both in the US and globally. In answer to the question "what should we do?" I think

---

7 Luxemburg 2008: 89.
8 Editor's note: There is no available reference for the quote, but according to the author Zinn was often heard using it during his talks.

Luxemburg would tell us to participate in the social movements, learn from them, take them into the labour movement, raise the profile of socialist politics and build socialist organization *where and how we can*. The gap between the "dramatic growth of socialist consciousness" and the "organized socialist movement" is immense, but there are opportunities to make connections and nurture developments wherever we find ourselves. For me that means working as a socialist within my union, joining with others to build rank and file, class struggle, social justice unionism. This would include such concrete measures as pushing for union solidarity with the Boycott, Divestments and Sanctions and Black Lives Matter movements, and bringing union contingents to protests. I know from our conversations lately that you are not organically connected to movements as you have been in the past. But your experience and knowledge remain invaluable, and you continue to write, and relate to struggle in your community and workplace, in ways that are important and meaningful.

I am a little behind you with end-of-the-semester and spent the last week scrambling to submit grades and take care of a million and one administrative tasks. The workload at the University of Vermont has been increasing steadily, and more dramatically this year due to the pivot to remote-everything and a squeeze on productivity that has hit staff and non-tenure-track faculty the hardest but has negatively impacted all faculty. In keeping with a wider trend in higher education, the administration over the past year has taken the shock doctrine approach to the pandemic, laying off lecturers and announcing draconian program and department closures despite the university's immense wealth. The cuts provoked a year of struggle from unionized faculty, staff, students, and community members. Management have recently reversed some of the worst measures because new student enrollments are much higher than they anticipated, but it is clear that the battle will be ongoing. The current campaigns have been able to change the public narrative, but they lack power – we would need a faculty strike in order to reverse the administration's restructuring plans. Luxemburg's analysis of the trade unions is remarkably relevant, over a century later. The conservatizing effect of the trade-union officialdom that she described in *The Mass Strike* – leading to "bureaucratism and a certain narrowness of outlook"[9] – continues to weigh down the labour movement. And yet the revolutionary potential of the rank and file continues sporadically to provide an alternative, as in the great wave of illegal strikes by teachers in the "red state revolt" of 2018-19.

I certainly share your skepticism towards the Biden administration. You talk of "new proposals that reflect some of last year's deepened radicalization" tempered by "compromises." I would go further, in fact, and argue that the "leftward adaptation" of the Democratic party leadership is better understood as a pernicious reorientation away from the radical demands of the mass movements – defunding the police, Green New Deal, Medicare for all – into pro-corporate liberal measures which are all part of shoring up US capitalism against its global competitors, namely China. Ashley calls this "Imperialist Keynesian." I completely agree with you that hope for humanity and the Earth itself will only come 'from the bottom up' – which means that movements have to stand up against the Democrats and pose genuine alternatives to the far right. Again, Luxemburg has much to offer here, particularly

---

9 Luxemburg 2008: 177.

her recognition that the domestic and international spheres, and the economic and political, are inextricably connected facets of the accumulation of capital. Rather than looking to the Democratic party to provide social change, we need independent struggle that can push for genuine reforms.

There are some current examples of these kinds of independent struggles. The Palestine solidarity movement is one such. A 'ceasefire' is now in place, but only after Israel's war on Gaza inflicted unimaginable misery on Palestinians, destroying hospitals, schools, homes, water and electricity supplies. Protestors are holding Biden accountable for his defense of Israel. Similarly, the Black Lives Matter movement has come out against Biden's George Floyd Act because it moves away from the systemic demands raised by the movement in favor of "incrementalist reforms" that fail to address the root causes of police racism.

This is the approach that must animate the struggle for climate justice in the face of the "existential crisis" we now live with. The work of Pittsburghers for Public Transit strikes me as a model for Green New Deal activism, because it combined environmentalism and labour politics while orienting on coalition building and mass actions. I can see why you are proud of your participation in those struggles. It is hard for me to see the forces that could make this happen on a national level, at the moment, but certainly environmental activism has erupted in mass struggles globally in recent years, and will no doubt continue to do so.

I can understand, too, your growing sense of urgency in the face of growing older amid the "wreckage" of so many organizations and movements. Luxemburg provides helpful frameworks for both sets of anxieties – those looking backward and those looking forward. I think of her responses to the epic crises she lived through. She always maintained a bigger view of the sweep of history – the "objective historical significance" as she would say. And she had a remarkable capacity for what is currently referred to as mindfulness. As she wrote to her beloved Hans Diefenbach in March 1917 from Wronke prison: "I am attached to the present moment and the beauty that it offers."[10] She was able to draw sustenance from the natural world even in the least promising of circumstances: she told her friend Luise Kautsky to "look for the honey in every blossom"[11] even while her own exposure to the natural world was limited to the prison yard.

So, I am happy to know that you and Nancy have been walking together and finding pleasure in nature. I know too that you find much joy in your grandchildren. Your beautiful photos remind us that the next generation will continue the struggle, and that nature finds a way to repair and replenish against all odds.

I have very happy memories of walking with you and Nancy and Ashley in the woods at Rock Point on the shores of Lake Champlain. In the last year we have walked there most days. This spring has seen a riot of spring flowers: squill, trillium, violets, columbine, periwinkles, anemones. I am sad to say that my capacity for walking has deteriorated since we last met, as my MS has progressed in the last couple of years. I can no longer go for the long walks that I used to enjoy, but I

---

10 Luxemburg 2013: 382.
11 Ibid: 393.

have found that I can manage two shorter walks, of around a mile each, spread out over the day. I again find myself drawing on Luxemburg's spirit of embracing and appreciating all aspects of life, rather than dwelling on adversity.

I am certainly appreciating the fact that I am not teaching this summer and so will have time to return to Volume 5 of the *Complete Works*. Like you, I find this work deeply satisfying, and I am so glad to have you as a partner in it all.

In comradeship and friendship,

Helen

I don't know myself why
it is that a beautiful poem,
especially by Goethe, so
deeply affects me at every
moment of strong excitement
or emotion. The effect is
almost physical. It's as if
with parched lips I were
sipping a delicious drink
that cools my spirit
and heals me, body
and soul.[12]

12 "I don't know myself why it is that a beautiful poem, especially by Goethe, so deeply affects me at every moment of strong excitement or emotion. The effect is almost physical. It's as if with parched lips I were sipping a delicious drink that cools my spirit and heals me body and soul." (Luxemburg 1978: 220)

Dear Helen,

It was good to get your letter. I am going to respond in two parts. The second part will focus on personal specifics (which also interweaves, for people like us, with political specifics). This first part will be more sweepingly political, but hopefully not overly abstract.

Some of what we have been saying to each other makes me want to turn to our comrade Rosa to ask her about her life as an activist. In the massive and already highly organized German Social-Democratic Party, her experience seems to have been as a writer, a lecturer, a teacher, and a high-level participant in discussions and debates – but all within an organizational context incredibly different from ours. In some ways closer to the context in which we find ourselves must have been her youthful efforts to help build the much smaller Marxist organization in Poland, connected to an embryonic labour movement with fluctuating fortunes.

"What were you guys doing to build up the organization and movement? What were your mistakes, how did you make gains, what are organizing and activist insights you can share?" There are hints in the mass strike pamphlet and in her correspondence (though we don't yet have enough of that!), but she left no memoirs. In contrast, Lenin's massive correspondence is available, and we have the richness of Nadezhda Krupskaya's invaluable *Reminiscences of Lenin*, but I wish it was possible to consult Luxemburg on such stuff. From Paul Frölich's biography of Luxemburg we have this wonderful word-portrait:

> Everyone felt the strength of her personality. In conversation her face reflected the range of her ever-changing impulses and feelings, from earnest meditation to unrestrained joy, from sympathy and kindliness to asperity and sarcasm. [...] Her large, dark eyes dominated her whole face. They were very expressive, at times searching with a penetrating scrutiny, or thoughtful; at times merry and flashing with excitement [...] To the end of her life she retained a slight Polish accent, but it lent character to her voice and a special zest to her humor. Because she was sensitive to the moods of others, she knew when to remain silent and to listen [...][13]

I imagine this wonderful person not as 'The Great Rosa Luxemburg' but as a very human comrade in small organizing meetings where we are planning on what to do next – a recruitment effort designed to draw in this and that specific person, creating a discussion-group or reading-group, developing a campaign that includes leaflets and demonstrations and a push to actually win a winnable goal – for, as she put it, the pathway to social revolution is paved with accumulating reform struggles that build the consciousness and the organized strength of the working class.

'The working class' is all-too-often a dreadfully idealized and inhuman abstraction – something that is worshipped by some on the Marxist Left, with others abandoning Marxism because they conclude this powerful abstraction 'no longer exists.' In

---

13 Frölich 2010: 162.

fact, that thing *never* existed. It has always been a massive and diverse collection of 'imperfect' living individuals like ourselves who are dependent on the sale of our labour-power (physical, mental, intellectual) in a variety of occupations, dominated by those who control and profit from our various labours. But what does the abstract 'working class' think and feel and want? That misses the reality Luxemburg put her finger on in a 1917 prison letter to her friend Mathilde Wurm:

> There is nothing more changeable than human psychology. That's especially because the psyche of the masses, [...] the eternal sea, always bears within it every latent possibility: deathly stillness and raging storm, the basest cowardice and the wildest heroism. The masses are always what they *must* be according to the circumstances of the times, and they are always on the verge of becoming something totally different from what they seem to be.[14]

We ourselves are elements within this mighty swirl.

What some of us are wrestling with right now is how to draw more and more of us together into small but growing (and eventually extensive) communities of mutual support, of consciousness, of resistance and struggle. Luxemburg with many co-thinkers and comrades once helped achieve something like that – a vast and vibrant revolutionary collective which had a genuine possibility of bringing to birth a new world from the ashes of the old. We are now engaging in one of the further cycles of rebuilding and reanimating – in contexts that are new and different from Luxemburg's, but not entirely new and different. So what can we learn from Luxemburg and others about how to do it?

Despite the hints, outlines, insights and sketches we can retrieve from the experiences of these wondrous but long-dead comrades, there are layer upon layer of difficult work that *we* must do – it is so hard that I sometimes despair. But I have found, over the course of my life, that I cannot stop. Time and again, after I conclude that defeat must be accepted, after I am finally convinced that there is no option but to withdraw from the effort – I find myself pulled back into the same struggle to which Luxemburg and others devoted the whole of their lives.

I have learned some things over the years, sometimes the hard way:

- we cannot accomplish what must be accomplished simply by reading and reciting what our Revolutionary Heroes said long ago;
- we cannot accomplish what must be accomplished simply by thinking Correct Revolutionary Thoughts and talking about them in discussion groups, articles, books, meetings and conferences;
- we cannot accomplish what must be accomplished by 'proving' to ourselves and our friends they we represent Correct Revolutionary Thinking, and that those not measuring up to our particular Correct Principles demonstrate our superiority and their inferiority;
- we cannot accomplish what must be accomplished by simply play-acting, assuming the roles of Revolutionary Heroes in morality plays constructed in our imaginations;

---

14 Luxemburg 2013: 374.

- we cannot accomplish what must be accomplished by simply being loyal, with closed eyes, to idealized leaders, organizations and regimes that assure us they represent Revolutionary Truth.

In fact, we must admit the possibility that we may not accomplish what must be accomplished, that rather than moving forward to the socialism Luxemburg envisioned, humanity will experience a downward slide into the worst barbarism, with civilization replaced by a vast cemetery. Often in my conversations with friends about this, I refer to post-apocalyptic films – *Children of Men* and *The Road* – as containing the more likely possibilities facing us.

But to the extent that we can achieve the better future for which Luxemburg and her comrades were reaching, I am convinced this can be accomplished only through real struggles for the freedom and well-being of real people who exist in the here-and-now.

If climate scientists are right, we have only a few decades to accomplish what needs to be accomplished. At the age of 74, I am confident that I will be one with Rosa Luxemburg (among many others) in not seeing how it all turns out. But I find meaning in my life through being part of the long collective process of struggles to allow for a future of growing freedom, genuine community, and creative labour for humanity.

In our struggles, we have much to learn from the genuine revolutionaries who went before – and I very much believe this includes Rosa Luxemburg and the other activists and fighters whom she respected. But I also believe that, like them, we find ourselves facing a situation in which we are thrown back on our own devices, collectively growing and learning through the fumbling experience of trial and error accumulated in our own time. We need to build up and learn from our own body of collective experience in the world we are part of.

The specifics, including important nuances of difference (though I find I pretty much agree with everything you are saying) in how you and I are discussing the nature of the Democratic Party, relate to this learning experience – not simply for you and me, but for thousands and millions of others. The two of us are of the same mind, I think, in our agreement with Luxemburg's insistence on the necessity of mass action, not electoralism, as being the decisive element in determining the future. She put it well:

> […] bred-in-the-bone disciples of parliamentary cretinism […] have sought to apply to revolutions the home-made wisdom of the parliamentary nursery: in order to carry anything, you must first have a majority. The same, they say, applies to a revolution: first let's become a "majority." The true dialectic of revolutions, however, stands this wisdom of parliamentary moles on its head: not through a majority, but through revolutionary tactics to a majority – that's the way the road runs.[15]

It is the "revolutionary tactics" characteristic of the Occupy Wall Street movement and the Black Lives Matter movement that have tilted consciousness and politics

---

15 Luxemburg 2004: 289.

leftward in this country of ours. There has certainly been a dialectical interplay between such mass action politics and electoral politics – as demonstrated by the Sanders campaigns, the election of "the squad," etc., not to mention the overarching opportunistic fake-radical maneuvers you point to. But the *primary* force is the building up of independent mass action, which sometimes assumes explosive proportions.

May 29, 2021

Here is the more 'personal' component of my response to your letter, from which our shared revolutionary commitments are naturally inseparable.

Among the passages in Luxemburg's letters that I love is this one, from a prison letter to Hans Diefenbach:

> […] Everything would be much easier to live through if only I would not forget the basic rule I've made for my life: To be kind and good is the main thing! Plainly and simply, to be good – that resolves and unites everything and is better than all the cleverness and insistence on 'being right.'[16]

These are qualities that I identify with you. What I remember as my first contact with you precedes our initial phone conversation. It was when I read in the old *International Socialist Review* your engagement with my book *Marx, Lenin and the Revolutionary Experience: Studies of Communism and Radicalism in an Age of Globalization*. With this book I had decided to "trust my own voice," as you put it. In doing that, I went far beyond the orthodoxies and rules of conduct I had learned on "the revolutionary left" (such as it was) – about how to deal with those having opposing viewpoints, how to deal with issues that many on the Left preferred to ignore or deny, how to deal with religion and heresies, all in the context of what it meant *to me* to remain a revolutionary.

It was a book in which I consciously violated numerous boundaries of what some would deem 'political correctness.' I pushed against anxieties around what 'the comrades' would say (or what Lenin and Trotsky might say) about *what I had to say* or about the way I said it. Part of me was scared to send that book out into the world. I would be an easy target for sharp-minded polemicists (including among old friends and comrades) concerned to demonstrate their superiority over my 'jumbled petty-bourgeois confusions,' etc. Perhaps I was saved from this because only relatively few people bothered to read it. I was astonished, in reading your review, that you had actually read what I had to say, understood it, and responded to it as a kindred spirit.

I feel anxious about what you say regarding declining stamina for long walks through the wooded hills by Lake Champlain – I very deeply want you to be able to go as far and wide as you would like. Also, I daydream about you and Ashley and Nancy and me going for another such lovely walk as we took a few years back. Of course, taking it in a couple of one-mile stints – with rests and perhaps even time for a little picnic – is an appealing variant of that daydream. It would offer a truly

---

16 Ibid: 378.

fine opportunity for relaxed (though perhaps also animated) conversation not only of ideas, but especially about what we have been doing politically, and how we are sizing up those experiences. Perhaps we can do that soon, at the end of this summer or surely next spring. Or perhaps we shouldn't wait – we could take advantage of Zoom to actually see each other's faces as we share our thoughts and impressions.

I wonder how Luxemburg would have felt about Zoom. Surely, she would have been delighted to see and talk with many friends and comrades throughout Germany and Poland and Russia. (I imagine her Zooming with Lenin – as she put it: "I enjoy talking with him, he's clever and well educated, and has such an ugly mug, the kind I like to look at."[17]) Surely, she would have been frustrated with the limitations imposed by Zoom – the replacement of sensual contact in the natural world by flat images on screens. I imagine she might also have found it intolerable to the extent that it eroded the experience of corresponding through the lengthy, rich letters that obviously meant so much to her. It wouldn't be the same for us engaging with her "correspondence" by watching recordings of old Zoom calls (with inferior English translations streamed across the bottom).

I must confess that I value very much the kind of correspondence we have been able to have as part of this project. But one way or another, I am eager to have the kinds of conversations with you indicated above about aspects of our political work. For example, I am quite eager to hear about your experience with the state labour council. I have much to tell you, as well, about a newly formed Pittsburgh Green New Deal project that is breathing new life into the activist element that has been essential to who I am.

Then there is the promise of the Tempest Collective (a scrap from the disintegrated International Socialist Organization), and the limitations of the same. I have also connected with another political collective called Left Roots (self-identifying as "a national formation of Left social movement organizers and activists who want to connect grassroots struggles to a strategy to win liberation for all people and the planet"). And there are certainly other fragments of a potentially recomposed new Left for us to compare notes about.

And of course, now that our teaching is done for the summer, we will also be able to turn our attention, once again, to our joint effort of preparing volume 5 of *The Complete Works of Rosa Luxemburg* which will become not only an enduring contribution to scholarship, but especially a rich resource for revolutionary activists of the future.

It will be a joy to connect with you in all these ways.

Warmest regards,

Paul

---

17 Luxemburg 2014: 298.

Every line of your wondrous pen has taught the German proletariat that socialism is not only a question of the knife and fork, but of a cultural movement and a great and proud worldview. [18]

18 "Every line of your wondrous pen has taught the German proletariat that socialism is not a question of the knife and the fork, but of a cultural movement and a great and proud worldview." (Luxemburg 1987: 104)

Dear Paul,

Your reflections on Luxemburg as an activist, an imperfect individual, and a human comrade form an important corrective to various attempts to heroize (or demonize) towering revolutionary figures. At the same time, picturing her in distinct contexts – her youth in occupied Poland at a time when the working-class movement was slowly regenerating after dreadful repression, and socialists operated in conditions of illegality; the years in Berlin with the SPD growing into a "state within a state"; her long periods in prison – enables a historically grounded engagement with the circumstances that shaped her. This dialectical interplay between the individual and the societal is constantly on my mind as I research and write about Luxemburg.

To escape the "revolutionary hero" I tend to conceptualize her as someone who was able to crystalize and express the revolutionary aspirations of the broader movement which in turn represented a pinnacle of political struggle. As we have often discussed, Luxemburg stayed very close to working class struggle throughout her life, unlike many of the reformists who were oriented on the *Reichstag* and electoral politics, or the union bureaucrats who prioritized the institution over the struggle. Her actions and writings came out of and were guided by collective practice.

Recognizing this does not diminish those qualities that emerge from biographies, witness testimony, her correspondence and writing, but it shifts attention to the broader collective – all those largely anonymous figures who were leaders and participants in the mass strikes and revolutionary upheavals that marked the age and without whom Luxemburg could not have become the formidable political thinker and actor she was.

The same set of questions, which I suppose could be categorized under "subjective and objective factors," lie behind your discussion of "the work we must do" in the current conjuncture. Like you I don't see it as an option to withdraw from engagement with the world – as you say, even when you feel the most pessimistic, you are drawn back into political struggle. I would not argue with any of your negative examples – ways we will NOT accomplish what must be accomplished! I would add one more: "we cannot accomplish what must be accomplished by throwing ourselves into activism without being guided by history and theory." All too often theory and praxis are separated, with one prioritized over the other, while Luxemburg understood them to be dialectically connected and inseparable. But I would also add that even if we had the best strategy in the world, history is going to be determined by far bigger forces.

Not long ago an old friend and long-time comrade told me that they were pulling back from activism because they believe that our side is going to lose: Luxemburg starkly presented the options for our future as socialism or barbarism, it is increasingly clear that the latter is already the reality for much of the world, and global capitalism is now threatening the very planet itself. I told my friend that whether or not they as an individual believe that resistance is futile, people around the world will continue to struggle as long as there is oppression and injustice. Just think of the return of the mass strike 100 years after Luxemburg's death, in Algeria, Chile, Colombia, Iraq, Lebanon, Sudan. And the remarkable global outpouring of the movement for Black lives that swept the world last year. Or right now, people in Columbia, Haiti, Palestine, resisting against the odds. The question is shall we as individuals do what we can to support and amplify those struggles, or make our peace with the system and try to shut out the horrors? It's unlikely that the actions of you, me, or any other individual will greatly impact the great sweep of history, but we can still use what resources, experiences, and energy we have to help build "real struggles for the freedom and well-being of real people who exist in the here-and-now" and make connections with global struggles beyond our local arenas. Our efforts are going to be more successful if part of a collective project, and if they draw on the lessons – positive and negative – of the revolutionary socialist tradition. That's why I think the Tempest collective is worth pursuing. It's currently a small group of people, but everyone is embedded in local struggles, and has a commitment to building "communities of mutual support, of consciousness, of resistance and struggle."

I'm glad you remembered the review I wrote of *Marx, Lenin and the Revolutionary Experience*. I did have a profound connection with that book. I love its range and eclecticism, and especially its interest in culture. Your engagement with plays and poems and fiction affirms my conviction that literature and the arts have an outsized role in the struggle for liberation and can capture elements of social forces that are beyond other forms of discourse. I remember you citing a Marge Piercy poem – "We are trying to live/As if we were an experiment/Conducted by the future" – that captures the spirit of the 1960s movements. This is very much in line with Luxemburg's approach to culture. As you know, my research for several years now has focused on her awareness of the power of art both to reveal historical truths and to provide sustenance and inspiration. This is an area that has been sadly neglected.

Marx, Lenin and the Revolutionary Experience also continues the project at the heart of much of your work, of liberating the revolutionary socialist tradition, and particularly the contributions of Lenin, from the barrage of disinformation that has attempted to bury this legacy. I appreciate the way you give a fuller, more complex picture of Lenin than the caricature of a grey, unsmiling ultra-Bolshevik, and in the process break with the tired 'good revolutionary/bad revolutionary' opposition between Luxemburg and Lenin. Sexism has colored the way Luxemburg is described, obviously by the rightwing misogynists of her time, but also by many more friendly contemporary commentators who portray her as the caring, gentle soul in contrast to the steely, hard Lenin. This does a disservice to both figures, who were comrades and collaborators on the revolutionary left.

I remember conversations we had when *The Letters* were first published by Verso about the disproportionate interest in her personal life. Much as I value the insights provided by the correspondence, I am also made uncomfortable reading lines that clearly were never meant to be made public, and I have qualms about reviews that dwell on the most intimate subjects, particularly her romantic partners. It troubles me on two levels – first because I think public figures have the right to some privacy, and second because of the gender differential. This is why I've never been comfortable referring to Luxemburg as "Rosa": nobody refers to Marx as Karl or

Lenin as Vladimir or Benjamin as Walter. The editors of *Creolizing Rosa Luxemburg* provide a compelling explanation of why they chose to use "Rosa" despite the sexist baggage, but in most contexts, I would not do so.

I attach two photographs from the trip to Berlin I took with Ashley in January 2019. It was a fascinating and moving experience to be there for the 100th anniversary of Luxemburg's murder. The city was abuzz with scholarly and political and popular events to recognize and assess her legacy, showing that she remains a tangible living presence.

The city itself has many memorials to her. My mixed feelings about them were illuminated recently when I read an excellent article in *The Guardian* by Gary Younge, "Why every single statue should come down." Did you read it? He explores the recent global spate of toppling statues of colonizers, racists, and slave traders, and defends this against both conservative and liberal critics: "I think it is a good thing that so many of these statues of pillagers, plunderers, bigots and thieves have been taken down. I think they are offensive."[19] But he takes issue with various proposals to replace them with statues of individuals from marginalized and underrepresented groups, including storied freedom fighters, and instead argues that statues of individuals always represent the most conservative and lazy form of public memorialization because they "elevate an individual from a historical moment and celebrate them" and in the process risk fixing and distorting their dynamic and complex legacies. He argues instead for alternative ways to recognize and engage with historical figures.

---

19 See Younge 2021.

Along those lines, the Luxemburg memorial that I found the most powerful was in Rosa-Luxemburg-Platz, where the pavements are lain with quotations from her work. I can't help thinking she would have been appalled by the prospect of her likeness cast in bronze, or of a city plaza named for her. But perhaps she would have looked more favorably on her words being etched in stone.

Gary Younge's essay is animated by the belief that history is made not by great individuals but by the collective struggles of largely anonymous people. As we've discussed, this principle is at the heart of Luxemburg's life and work and is perhaps her most important legacy for our time. Principled advocacy for socialism from below seems especially urgent because we are seeing not only new forms of reformism but also a resurgence of Stalinism. And then there is campism – tolerating or denying the atrocities of ruling classes in, for example, Syria or China, because the regimes are antagonistic to the US empire. These developments are alarming for so many reasons. All varieties of "socialism from above" that bypass the central Marxist tenet of self-emancipation of the oppressed and look instead to capitalist governments and states to rule "on behalf" of the masses, have had catastrophic consequences. German Social Democrats in power in 1919 reined in the revolution and murdered revolutionaries, including Luxemburg. And governments claiming the mantle of communism have a long record up to the present of the kind of violent repression and exploitation that was anathema to Luxemburg. More than anything, Luxemburg conceptualized the world through the lens of class, not nation: perhaps more than any other leading figure in the Second International she refused to give radical cover for any capitalist state, even if they were the lesser evil on the world stage.

I share your daydream of reconnecting – hopefully on the shores of Lake Champlain – and I second your proposal of shorter walks punctuated by long rests and conversation. And until we have arranged the details, we should indeed organize at least a virtual visit. I'm inclined to agree that Luxemburg would have embraced Zoom as another tool for global organizing but would have sharply felt its limitations. It is astonishing that she and others in the mass socialist movement managed to stay so connected and in close communication despite their sole reliance on mail, especially given frequent physical and social restrictions. Judging from their correspondence, the postal service was frequent and rapid: They sent each other drafts of papers, read and returned with comments with remarkably quick turnaround. In contrast it is taking me a long time to finish this letter. As I said at the start, I feel out of practice. We are so used to brief, ephemeral email messages and texts. I worry about the loss of hand-written communication for posterity. I'm not even sure that recordings of old Zoom meetings – limited as they are – would have much of a shelf life.

I too have valued the exchange. It is unusual to have this kind of sustained back and forth in writing, and the medium encourages more reflection and analysis than is typical in a phone call or in-person visit. The fact that it takes some time makes me all the more appreciative of Luxemburg's lengthy, eloquent missives covering everything from party politics to Marxist theory, to observations about flora and fauna, to the activities of her cat.

On that note, the final photograph is of Siberian squill (scilla siberica) in the woods at Rock Point. They are the first sign of spring around here, and every year it is astonishing to see waves of bright blue appear after months of snow followed by dreary mud season, which always feels like it will last forever. They are another seasonal reminder of the promise of change and regeneration.

Now, back to Volume 5!

With love and solidarity,

Helen

References

Chomsky, Noam (2020), "Forward," in Stan Cox, *The Green New Deal and Beyond*. San Francisco: City Lights Books.

Cliff, Tony (1959), "Rosa Luxemburg." *Marxist Internet Archive*. Accessed on 30.08.21, at https://www.marxists.org/archive/cliff/works/1959/rosalux/2-reforrev.htm.

Frölich, Paul (2010), *Rosa Luxemburg*. Chicago: Haymarket Books.

Gordon, Jane Anna and Drucilla Cornell (2021), *Creolizing Rosa Luxemburg*. Lanham: Rowman & Littlefield.

Le Blanc, Paul (2006), *Marx, Lenin and the Revolutionary Experience: Studies of Communism and Radicalism in an Age of Globalization*. New York and London: Routledge.

Luxemburg, Rosa (1978), *The Letters of Rosa Luxemburg*. Ed. Stephen Eric Bronner. Boulder: Westview Press.

Luxemburg, Rosa (1987), *Gesammelte Briefe. Band 5*. Institut für Marxismus-Leninismus beim ZK der SED. Berlin: Dietz Verlag.

Luxemburg, Rosa (2004), *The Rosa Luxemburg Reader*. Eds. Peter Hudis and Kevin B. Anderson. New York: Monthly Review Press.

Luxemburg, Rosa (2008), *The Essential Rosa Luxemburg: Reform or Revolution & The Mass Strike*. Ed. Helen Scott. Chicago: Haymarket Books.

Luxemburg, Rosa (2011), *The Letters of Rosa Luxemburg*. Eds. Georg Adler, Peter Hudis, and Annelies Laschitza. London and New York: Verso Books.

Neale, Jonathan (2021), *Fight the Fire: Green New Deals and Global Climate Jobs*. London: Resistance Books.

Younge, Garry (2021), "Why every single statue should come down." *The Guardian*. Accessed on 15.08.2021, at https://www.theguardian.com/artanddesign/2021/jun/01/gary-younge-why-every-single-statue-should-come-down-rhodes-colston.

Uncurbed revolutionary energy

and wide human feeling –

that is the real breath

of socialism [20]

20 "Uncurbed revolutionary energy and wide human feeling – that is the real breath of socialism." (See Cliff 1959)

2. Michael Löwy
&
Małgorzata
Kulbaczewska-Figat

Dear Malgorzata

I'm very interested to learn how you discovered Rosa Luxemburg in the Polish context. In this first message I will tell you something about my own relationship to her, which began many decades ago, in Brazil. I'm very old, born in Brazil in 1938, from Viennese Jewish parents who emigrated to São Paulo in the 1930s. My mother, Hedwig Löwy, had social-democratic sympathies, but she had brought with her to Brazil an edition of Rosa Luxemburg's prison letters from 1928, published (in German) by the International Communist Youth. That was my first contact with her, more of a personal than of a political nature. But soon after, around 1955, I met the economist Paul Singer, a few years older, also a Viennese Jew, who introduced me to her political writings. He became my mentor, and I followed him when, in the same year, a small group of people founded the Internationalist Socialist League, a "Luxemburgist" organisation: a very exotic thing in Brazil, where most of the Left was Stalinist and Nationalist! I really fell in love with her: with her beautiful face, her indomitable character, her tragic life story, her revolutionary writings, her love of freedom, her wonderful *Prison Letters*. It is a love story which lasted all my life…

I must confess that I never understood her economic writings, but I avidly absorbed all her political essays and pamphlets that I could get; some of them I found in Brazil, but others I discovered when visiting Paris for the first time in 1956. I greatly enjoyed her polemical writings against Bernstein, or her criticisms of Lenin and the Bolsheviks. Her unique combination of an uncompromising revolutionary spirit, with a profound commitment to freedom, pluralism and democracy seemed to me the only true meaning of socialism. In one of the pamphlets I bought in Paris there was a drawn portrait of her which I framed, and put on the wall in our headquarters (a room 3x5 meters): she was our guiding star!

During the years 1956-1960 I studied social sciences at the University of São Paulo, but what really interested me was political activism, Marxist theory and… Rosa Luxemburg. I became interested in the early writings of Marx, and decided to write a PhD on "Young Marx's Theory of Revolution." During those years I had become acquainted with the writings of Lucien Goldmann, an unorthodox Marxist humanist philosopher and social scientist, which I liked very much. In 1961 I got a French scholarship and went to Paris to do my doctorate under Goldmann's supervision. My PhD was in fact a… Luxemburgist interpretation of Young Marx (1842-1848), emphasising the idea of proletarian self-emancipation, against all leftist politics based on the idea of an emancipation "from above," by a Great Guide, a Supreme Saviour, or an Enlightened Vanguard. I tried to connect Marx's philosophy of praxis – in revolutionary action, the change of objective social conditions coincides with the transformation of subjective consciousness – with the idea of self-emancipation of the oppressed. Lucien Goldmann had some disagreements with me, but the thesis was finally approved unanimously in 1964, and published a few years later in a collection of books edited by a "Luxemburgist" historian, Georges Haupt (a Hungarian-Romanian Jew).

In 1970 I published two pieces on Rosa Luxemburg in an issue – edited by G. Haupt – of the leftist Journal "Partisans." But my first significant essay on her is a piece from 1973 on "Socialism or Barbarism": I tried to argue that this motto from 1915, in her *Junius Pamphlet*, was a turning point in the history of socialist thought. For the first time, socialism was not seen as the inevitable result of the capitalist contradictions, a future determined by the laws of economy, or the dialectics of history, but an objective possibility, which depended on several subjective factors: the consciousness, organisation and will of the exploited classes. I saw her argument as prophetic, since the defeat of socialism in Germany in 1919 led, a few years later, to Nazi barbarism.

In spite of being a "Luxemburgist" to the marrow of my bones, I had one (important) disagreement with my heroine: I agreed, against her, with the Leninist argument for the people's right to self-determination. I very much admired Luxemburg's internationalism, and her stubborn opposition to war and "national defence" in 1914, but I did not agree with her rejection of the right to separation and independence of national communities – including, of course, Poland! In 1973, my friend Georges Haupt proposed that we publish together an anthology of *Marxists and the National Question: 1848-1914*. We worked on it together, selecting texts by Marx, Engels, Otto Bauer, Rosa Luxemburg, Lenin, Stalin, etc. But we disagreed on the issue of Rosa Luxemburg vs. Lenin: so we decided he would write the introduction, and I the conclusion, with somewhat different perspectives – his piece a historical narrative, and mine a theoretical reflection – and somewhat different appraisals of Luxemburg's stand on the national question.

Throughout the 1970s Haupt published several volumes of Luxemburg's correspondence with Leo Jogiches, and several others: extraordinary documents of human feeling, love, rage, tenderness, compassion, friendship, irony. I could not but admire and love the extraordinary human being behind these writings...

During the next few decades I continued to write papers on Rosa Luxemburg. I will not bother you with the list... I also joined an International Association of Rosa Luxemburg Studies, and participated in several of its international conferences. But only recently, in 2018, I decided to collect in a book most of my writings on her. The book is called *The Burning Spark. Essays on Rosa Luxemburg*, and was published in French and German.

Since my youth, I have added many figures to my personal pantheon: Georg Lukács, Che Guevara, Leon Trotsky, Ernst Bloch, Franz Kafka, Gustav Landauer, Walter Benjamin – and many others. But Rosa Luxemburg remains for me the most shining star in this constellation.

I do not know much about you... I suppose you are much younger than me. And of course, your experience with Rosa Luxemburg, in Poland, must be very different from mine, in Brazil and France. Or, perhaps, not? So, please, tell me your story!

In friendship,

Michael

Rosa Luxemburg, The Eternal Spring

Dear Michael,

Thank you very much for your letter. It was absolutely moving to read that you fell in love with Rosa Luxemburg... her character, her external beauty as well as the beauty of her writings. Would I be able to say the same? For sure, I can say that Rosa – Róża in the original, Polish language – has been an inspiration for me. Perhaps not the first and greatest, but a very particular one, and a very close one indeed.

I was born in 1990 in Toruń, a city in central-northern Poland, in a family that was definitely left-leaning but which did not really encourage me to get involved in politics. My childhood and early youth were, by the way, a very bad time to be even interested in socialism, revolution and social changes, not to mention becoming an activist. The "real socialism" in the Eastern Bloc had just collapsed. Hardly anyone defended Marxist theory as a tool of analysis or said aloud that the revolution and socialist experiment, despite all the mistakes that had been committed, had reshaped Eastern Europe and brought things that had never been seen there before: education and healthcare for everyone, no illiteracy, affordable housing, industrialisation and modernisation of the economy. I was too small to remember the transformation times, but I talked enough to people, doing my journalist work, to grasp the spirit of that time: on the one hand, a breath-taking enthusiasm for capitalism and the new possibilities, on the other – insecurity, privatisation, destruction of whole branches of the economy. And hardly any conscious voice from the Left. Polish Social-Democrats, a post-communist party, were busy doing business or trying to get accepted by the new elites. Of course, there was always a part of the society who did not want neoliberalism and believed that socialism, which gave basic equality and security, could have been reformed and saved. But no one represented them. Instead, the public debate was a mixture of Catholic conservatism and a blind enthusiasm for the free market... A real irony: Poland, where Rosa Luxemburg was born, became one of the worst places to find out about her and study her legacy. Even today, she is a hero for left-wingers (at least the more courageous ones) and an anti-hero for the right-wing, both liberal and conservative, for being 'unpatriotic' and believing in world revolution rather than fighting for an independent Poland. (There is no worse sin for the right-wing in Poland than thinking outside of patriotic/ nationalist categories...)

That said, I could never have found out about Rosa. I could have completed higher education in Poland and never realised that one of the most brilliant critics of capitalism was born in Zamość, in the eastern part of my country. Or, at best, I could have just heard of her as one of the menacing Communist figures who built an unworkable utopia and deprived us all of freedom for almost a century. Basically, this did not happen thanks to a set of circumstances. My mother is a history school teacher and she has had loads of books and textbooks, including old, socialist-era textbooks. I loved reading them – and this is how I bumped into a photo of Rosa and a summary of her life for the very first time. The description was not 100% accurate, as it was necessary for the author to focus on her disagreements with Lenin on nationalities... but nevertheless. I read about a woman revolutionary who fought for her beliefs all her life and ultimately sacrificed her life for such values as liberty and equality of all the people. How could I not respect this?

Later on, when I joined my first left-wing organization (again – inspired by both books and talking to my father, a trade union activist), I got acquainted with Rosa's writings in much greater detail. She was not my first and greatest inspiration – in fact, Leon Trotsky was – but the more I read, the more I was stunned by how able she was to describe the nature of capitalism, monetising more and more areas, unable to survive without opening up new markets, exploiting the peripheral areas. I was amazed by how she could prove that social-democratic parties would not stand up and fight when there would be a real chance to undermine the system. (The question of social-democracy being a part of "liberal parliamentarianism" rather than a moving and energetic force has become painfully familiar in modern Poland, too). And finally, discovering her prison letters made me realise that we had a lot in common. Love for plants. Ability to see beauty around, even in unfavourable circumstances... The desire to be a part of a revolutionary movement, for socialism is the only path that would save humanity from destruction – and at the same time, a feeling from the *Junius Pamphlet*, that you have so brilliantly written about. That socialism has never been a necessity. That it might never become a reality, if a set of factors and conditions is not met.

I sometimes tried to imagine how Rosa – an intelligent and strong woman – managed to get through in male-dominated political parties and circles. To what extent did she have to struggle to make her voice heard and not to be limited to women liberation questions? I wondered how she dealt with her comrades, who could have even been unconsciously repeating the gender stereotypes of the epoch. At another point I felt that we were, in a way, close to each other. For the stereotypes are not gone in Poland. This is another great irony: women are still being refused leading roles in political parties and movements – and yet the best known theoretician and activist born in Poland, who Rosa was without a doubt, was a woman.

Right now I am no longer a member of any political organisation. There is just no serious anticapitalist organisation in Poland that I could have joined with a clear conscience and a feeling that this is a step in the right direction. I wondered if I could become a member of a social-democratic party that seems, still, the best available option, but I realised that my disagreements with their program would be too serious to make a long-term co-operation possible. Nevertheless, since 2016, I have worked as a journalist for left-wing platforms. I have covered workers' fights in different countries of Eastern Europe, commented on political events in my country from a strong left perspective, written on workers' and socialist movements' history in Eastern Europe. I feel that this is what I can do here and now, to remain one of these people who believe in a better world and try to build it with their hands, even if the resources are modest and the enemy powerful...

Once again, Rosa Luxemburg keeps inspiring me not to give up. As I mentioned already, her memory is still being offended (I cannot find a better word for that) by right-wingers – but she has become a kind of icon for the younger generation of activists on the Left. Definitely she is no longer forgotten in Poland, even though a few years ago the town of Zamość removed the memorial plaque on the house where she lived (it was, in fact, ordered to do so by the Institute of National Memory, an institution that creates official politics of memory and has the right to say who must not be commemorated in public spaces). For the young social-democrats of Poland, Rosa has become a universal example of fighting for freedom, equality and democracy, for democratic socialism, with a revolutionary dimension, sadly, often being lost or underrepresented. But still! We are, at least some of us, rediscovering her. And this happens at a time when young women in Poland are marching against the anti-abortion law written by the Catholic fundamentalists...

I hope that what I have written will help you to get to know me better. There are decades of age and thousands of kilometres between us, but, I think, there is also a common belief that socialism is still not an impossible dream. Even if it is not a necessity either...

With friendship,

Małgorzata

Moim ideałem jest taki ustrój społeczny, w którym by wolno było z czystym sumieniem kochać wszystkich.[1]

1 "My ideal is such a social system, where it is possible to love every single person with a clear conscience." (See Leszczyński 2021)

March 30, Paris

Dear Malgorzata

Many thanks for your letter. It is quite remarkable the way you were able to discover and cherish Rosa Luxemburg in such a hostile, nationalist-conservative environment. It needs a lot of courage and an independent mindset! Yes, we are very different in age and cultural background, but Rosa helped both of us to find our ways. And I share your hope that someday, in the future, people in Poland will be able to read again and admire Rosa Luxemburg, in spite of her (wrong) views on national independence... What you wrote about young people's interest in her is a very positive sign.

Many years ago, I met Felix Tych, a Polish scholar who had published a bibliography of Rosa Luxemburg's complete works. He intended to publish all her writings, but was not able to do it. I wonder if someone is trying to have some of her works published today in Poland. This year, in the context of her 150th anniversary, I have been often asked how Luxemburg's ideas relate to present struggles and aspirations. Of course, our times are very much different from hers, and we must deal with new problems that she could not know about. However, capitalism is still the name of the game, and socialism still the only real challenge to the system.

The danger of ecological catastrophe is one of the most evident differences between our age and hers. In my view, the ecological crisis and climate change are *the* key political and moral issues of our times. For the first time in history, the conditions for human life itself are being threatened. What do you think of the ecological movement in Poland? I know the rulers in the country are opposed to any ecological initiatives and refuse to discuss the need to phase out coal production. Of course, the same applies, in spite of a "Green" rhetoric, to Germany and the other European capitalist countries. This is a very serious problem, since coal and oil – the fossil energies – are the main providers of CO_2 emissions responsible for climate change. Obviously, during Luxemburg's lifetime, this issue was not so relevant, and there was no reason to take ecology as a serious political challenge. However, in spite of this inevitable limitation, I think her writings can inspire the present ecological movement, in several aspects.

First, because she was one of the few socialists of her time with a deep affection for natural life. You mentioned her love for plants: indeed, she spent some of her time collecting leaves and flowers for her Herbarium. She also had a passion for birds – whose flight she followed from the barred windows of her prison – a deep compassion for animals being mistreated or tortured by people, and she was enraged by the extermination of certain species – e.g. buffalos in the United States – by well-armed hunters.[2] Her letters from prison document this rare "naturalist" sensitivity. Socialism today has no future if it does not include respect for Mother Nature, and for all forms of life on the planet.

2 Editor's note: Neither the author nor the editor have been able to identify the precise quote, but according to Michael it is not the quote about the Romanian buffalos, as published in the *Letters*.

Second, because of her internationalism. She always considered all problems and conflicts from an internationalist viewpoint, rejecting the disastrous ideologies of nationalism and xenophobia. Climate change is a planetary threat, which cannot be confronted in the narrow limits of "national interests." Capitalist governments refuse to take the radical ecological measures urgently needed, in the name of "our national economy," "the competitiveness of our industries," or our "American (or other national) way of life." In contrast, the new youth movements around ecological issues are global and international: Fridays for Future, Students' Strike, and several others have been able to mobilise hundreds of thousands, if not millions, all around the world. In this sense Greta Thunberg is a sort of improbable heir to Rosa Luxemburg's internationalism.

Third, because the Ecosocialist perspective, which is the only real alternative to ecological catastrophe, cannot be achieved without a revolution, and this revolution cannot be successful without freedom, democracy, pluralism and universal suffrage – as Rosa Luxemburg always insisted. This does not mean that partial ecological reforms cannot be obtained, but, as she had argued since 1899, only a revolutionary movement can wrest power from the hands of the ruling classes – the necessary condition for the radical social and ecological change needed.

Fourth, because we know that the economic or ecological crisis will not lead, by themselves, to the destruction of capitalism. As you emphasised in your letter, Rosa Luxemburg argued there is no "historical necessity." We cannot wait for the conditions to ripen, or for the system to break down: we have to act here and now, if we want to prevent the worst from happening. In her *Junius Pamphlet* from 1915, Rosa Luxemburg raised the famous motto "Socialism or Barbarism;" the choice today may be even more dramatic: "Ecosocialism or the Destruction of Life."

Let me know what you think of the relevance of Rosa Luxemburg's ideas to present movements of protest and struggle, or to the dreams of the youth today for a different world – in Poland and elsewhere. She was not much of a feminist – she believed she could leave the issue for her friend Clara Zetkin – but her idea of the self-emancipation of the oppressed could perhaps be of interest for the wonderful women's movement in Poland...

With my friendship,

Michael

PS: I'm in good health, thanks. I already got two doses of anti-Covid vaccine. But the pandemic is getting worse and worse in most European countries. Take care, young people may suffer from it too.

"La fraternité mondiale des travailleurs
est pour moi ce qu'il existe de plus
haut et de plus sacré sur terre, c'est
mon étoile guide, mon idéal, ma patrie
Je préfère perdre ma vie, plutôt qu'être
infidelle à cet idéal!" [3]

3 "The fraternization of the workers of the world is for me the highest and most sacred thing on earth; it is my guiding star, my ideal, my fatherland. I would rather forfeit my life than be unfaithful to this ideal!" (See Luxemburg 1916)

Dear Michael,

Thank you very much for all that you wrote. In fact, I could not agree more with what you wrote on Ecosocialism, and the ecosocialist revolution, as the only hope left for humanity. The Left has argued for over a century which way should we go: the way of revolutionary change or the road of reforms, a slow transformation of the system from inside. Right now, there is no more time left for debating – the planet has been destroyed in such a manner that no partial changes and no local initiatives can bring real change. Even worse, as you pointed out, local initiatives are being blocked or stopped due to "national interest," "the need to be attractive for investment," and the biggest players do not want to give up their profit – even though we all know that we just cannot continue this way. We are already living in the century of barbarism, we are making the barbarism even worse – are we, as humanity, still able to save ourselves? I want to believe that at least some of us are determined not to wait for the catastrophic outcome without trying to prevent it. There is a hope in the ecological movements of youth who are able to understand, better than older generations, that unlimited consumption will not last forever.

You asked me about the Polish ecological movement, which has been developing in recent years as a reaction to the most outrageous moves of the Polish government: permission to cut down trees and forests in Poland on an unprecedented scale, including in the most valuable forest in the country and perhaps in Central Europe (the Białowieża National Park), or a complete refusal to invest in new sources of energy, phase out coal mining and transform industry in the region where most of the mines are located. Without a doubt, the brave and sensitive people who get involved in ecology are doing a great thing. What we miss, however, is an unequivocal anticapitalist face of the movement – just like we were missing someone who would say what Rosa Luxemburg said, putting the environment question in a general context. Some of the activists understand that it is capitalist pursuit of profits that led us to the blind alley we are in now. Others just condemn the wrongs of today, without adding the conclusion: that ecosocialism would save us. Not a regulated capitalism or a set of reforms eliminating the worst policies. We definitely miss here in Poland – and not only, I think – someone like Rosa Luxemburg who would point out: it is the capitalist need of getting more and more markets, more and more mechanisms of profit that is guilty of the planet's destruction. We will never save the planet by changing personal habits, like some liberals tell us to, but allowing the great companies to keep poisoning us and the environment. I can imagine that Rosa Luxemburg would be now doing all in her power to unite the ecological movement with the workers' movement. She would attack both the insensible tech giants and those "liberal ecologists" who – we have people like that in Poland too – just tell the industrial workers that their mines and factories must be closed... but offer them no real alternative, no other options to gain a living. Rosa was able to combine compassion and love for people and for the planet. And, I believe, this compassion and willingness to love could lead us in fighting for a better world today as well.

I would also say that the key element of Rosa's legacy that may be useful for today's movements would be her capacity to analyse things broadly and set priorities. She never lost capitalism from the horizon, as the ultimate frame of destruction. She was able to see that without the removal of the very essential mechanism of exploitation we would never get rid of many other conflicts, which are deliberately used and inflamed by the exploiters and the politicians standing by their side. In a world where many left-wing movements seem to be no longer able to defend socialist ideas and perspectives, or wander towards identity politics being the only actual point of interest, Rosa could serve as a powerful reminder that real equality, diversity and brother/sisterhood can be achieved only through a revolutionary reconstruction of the economy. This is important from the point of view of the women's movement too, the newly strengthened Polish women's movement and other similar mobilisations as well. For yes, women share an experience of being considered worse, of facing stereotypes and violence, but on the other hand – the perspective of a businesswoman who stands up for her woman rights is not the same as the perspective of a woman worker who experiences discrimination in different fields. The first one may be touched by anti-woman legislation, but her capital and connections could strongly help (for instance, in getting an abortion in a neighbouring country if it is banned like in Poland now) – the other one may count on the solidarity of other working women only. And yet right-wing governments, like the one in Poland, tend to stir up public quarrels (not debates) over lifestyles, family models or even basic human rights, so that the attention of society is turned away from questions such as low wages, violations of the labour code or the incompetence of the state in fighting the pandemic. Here we can be brilliantly inspired by Rosa – her capacity to see the broad picture and define the real sources of conflicts and misery. Yes, her concentration on economics only led her to wrong conclusions on nations, the vivacity of national sentiment, the will to get and to defend a national territory (after multi-national empires failed to give a true sense of security and belonging to a dozen nations, including Poles, and, we could even say, the working people of Poland in particular). However, is the modern mainstream Left even more wrong in refraining from challenging capitalism fundamentally, as Rosa and her generation did, and putting too much hope in granting more personal and identity rights to single human beings? Even rainbow capitalism, inclusive and smiling, remains capitalism...

Capitalism is still the name of the game, and we as humanity are losing this game. One more inspiration from Rosa Luxemburg is that capitalism would not give up, realise its mistakes, put on a more human face. This is a system that survives only through permanent growth, and we are much closer to the ultimate margin of this growth than a hundred years ago. If not forced to, if not pressured by a mass movement, it will continue to kill and destroy. Rosa's life shows us how uneven the forces are: on one side, all those who profit from the system and would defend the status quo, on the other, all the oppressed, often confused, demoralised by harsh everyday conditions or unsure why and how should they join the fight. And yet... if we give up, we will inevitably succumb to barbarism and welcome our self-destruction. Rosa did not give up. Could we be able to find the strength she had?

With friendship,

Malgorzata

PS: Good to hear that you have already been vaccinated. Sadly, I do not even imagine when my turn will come: my country has not yet started to vaccinate people under 55 years of age (excluding medical workers and teachers) and even my parents are still waiting for the vaccine, not to mention me! Luckily, I am able to do most of my professional duties online... and I want to hope that my journalism has any value in modern times, where people are struggling for survival, literally.

A Dream that Never Dies

References

Leszczyński, Adam (2021), "150. urodziny Róża Luksemburg." *Wyborzca*. Accessed on 30.08.21, at https://wyborcza.pl/alehistoria/7,121681,12130297,150-urodziny-rozy-luksemburg-idealem-jest-ustroj-spoleczny.html.

Luxemburg, Rosa (1916), "Either/Or." *Marxist Internet Archive*. Accessed on 29.08.21, at https://www.marxists.org/archive/luxemburg/1916/04/eitheror.htm.

Luxemburg, Rosa (2004), *The Rosa Luxemburg Reader*. Eds. Peter Hudis and Kevin B. Anderson. New York: Monthly Review Press.

Zastój, deptanie w miejscu, zadawalanie się
pierwszym osiągniętym celem
są niedopuszczalne w rewolucji.[4]

---

4 "To stand still, to mark time on one spot, to be contented with the first goal it happens to reach, is never possible in revolution." (Luxemburg 2004: 287)

3. Rebecca Selberg

&

Maureen (Mo) Kasuku

Dear Maureen,

How happy I am for this opportunity to exchange thoughts on Rosa Luxemburg with you! There are many things that separate us – things that today seem extremely important to the feminist and socialist movement, and for good reason: nationality, race, age, social experiences and structural positions in the world system. But I do feel close to you, especially since you wrote in an email to me that despite our current personal struggles, which make it a bit tough for both of us to take this project on at this particular time, "we will make Rosa proud." I found that sentence and its sentiment so encouraging and beautiful. I grew up in a very small family – only my mother and my sister, and despite living in a welfare state there is a certain vulnerability in having so few people to depend on. But I also grew up in a movement where there were many other parents and aunts and uncles and cousins, an extended family in struggle. And through them I realized that once you belong to a movement you also belong to a history of dreamers and organizers and we strive to make them proud, those who came before us, and to always remember them and their dreams. "*Die Toten mahnen uns*" – the dead admonish us. Rosa – a short, partly disabled political refugee belonging to a persecuted religious minority, iron-willed and with a sharp, clear mind – is like an aunt who connects us in kinship, spanning the vast distance between Kenya and Sweden. Let's make her proud!

I read some of Rosa's letters recently, in Swedish translation, and there is one letter in particular which resonated with me. In it, Rosa is lecturing her dear friend Mathilde Wurm, who I guess is complaining and whining about the state of affairs. Rosa tells her in a very sharp tone (I would have cried if someone wrote such a thing to me) to stop it; how lucky we are, Rosa writes, "that world history up to now was not made by people like all of you, because otherwise we would have had no Reformation and would probably still be sitting under the ancien regime."[1] How that must have stung poor Mathilde! But then Rosa goes on to encourage her friend: be human, it is what matters the most, she says. And being human means being firm and clear and happy – yes, happy despite everything, because crying is a thing of weakness. "To be a human being," Rosa writes, "means to joyfully toss your entire life 'on the giant scales of fate' if it must be so, and at the same time to rejoice in the brightness of every day and the beauty of every cloud."[2] She wrote this in 1916, when WWI was raging and German Social Democracy and the Second International were falling apart and only three years before she would be murdered by proto-fascists.

I thought this was positive thinking so very different from the kind we are fed daily through contemporary pop culture. US sociologist Arlie Russell Hochschild wrote a book about the industry of positive thinking (self-help books, life coaches, executive speakers, etc.) that feeds on the idea of the power of imagination. If you fail, it's because you were too negative, and it's your own fault for not believing in

---

1 Luxemburg 2013: 362.
2 Ibid: 363.

yourself. This, of course, is a narrative that performs a magic trick: it hides structural inequalities and places the blame with individuals for being stuck in hopeless situations. If you're exploited, it's because you lack drive. It's the worst aspect of capitalism – commodifying even the lie of inequality.

Rosa's positive thinking is also very different from what I find to be a strong identification with victimhood in some parts of the (US/European) feminist movement, where emotions, vulnerability and trauma take up much space at the moment. I do believe it is central for feminists and socialists to talk about trauma, about suffering, but I sometimes wonder if maybe we need to re-center the movement around the kind of optimism that Rosa embodied. I guess this optimism is about "socialism or barbarism" and "don't mourn, organize." If you really do believe that it is either barbarism or *frihetlig/freiheitlich* (free) socialism, then you must move forward, you must be human and you must find beauty in the struggle of existing, and existing in a state of struggle for the dead, for the living, and for those to come. You simply can't afford to get stuck in the pain.

I feel weak most of the time, and certainly in comparison to Rosa – such a force! She saw things so clearly, and she was so productive and inquisitive. I look at my life and the world around me – the political situation in Sweden is quite dreadful at the moment – and I just… don't know, you know? But then I realize that Rosa was also in doubt, she just knew she had to continue anyway.

This is where I am now, my dear friend, contemplating this powerful idea of being human and finding joy in spite of it all – how to balance a sound negativity and anger with the kind of positive spirit that pushed Rosa forward, forward.

Med bästa hälsning och handling,

Rebecca

Men att offentligt högljutt dundra om
"individens frihet" och i privatlivet på
grund av vansinnig passion förslava
en människosjäl – det begriper jag inte
och förstår inte. I detta fall saknar
jag de två grundelementen i den
kvinnliga naturen: godhet och stolthet. [3]

3 "But to publicly, loudly shout about 'individual freedom', and in the private life, due to mad passion, enslave a human soul – that I cannot understand. In this case I miss the two basic elements in the female nature: goodness and pride." (Luxemburg 1987: 158)

April 18, 2021
Nairobi, Kenya

Hujambo Rebecca,

It's Sunday morning here in Nairobi. I'm reading your letter for the millionth time. I am at my mother Aliviza's house. Nursing her back to health after a bout of Covid-19. She's much better now and in good spirits. She keeps asking *"unasoma nini?"* (Kiswahili for "What are you reading?") I tell her it's a letter from my comrade in Sweden. She says you should visit someday. *Karibu Kenya* Rebecca!

Like you, I grew up in a small family. Detached from many of my relatives because of classist reasons. We were/still are considered 'too poor' to be invited to 'family' social events. This bothered me for years, but I found camaraderie with the amazing socialists and feminists in my hometown and we are putting in the work to change our material conditions for the better. Rosa would be proud. No time for moping around. We are organizing like crazy! And one of the ways we are doing it is by providing localized political education sessions to the masses, equipping them with an ideological understanding of socialism, to combat fascism & capitalism.

Rosa once said that "the most revolutionary act is and forever remains 'to say loudly what is'."[4] And these political education sessions allow the disenfranchised working-class people in the grassroots to express themselves amid the turmoil surrounding them. We are living in a police state. Literally. We are surrounded by police as we go about our daily business. These agents of the state – violently enforcing an unscientific curfew and lockdown that has ruined the livelihoods of millions of poor working-class people and exacerbated poverty – have wrought havoc; and speaking up as a form of resistance has dire consequences.

Recently, a vocal social media activist was arrested on the frivolous charge of "cybercrimes." Many believe it was his fervent campaign to get the state to provide some form of welfare safety nets for the workers who have lost their jobs.

The state has its priorities misplaced and has dedicated resources to forcing down our throats a referendum no one asked for and, by the president's own admission, the country loses Ksh 2 billion a day. As Kenyans sink further into poverty.

Everything seems terrible right now but reading Rosa's letter from prison to Stefan Bratman-Brodowski in September 1918, in which she reflects on the arrest and execution of hundreds of Left Social Revolutionaries in Russia and still manages to stay optimistic, is the morale boost I needed to get through this.

You talk about re-centering the movement around the kind of optimism Rosa had. Instead of incessant mourning and becoming fodder for right-wing memes popular here in Kenya, we dust ourselves off, roll up our sleeves and strategize. That's what Rosa would have wanted for us.

---

4 See Brie 2019.

Heck, I could easily be reading an Arlie Russell Hochschild book and "manifest" my way out of the hot mess that is Kenya today but that's not what Red Rosa, a materialist through and through, would recommend.

Nobody expected a walk-in-the park revolution, but neither were we prepared for how hard the state would hit back at any form of dissent. I know for sure that we are not outnumbered. Just out-organized. That's why studying comrade Rosa is crucial for me. This woman was living with a disability and had to deal with virulent sexism and still managed to lead the German workers' uprisings. I will forever be in awe!

Here we are dear comrade, continents apart, reflecting on the life and times of Rosa amid the death throes of capitalism. Remaining human and vulnerable in spite of the violence surrounding us. Rosa has brought us together 150 years after she made her debut. Who would've thought! Two socialist feminists coming together. Sharing, plotting, organizing, reflecting and most importantly, hoping that our letters will be read in a post-capitalist world. I have faith in the masses.

Tuko pamoja mwenzangu (We are in this together).

Always in solidarity,
Mo

The masses are the crucial factor.
They are the rock on which the
ultimate victory will be built. [5]

5 "The masses are the crucial factor. They are the rock on which the ultimate victory will be built." (Luxemburg
2004: 378)

April 30, Lund

Dear Mo,

I am so encouraged by your letter! I feel your power! Your words make me think of this beautiful line from the Swedish version of the Italian song *"Bandiera Rossa"*: *"för alla lika är världen till."*[6] It can be translated as "the world belongs to all equally." I sense how you fight for your world, and for our common world, even if we are – in one sense – worlds apart. I'm by your side, comrade.

I too have cared for my mother Barbro during this pandemic. The isolation hit her hard and she suffered a heart attack, made worse by the fact that she refrained from going to the emergency room when the first symptoms set in. Luckily my sister, who is a nurse, immediately identified the severity of the situation when my mom finally called her up to complain about chest pains and nausea.

Just a few weeks before this, my mother talked about not feeling right in her body. She also said, "you know, Rebecca, life expectancy is getting higher for everyone except working class women" – and she was right! Numbers support it; workers are losing out on life, while middle class people can expect to live longer than ever. My mom, who worked in factories and in cleaning all her life, could suddenly see and feel her life cut shorter by exploitation. When she was taken away by the ambulance, this is what I thought of: if I lose her now, it is to the system of oppression. She suffered a malaise that is typical for people whose hard work and poor conditions have settled in their veins. I was so angry at the world! And yet, I know that there is almost a 20-year difference in life expectancy between the people of Kenya and the people of Sweden. This is the coloniality of power. We must struggle against this system of oppression, because we are fighting for life:

Kom med förtrampade, och slåss för livet	*Oppressed, join us and fight for life*
Vår kamp för frihet	*Our struggle for freedom*
är också din[7]	*Is your struggle too*

The pandemic, of course, has exacerbated inequality. In Sweden, migrants have suffered the hardest, along with working-class women. And now we clearly see the brutal effects of imperialism in the distribution of vaccines, with core countries hoarding and prioritizing citizens who are not at risk, while peripheral countries can't access vaccines to distribute to their most vulnerable people. The WHO called it "an outrage," and said the uneven distribution of vaccines is "grotesque." In the *Junius Pamphlet*, Rosa writes about how there exist "two social orders, of traditional agricultural landlordism, of super-modern, super-refined capitalist exploitation, at

6 Lyrics by Lars Forssell, here in interpretation by Dutch-Swedish singer Cornelis Vreeswijk: https://www.youtube.com/watch?v=9i0GQiOP9cE.
7 See footnote 58.

62

one and the same time."[8] I think about the vaccines and the entire response to the Covid-19 pandemic as these two social orders materializing clearly – the durable political structures of colonial power; the reproduction of inequalities of risk (risks accumulate, as sociologists say, at the bottom); and the high-tech, fast-paced, hard to grasp super-refined capitalist order. Our fight is a complex one: we must envision a free world in which humanity's vast knowledge and technical capabilities are placed in the hands of the masses, and produced in service of all equally. I find Rosa Luxemburg such an inspiration here, as well as your words, speaking of everyday struggles.

My dear friend, I hope your mother is feeling better and stronger; I hope you get the chance to rest and enjoy the beauty around you.

Solidariska hälsningar,

Josune

---

8 Luxemburg 2004: 339.

/ ett oupphörligt växelspel mellan politisk agitation och yttre händelser har den pågående revolutionen flammat upp i enstaka explosioner eller i stora proletära enhetsaktioner. Bakgrunden är den stora ekonomiska kamp som med sin utgångspunkt i januaris generalstrejk alltjämt pågår.[9]

9 "Thus the great economic struggle that proceeded from the January general strike, and which has not ceased to the present day, has formed a broad background of the revolution from which, in ceaseless reciprocal action with the political agitation and the external events of the revolution, there ever arise here and there now isolated explosions, and now great actions of the proletariat." (Luxemburg 2008: 137)

Mwenzangu Rebecca,

These past 3 weeks have been...surreal to say the least. If it's not one thing, it's another. Mother got well and just as everything seemed to be going well, a friend called me in distress. She had just received an eviction notice. Her landlord wanted her out of the house as he "had found a prospective tenant willing to pay extra cash for her tiny studio flat and unlike her, won't be late with the rent." With a six-month old baby and an unstable job, moving out as you can imagine was going to inconvenience her majorly.

Then came the call from one of my party leaders telling me about a land grab involving one of our cells in Kayole Nairobi. As I'm writing this, we are preparing for a major protest against the state agencies facilitating the illegal occupation of this public piece of land on May 1st, International Workers' Day. I'll let you know how it goes.

I am continuing this letter a few days later and I am happy to report my friend got alternative accommodation on short notice but she's going to have to chase her rent deposit for the foreseeable future. Nairobi landlords are notorious for refusing to refund rent deposits.

All these stresses can have you dead at a very young age. Your mama is right. The working class are dying at an alarming rate. Capitalism is killing our people, Rebecca, and I am afraid the vaccine apartheid is going to aggravate everything.

It is disgusting how stupid patents and money have been prioritized over the lives of human beings amidst a raging pandemic. And I just know the Kenyan government will deregulate vaccine prices and let the "free market decide." You know what that means for the poor working class. I've never wanted a socialist revolution this badly. It's literally a matter of life and death at this point.

It is a truism that Africans will be the hardest hit if the so called "vaccine passports" become globally mandated. As if Africans do not experience enough prejudice the world over. Now this. There goes my dream of ever visiting *Lichtensteinbrücke* or seeing you at the University of Lund.

What would Rosa say to me at a time like this? Probably what she wrote to Sophie Liebknecht on Christmas Eve 1917:

> And in the dark I smile at life, as if I knew some sort of magical secret that gives the lie to everything evil and sad and changes it into pure light and happiness. And all the while I'm searching within myself for some reason for this joy, I find nothing and must smile to myself again and laugh at myself. I believe that the secret is nothing other than life itself; the deep darkness of night is so beautiful and as soft as velvet, if one only looks at it the right way; and in the crunching of the damp sand beneath the slow, heavy steps

of the sentries a beautiful small song of life is being sung - if one only knows how to listen properly. At such moments I think of you and I would like so much to pass on this magical key to you, so that always and in all situations you would be aware of the beautiful and the joyful, so that you too would live in a joyful euphoria as though you were walking across a multi-colored meadow.[10]

How profound and beautiful. At her lowest moment, just two years before her death, Rosa still found joy in the darkest of places. My friend, I am going through a really dark phase right now. Some things I just cannot put into words. But every day, I pick myself up and roll up my sleeves because there's work to do. I gain strength from my comrades all over the world.

So let's walk across the multi-colored meadow together, Rebecca. As *"Auf, Auf zum Kampf"*[11] plays in the background, I hope you have your dancing shoes ready. Hjalmar sent me this song when he first reached out. I really enjoyed it. It's a "bop" as my sister Akinyi would say. Have a listen.

Pass my regards to your family. And remind mama to take it easy. She works too hard.

In solidarity always.

Kwaheri kwa sasa (Goodbye for now)

MD

PS: My comrades and I attended the May 1st protest. The police gave us a hard time but we made our demands known. Check out this pic of us on site.

---

10 Luxemburg 2013: 455.
11 Listen at https://www.youtube.com/watch?v=OoGG__ihnVQ.

Dear Maureen,

I am working too hard and I know it. But there are so many things I want to do! And so little time. And so many things I have to do, whether I want to or not. I wonder if work was harder for Rosa, or easier. How was the sense of time for her? Did the weeks fly by? Was it suddenly sabbath, again? Was she suddenly a bit older, a bit more tired? She had such a short time on earth; I wonder if she sensed it. They took her time, the murderous bastards. But she had already made her mark on the world. Rosa Luxemburg is timeless. They can never truly take someone like that.

Time, that is what I'm thinking about right now. I'm short on time. I'm full of ideas; I have all the material things I could ever need; I have a steady salary, a prestigious job, I'm a white lady with a PhD in a racist world that fetishizes 'accolades.' But I feel as if I'm constantly underperforming. Oh, how I complain; Rosa would scold me! But it's a special kind of hell to feel inadequate all the time. I also think it is a gendered experience. Mothers always seem to feel inadequate.

I steal time from wage work by reading *Reform or Revolution*, and it's amazing how contemporary it seems. I absolutely loved this remark:

> No coarser insult, no baser aspersion, can be thrown against the workers than the remarks: 'Theocratic controversies are only for academicians.' Some time ago Lassalle said: 'Only when science and the workers, these opposite poles of society, become one, will they crush in their arms of steel all obstacles to culture.' The entire strength of the modern labour movement rests on theoretic knowledge.[12]

It is essential for us to discuss the theoretical underpinnings of our activities, of our movements. Yes! Let's make time for that. One aim of our movement should be to make sure everyone has the time to really think about things. I am so privileged in that I am, to a certain degree at least, paid to think, to read and analyze. But something has to come out of this thinking – something tangible, something measurable. "Output," it's called, and output needs to be quantified and ranked: preferably in journal articles (weighed and measured in terms of 'citations' and 'impact factors'). So, it's not free thinking, it's commodified thinking, it's thinking with an eye towards producing an object to be measured. This is the system I'm in, and of course, it is much better than being in a sweatshop. But it is also, in some form, turning thinking into a sweatshop-like activity; producing something for someone else's benefit. I can climb if I produce, so there are social and monetary rewards in it for me. I am not totally alienated from my products because I'm paid back in this 'merit-based' system; I'll get a fancier title and more status. But when I read Rosa's texts, I wonder what it would be like to exist outside of a system of quantifiable results.

But anyway, I'm reading *Reform or Revolution* on time that I steal for myself and for us, dear comrade. Where are we, then, in terms of reform or revolution? Well,

---

12 Luxemburg 2008: 42-43.

from a Swedish viewpoint, I could only wish for a Social Democracy that actually still believed in reforms! "*Utan reformer ingen revolution, utan revolution inga bestående reformer*" [Without reform no revolution; without revolution, no lasting reform]. Luxemburg was right: we were not able to reform our way to socialism. However, the Swedish labour movement was able to move a whole nation from abject poverty to incredible wealth (not by itself; the wealth was also built on domestic and foreign colonial extraction, as always). But "reform" today means invariably regression, making it harder on the working class to survive. "Reform" used to mean something was going to be made better for the broad masses; such as the Swedish housing reforms in the 1960s, which managed to build one million affordable and modern apartments in ten years, wiping out the problem of lack of housing for the working class. Nowadays, housing is a huge problem in Sweden, for the working and the middle class. The housing market has been "reformed," but ever since the onset of the neoliberal era, "reforms" seem only to mean "making life harder to live." Swedish Social Democrats have a proud history and a shameful legacy: reforms for the good of the people, and later reforms to undo those reforms, to the benefit of the wealthy.

Rosa, in her book on the concepts of reform and revolution, took the fight to the Social Democrats, especially Bernstein, of course. It's a remarkable text! Bernstein thought capitalism was so adaptable, so able to overcome its crises, that it was pointless to wait for the cataclysmic event that would bring the system to its knees. We are soon in a post-pandemic state (*ojalá*) and we see the inherent contradictions in the system everywhere, but we also see the incredible ability among those in power to save the system off the backs of workers, especially workers in the Global South. But I see the contradictions here too. I work and I work and I work and I am grateful, because while a few of us in the Global North get to enjoy steady employment and good wages, some of us are in a state of perpetual unemployment and under-employment. Some work too much and are always close to being unable to reproduce themselves; some work too little, and don't have the means to reproduce themselves. This is an inherent contradiction: the reproductive capacity of the system is failing. Culturally, those who work are integrated into an exploitative system which gives them possibilities to lead comfortable lives uncomfortably; despite relatively high wages, we owe our lives to the banks, because the middle class is not comfortable enough to buy houses at market price. So, we borrow. And here is another contradiction: "Credit is," according to Rosa, a "particularly mighty instrument for the formation of crises." "It introduces," she writes, "the greatest elasticity possible; it renders all capitalist forces extensible, relative and mutually sensitive to the highest degree." And so it "facilitates and aggravates crises, which are nothing more or less than the periodic collisions of the contradictory forces of capitalist economy."[13]

In 2008 the financial crisis hit and our home, a modest two-bedroom apartment in Lund, was suddenly extremely costly. Yes, we felt the periodic collision of the contradictory forces of capitalism, and it shook us! I was expecting my son at the time, and worried sick about not being able to afford our apartment anymore, as interest rates shot up. The British Marxist David Harvey has said that "debt-incumbent home-owners don't go on strike."[14] That's right, we don't.

---

13 Luxemburg 2008: 48-49.
14 See Harvey 2010 (Min. 3:08).

Truth is, I live in a social democratic country which has been severely neoliberalized because the reforms the proud Social Democratic labour movement produced didn't withstand a coordinated attack by capital. And the Social Democratic party bowed. Rosa Luxemburg would point to her text and say: yes, of course, I told you so! Everything is being sold out. We have a unique system in Sweden now whereby public funding is funnelled into private corporations who make gigantic profits off of taxpayer money! You can open up a school, get paid in tax dollars (well, it's Swedish Crowns, of course) for each student, and then simply cut services and slim down costs. You can also cater specifically to well-off students who are in no need of special education teachers or the like, which municipal schools are required to have. Then you're left with a nice sum which you take home as profit and dole out to shareholders. It's absurd, it's organized theft, it's an incredible socialism for the rich, and it was a system – absolutely unique to the world – condoned by the Social Democrats. They can't even get themselves to part with it now, even though it is becoming evident that the system is extremely short-sighted and expensive.

To stay afloat in this neoliberal land, I spend all my time working, selling my labour power, which is mental and not manual but certainly sits in my body (I grind my teeth, I have constant headaches, my shoulders hurt, my back is in pain). I work and try to argue that my work is activism, when in truth it's not, because we need to take to the streets; we need street activism alongside theorizations of the current state of affairs. I thank Rosa for making it so clear that theory is essential. But I am too tired to theorize and too tired to take to the streets. And so, I feel inadequate again.

To the rescue comes: Bertolt Brecht, *"Till en kamrat."* I love this poem so much, I think maybe it is my favorite piece of writing in the whole world:

We hear: you no longer want to work with us.
You're too broken. You can no longer run about.
You're too tired. You can no longer learn.
You're finished.
No one can demand of you that you do more.

Then know this:
We demand it.

If you're tired and fall asleep
No one will wake you and say:
Get up, there's food on the table.
Why would there be food on the table?
If you can no longer run about, then
You must lie down. No one
Will look out for you and say:
There's been a revolution, the factories
Are waiting for you.
Why would there have been a revolution?
When you're dead they'll bury you
Whether you're to blame for your death or not.

You say:
You have fought too long. You can fight no more.
Then hear this:
Whether you are to blame or not
If you can no longer fight, you will go under.

You say: you have hoped too long. You can hope no more.
What did you hope?
That the struggle would be easy?

That's not how it is.
Our situation is worse than you thought.
It's like this:
If we don't perform the superhuman, then
We're lost.
If we cannot do what no one can demand of us
We will go under.
Our enemies are waiting for us to tire.

When the fight is at its fiercest
Then the fighters are most tired.
The fighters who are too tired will lose the battle.[15]

Well, this was perhaps a bit pessimistic! I apologize. What happened with that land grab that you wrote to me about? And is your friend settling into a new apartment? I suppose we are worlds apart, there is a vast geographical, political, economic, social and cultural distance between us, but somehow the struggle is the same. The pain is the same. The hopes are the same. The struggle is hard and we are tired but we can't be more tired than those we struggle against. We can't lose.

All my best to you and yours,

Rebecca

---

15 Editor's note: *Vielen Dank* to Tom Kuhn for rendering this poem into English especially for this book.

The Rocks in my Childhood Village

Dearest Rebecca,

I know too well what it means to be short of time as evidenced by how excruciatingly long it takes to get back to you. I hate that too much of my time and labour is spent in work I consider alienating. I once heard that time flies by when you are enjoying yourself. But the opposite is true for me. I feel like my time is being stolen by work that is, quite frankly, not useful. Rather bleak, but that's just how I feel. I too wonder what it would be like to exist outside of a system of quantifiable results. To be able to create without having to worry about KPIs and profits. I no longer take pride in the labour I produce even though it is crucial for my survival. And I don't use the word survival lightly. Working for a subsidiary of a major media house in Kenya might seem like a dream to most but it's not all glam. There's a lot of churn-and-burn pressure with no financial incentives to show for it.

I feel like I am confined in a box, Rebecca. The way things are set up here for me, it feels like I am in a prison of sorts. Hyperbole perhaps. And this is in no way a trivialization of the experiences of those in the carceral system. I often think about how Rosa courageously and closely regarded the small space of her prison. She showed how confinement can turn out to be an opening up of the world. Because she could not see past the walls, she found a world within. She found joy and purpose even in the darkest of times. Remember how she urged Sophie Liebknecht in her March 24th 1918 letter to check out a garden over a crucial political event. She wrote to Sophie asking her to go to the Botanical Gardens in Sonichka: "Towards noon when the sun is shining brightly, and let me know all you can hear. Over and above the issue of the battle of Cambrai, this really seems to me the most important thing in the world."[16]

I think Rosa was trying to tell Sophie (and Mo, 103 years later), that sometimes, you've just got to see the world before you demand that it changes. She was telling us to breathe a little, take in everything and then get down to business. And that's what I did this past weekend. I did not go to a botanical garden, but I put aside my party duties, ignored my work emails and I took long naps at my friend's new, modest studio apartment (see what mutual aid can do, comrade? She got her own place now!) The rejuvenation is what I needed to look into *Reform or Revolution* and with all that's been happening in Kenya, this really got me thinking: "Only the hammer blow of revolution, that is to say, the conquest of political power by the proletariat can break down the wall between capitalist society and Socialist society."[17]

As we grapple with the ripple effects of a devastating economic crisis and a raging pandemic with no end in sight, I am convinced that no reform of the current system will save us. To hell with elections. We need a complete overhaul. We need a revolution.

---

16 See Luxemburg 1918.
17 Luxemburg 2008: 65-66.

Of course, I am not naïve to the consequences of a revolution. I understand what it'll take. We are grounding ourselves in theory at Revolutionary Socialist League (RSL) and preparing ourselves and those that'll come after us for a socialist society.

You see, even the most well-meaning people in Kenya think like Bernstein. That capitalism is adaptable and a few nips and snips here is all it needs to function optimally. That all we need to do is "elect good leaders." That "fair" elections are the silver bullet to the stark inequalities in our country. And that we all need to just "work a little harder" to afford the most basic of things.

In fact, we've been told by others that we need to go the "Scandinavian way." But they don't have a friend like Rebecca who tells them that the "Scandinavian way" is Social Democracy that has been severely neoliberalized.

How can we reform a system that forces Kenyans to contribute to a medical fund that keeps expensive, private healthcare providers afloat? Reform a system that leads to the suicide of doctors who are overwhelmed and underpaid? Make adjustments to this system that locks out millions of children from accessing education and has the proletariat at the mercy of a workers' union led by an agent of the state? It's laughable that anyone would want to reform this.

I loathe these reform discussions in leftist spaces in Kenya and next time we have those long, boring webinars on the "way forward," which is really just circling back to capitalism, I'll share these words by Rosa:

> [P]eople who pronounce themselves in favor of the method of legislative reform *in place of and in contradistinction* to the conquest of political power and social revolution, do not really choose a more tranquil, calmer and slower road to the same goal, but a *different* goal. Instead of taking a stand for the establishment of a new society they take a stand for surface modifications of the old society [...] Our program becomes not the realization of *socialism*, but the reform of *capitalism*, not the suppression of the system of wage labor, but the diminution of exploitation, that is, the suppression of the abuses of capitalism instead of the suppression of capitalism itself.[18]

These reformist leftists are mostly petite bourgeoisie and perhaps are afraid that they might never get a chance to "climb the ladder" if we continue agitating for social equality. But many of them are facing the crisis you unfortunately experienced in 2008. Perhaps this is the wakeup call they need.

So what is to be done then, dear comrade? We are unionizing the masses in the grassroots. We've said to hell with establishment trade unions. We are making a radical workers movement. Educating the masses, agitating on social media and recruiting cadres. We know the road ahead is long and bumpy, but we feel adequately prepared. Rosa would be proud.

---

18 Ibid: 90.

I love corresponding with you, comrade, even though we are worlds apart, we share the same experiences. I think international solidarity is a beautiful thing and I am happy to let you know that I will be joining our comrades in Venezuela this coming week for the Bolivarian Bicentennial Commemorations. I'm sure I'll find someone to talk about Rosa with.

Asante sana (Thank you very much) for the poem you shared. I looked up Bertolt Brecht and I found this really interesting poem he wrote. It's alluding to unionizing and I love it so much. I found the English translation. Here's some of it:

None or all

Slave, who will set you free?
Those who languish in the depths
Will see you, comrade, in your plight
They will hear you when you cry.

You who are wretched, who will dare?
Those who can no longer bear
The misery must band together
And act today, throw off your fate
For tomorrow will be too late.
All or nothing. None or all.[19]

It is all of us or none, comrade Rebecca. Always remember that. I wish you love and light, my friend. Pass on my regards to your family. We've been keeping well here at home. I can't wait to tell you about my trip to Venezuela. I hope you can write back soon. Even if it's just to say hello.

Tuko Pamoja,
MD

---

19 See Brecht 2018: 669-669.

Mwenzangu Rebecca,

I just returned to Nairobi from Venezuela. I was attending the Bicentennial Congress of the Peoples of the World to promote a platform of anti-imperialist struggle. It was a really wonderful meeting, interacting with socialists from all over the world as we came up with anti-capitalist and anti-imperialist strategies and resolutions.

It was also a celebration of Venezuela's 200 years of independence from Spain. This historical landmark occurred through the Battle of Carabobo, where patriotic forces led by Simón Bolívar fought the Royalist troops on June 24, 1821. The struggle continues today against imperialist forces led by the U.S. who have imposed a crippling blockade on the people of Venezuela.

I haven't felt this rejuvenated and excited for the impending revolution in a long time. My faith in the masses was affirmed and I am eager to implement what I learnt in Caracas here at home. Rosa would be proud!

We had lengthy discussions on elections at the congress and concerns were expressed on the U.S.'s interference in Venezuela's electoral process. Some argued that elections had become a tool of subversion by the capitalist opposition determined to undermine the Bolivarian revolution. They posited that perhaps it was time for the Chavistas to serve the interests of the masses without having to participate in elections. I'm not so sure about this strategy but it had me thinking about Rosa's words in *Reform or Revolution*: "Democracy is indispensable to the working class, because only through the exercise of its democratic rights, in the struggle for democracy, can the proletariat become aware of its class interests and its historic task."[20]

I have faith in the people of Venezuela. I trust they'll make the right choice in the upcoming elections. It is in their interest to say no to agents of imperialism in their country through a democratic process. No underhand tactics by the U.S. will undermine the will of the people.

After the November 21st elections, I can't wait to show my solidarity by tweeting Rosa's, "Only the hammer blow of revolution, that is to say, the conquest of political power by the proletariat can break down the wall between capitalist society and Socialist society."[21]

My biggest takeaway from this congress is that we have to pursue the route of revolution earnestly. Our enemies are resolutely trying to maintain a system that is killing the masses from Caracas to Nairobi. And yet, we have Bernsteins in our midst trying to tell us we can reform this system. To hell with them! Revolution now!

20 Ibid: 94.
21 Ibid: 65-66.

I do trust you and the family are keeping well, comrade. Sending you lots of love.

Always in solidarity,
Mo

PS: I'm feeling horrid, comrade. I think I might be coming down with something. Maybe Covid. It might take a while to get back to you.

Being Human means throwing
(your whole life on the scales of
destiny when need be[22]

---

22 "Being human means throwing your whole life on the scales of destiny when need be." (Luxemburg 2013: 363)

Dear Comrade Mo,

How lovely it seems to travel and participate in a radical congress! Isn't it wonderful when you get to meet friends and comrades from all over the world? It shifts your perspective and the world seems brighter; a future to be won! A different world is possible!

I am curious about the strategies you discussed; did you come up with any concrete proposals to work on? And what will you take with you from the meeting in Venezuela to your important work in Kenya? It is absolutely wonderful to hear about the political work you do – I am especially intrigued by the strategies regarding unionization. In Sweden, the unions are increasingly bureaucratic in structure – Marx anticipated this, of course, and Clara Zetkin, too, in her scathing analysis of the Italian situation in the 1920s as the Fascist movement grew out of the workers' disappointment in the labour movement. There is a very strong bond between the Social Democratic party and the main blue collar labour unions in Sweden, which frankly is a problem as the Social Democratic party is veering farther to the right, losing all ability to even identify reforms highly sought after by the people. I'll tell you more about it. But it is also a problem because the unions lose sight of the bigger picture; they tend to support the Social Democrats no matter the broader consequences, and they are laser focused on achieving the smallest increase in wages or perks for their members. This, of course, is also something that Rosa discussed in *The Mass Strike*:

> The trade-union leaders, constantly absorbed in the economic guerrilla war whose plausible task it is to make the workers place the highest value on the smallest economic achievement, every increase in wages and shortening of the working day, gradually lose the power of seeing the larger connections and of taking a survey of the whole position. Only in this way can one explain why many trade-union leaders refer with the greatest satisfaction to the achievements of the last fifteen years, instead of, on the contrary, emphasising the other side of the medal; the simultaneous and immense reduction of the proletarian standard of life by land usury, by the whole tax and customs policy, by landlord rapacity which has increased house rents to such an exorbitant extent, in short, by all the objective tendencies of bourgeois policy which have largely neutralised the advantages of the fifteen years of trade-union struggle. From the *whole* social democratic truth which, while emphasising the importance of the present work and its absolute necessity, attaches the chief importance to the criticism and the limits to this work, the *half* trade-union truth is taken which emphasises only the positive side of the daily struggle.[23]

---

23 Luxemburg 2008: 177-178.

This could have been written today, certainly it speaks to the Swedish situation.

But I first wanted to let you know what I did yesterday evening, as I was feeling particularly depressed about the political situation in Sweden and in the world. I started by once again reading the Brecht poem you sent me; it is so powerful! The notion of really starting from the standpoint of the enslaved – of course, in one sense that is what Marx did, but it is also what feminists have done, and anti-racists – it is probably, to me, the most promising and inspiring intellectual endeavor. So, yesterday I wanted to feel, physically, the power of this Brecht poem, and I started thinking about my dear friend and comrade in struggle Nela Porobic Isakovic. We grew up together in the movement. She came to Sweden at ten years old, in 1992, from Bosnia and the horrific war that was ravaging Yugoslavia at the time. A few years later we met each other in the youth arm of the Swedish Left Party, the Young Left, and we instantly connected. We were always together! We drew so much strength from each other. And we had fun too, sometimes a little too much fun – we sure could drink together, and we always needed to pee at the same time, so we have spent some time together in restrooms at various bars; it is always good to go with a friend whom you can giggle with, right? I'm sorry if this is too much info but I promise you, some sharp analyses happen at nighttime in ladies' rooms at bars! Anyway, we also used to dance to Manu Chao.

Have you listened to Manu Chao? I guess he's French-Spanish, but he belongs somehow to the extended family of activists of the type who also embody that punk spirit. He put out a live album, "*Radio Bemba Sound System*", in 2002, and it is one of my absolute favorite records of all time. The music is a mix of punk, reggae, salsa, ska, and raï. And it is very political; Chao is close to the Zapatista struggle in Mexico. He sings from the perspective of the undocumented, of the disappeared, of the struggling, of *Pacha Mama* (the earth goddess in Inca mythology; I do believe Manu Chao, like many others, refers to Earth like this, as a way of reminding us to care for the planet). So, I turned on a live concert of his on YouTube and turned up the volume – luckily my kids were super tired from celebrating the first days of summer holidays, so they didn't wake up. Then I texted my dear comrade Nela and we discussed either withdrawing from the world by buying a small farm – or organizing a world revolution. We aren't suited to a farm, I think, so we'll probably continue trying for a world revolution, however far away that may seem at the moment.

Nela is back in Bosnia, and has been for a decade or so. She is doing wonderful work there, fighting right now for the rights of refugees passing through the Balkans on their way to Central and Northern Europe. The oppression and repression these refugees face is horrendous, and Nela is working with NGOs and activist groups to make a difference. She is tired, though, the work is really hard and it's an uphill battle; racism is rampant, as it is across Europe. She'll never give up. I told her once: in the future, you'll either be president of Bosnia, or a political refugee. She laughed and agreed. Yes, probably one of those. But yesterday, we sat on our couches, mine in Lund, southern Sweden, and hers in Sarajevo, central Bosnia, and listened to Manu Chao sing about the undocumented:

Solo voy con mi pena / Sola va mi condena / Correr es mi destino / Para burlar la ley /
Perdido en el corazón / De la grande Babylon / Me dicen "el clandestino" /
Por no llevar papel / Pa' una ciudad del Norte / Yo me fui a trabajar / Mi vida la dejé /
Entre Ceuta y Gibraltar / Soy una raya en el mar / Fantasma en la ciudad /
Mi vida va prohibida / Dice la autoridad [24]

I sang along and felt like screaming *PARA TODOS LA LUZ – PARA TODOS TODO* ("Light for everyone – Everything for Everyone") all night. I had that strange feeling of wanting to party to overcome my depression about where things are going. Perhaps that is what Rosa, as you so beautifully remark, had the ability to do: to enjoy life as a way of enduring life in the struggle. She watched birds and flowers; I need music, I need dance!

So, ok, where are we in Sweden? A lot has happened here lately. The political situation is this: Sweden has a parliamentary system based on proportional representation. Eight parties are in the national parliament (the threshold for representation is 4%). Historically, the majority has shifted along a left/right divide. However, the traditional blocs broke up after the 2018 election wherein neither the left of center nor the bourgeois coalitions were able to amass enough seats. The extreme right-wing party the Sweden Democrats (SD), founded by Nazis and now rehabilitated as just another party on the right, holds about 20% of the vote. The SD together with the Christian Democrats and the Moderate party, which is the old conservative party, holds close to half of the seats in parliament. The other half decided to form a coalition, the so-called January Deal, consisting of the Social Democrats (SAP), the Liberals, the Center party (which used to be the farmers' party but is now a hardcore neoliberal party, probably the most extreme in its economic positions) and the Greens. They agreed on 73 policy issues covering 11 areas, from the economy to the healthcare system to "integration" and housing. However, these parties don't have enough votes to get these 73 items through parliament; they need the Left party. This is the reformed communist party, consisting today of feminists, anti-racists and socialists. The Left party, recognizing that this coalition at least isn't as bad as a coalition involving the SD would be, agreed to passively support the January deal – but issued two warnings: they would not agree to relaxing labour protection laws, and they would never agree to abolish rent control. In Sweden, rents are subject to price control, and tenants have strong protection, making it difficult for landlords to evict people without just cause. This was a major systemic change which was enacted by the labour movement in 1942; one of the first and fundamental achievements of the Social Democratic labour movement which effectively changed the balance between working people and the owning class. However, the system of rent control has been a target of right-wing lobbying efforts for a long time. The bourgeoisie want to introduce so-called market-based rents, wherein each contract is negotiated between landlord and tenant; and since there is a severe housing crisis in Sweden, that would essentially give landlords all the power over housing, pushing us back to a pre-1942 situation. We would have a system like London, or perhaps Nairobi, wherein tenants are powerless and poor. Lobbying organizations

---

24 I go alone with my sorrow/Alone is my sentence/ Running is my destiny/ To evade the law/Lost in the heart/of the grand Babylon/ They call me "the clandestine"/for not having papers/To a city in the North/I went for work/I left behind my life/Between Ceuta and Gibraltar/I'm a streak in the ocean/a ghost in the city/my life is prohibited/say the authorities (Translation by the author).

on the right have suggested that there should be bidding for each contract, and also that tenants should only be allowed to hold a contract for a fixed number of years, after which there would be another bidding for the contract so that "anyone willing to pay more" would be able to take over. So, the Left Party said: these are our two "red lines," and if you cross them, we will no longer support the government and there will be a vote of confidence in parliament.

The reasoning behind the Social Democrats having agreed to right-wing policies is that if they don't, something worse will happen: the Center party and the Liberals may join the right-wing coalition with SD. So, last month, a parliamentary committee proposed market-based rents in new housing developments. Everyone understands that this is just the first step; soon enough, market rents will be introduced throughout the rental sector. The Left party stood their ground, and a vote of confidence was introduced in the parliament, which the Prime Minister lost, since the Sweden Democrats opportunistically took their chance to vote out the sitting Government. The Liberals, no longer a liberal party but a law-and-order party pandering to the SD base, have already announced that they have given up on the January deal and will now enter into a coalition with the Moderates and the Sweden Democrats. This means that for the numbers to add up, the Center party must agree to negotiate with the Left party. However, they argue that there are two extremist parties in parliament, the Left and the SD. So, they're not willing to negotiate with the Left party, creating a deadlock.

At the moment, the Left party is gaining significant support in this mess – more than 4000 new members in just a few days and increasing support in the polls. Also, and this is spectacular to witness: once the political issue being debated is about a proper political conflict like redistribution, the Sweden Democracts seem moot. They have nothing to add, nothing to say. They agree that they are against market-based rents, because they have to; their base definitely would lose out if the system changed. But it's not their question! They do try to argue, of course, that migrants are the problem – no migrants, more apartments – but it doesn't resonate. The Left owns this question. The party chair of the Left, Nooshi Dadgostar, has a background as a housing activist and she is in total control of the issue. This is fantastic, and it shows the weakness of center-left politics in Europe.

The great Swedish sociologist Göran Therborn wrote about this in the *New Left Review* blog recently, arguing that European social democracy got a second chance at power in the 1990s after the first "neoliberal shockwave." But they squandered this opportunity, Therborn writes, possibly forever, through "tone-deaf neoliberal adaptations." However, the Left hasn't stepped up either. While I'm hopeful about Nooshi Dadgostar being able to stand up to Social Democracy, she is also doing that precisely by mimicking industrial social democracy; she even quoted Tage Erlander, perhaps the most successful Social Democratic party leader and Prime Minister (1946-1969) ever, as she took the floor of the *riksdag*, the national legislature, on the day of the vote. Now, it's not that I didn't enjoy seeing a young woman of Iranian descent throwing the words of Erlander in the face of Stefan Löfven, the current party leader and PM; but like Therborn, I wonder if attempting to embody industrial social democracy is sustainable in the long run.

Erlander was interesting, and he is getting renewed attention in Sweden; just recently, the leader of the Reformists, a more progressive group within SAP, came out with a book on Erlander in which he argues that reformist socialism is the future. Well, of course a social democrat would think that, but what does it mean, now that reforms mean bending over for the bourgeoisie who constantly threaten to otherwise bend over for fascists? Erlander thought that taxation was an indication of how socialized a country was. The public sector was, Erlander argued, a way to introduce socialism under capitalism; if 80% of the GDP was represented by tax collection then a country would be in a state of socialism. I wonder, then, what we have in Sweden now, as private companies are profiteering from our schools? We pay taxes, and they are taken by investment firms who now view the Swedish welfare sector as a golden industry, with remarkable profits for shareholders! What is that, if not socialism for the rich?

Sweden was a country with the world's strongest Social Democratic party; the world's strongest trade unions; the world's most organized people – but also the world's most organized capitalist class. Despite this, we now have a perverse system of organized theft wherein social democracy paves the way for capitalists to get rich on the back of school children and the frail elderly. We went through a pandemic which illustrated just how catastrophic it is to sell out hospital pharmacies and introduce just-in-time systems for critical goods such as face masks and respirators. There is not a single reform which has not been the target of ingenious attempts at roll-backs. The SAP is at 28% in the polls; a party with roots in neo-Nazism will soon be on par with them. Reforms? Yes, please, but they're not enough. Rosa was right:

> The mystification is obvious. We know that the present State is not "society" representing "the rising working class". It is itself the representation of capitalist society. It is a class state. Therefore its reform measures are not an application of "social control," that is, the control of society working freely in its own labour process. They are forms of control applied by the class organisation of Capital to the production of Capital.[25]

I think that, for too long, the Social Democrats in Sweden got this mixed up; they thought that they were the State, and that the State did represent the "rising working class." And so, they believe whatever they do, whatever compromise they strike, whatever they concede, they do it as the State representing the People. But they no longer represent working-class people, they represent the powerful interests of the State, which is something else entirely. The disappointment leads people to give up on politics, and worse, to imagine that the true community is the Nation. That is the path of fascism. The Left must learn to recognize this always, and I think we will learn this lesson if we truly take in the wisdom of Luxemburg (and Zetkin, too).

Dear Mo, I am so happy that we have connected. I feel empowered by our exchange. I feel closer to the spirit of Rosa. We have connections now from Caracas to Nairobi to Lund to Sarajevo and across the world. On the one hand, I feel that the local situation in each country must take centre stage and that we should be inspired by Manu Chao: a transnational, eclectic and spirited resistance growing out of communities and barrios, speaking the language of each and all. On the other hand,

---

25 Ibid: 58-59.

I feel that maybe we should enter into a formal organization, a revolutionary force directly inspired by Rosa: The Rosa Luxemburg International. But then again, she would detest that kind of idolization, wouldn't she? The power of critique, that was Rosa Luxemburg. I don't know what the best way forward is, I only know that the only way forward is together.

My dear Mo, I hope you are feeling well. Do let me know what is going on in your life. Have you read anything new? And tell me this: would you like to dance with me sometime? Dance to the revolution, drink to the revolution, and the next day, work for the revolution!

Light for all, power for all,

Rosene

Masstrejken, som den framträder i den ryska revolutionen, är en sådan föränderlig företeelse, att den återspeglar alla faser av den politiska och ekonomiska kampen, och alla de olika stadierna i revolutionen.[26]

26 "The mass strike, as the Russian Revolution shows it to us, is such a changeable phenomenon that it reflects all the phases of the political and economic struggle, all stages and factors of the revolution. Its adaptability, its efficiency, the factors of its origin are constantly changing. It suddenly opens new and wide perspectives of the revolution when it appears to have already arrived in a narrow pass and where it is impossible for anyone to reckon upon it with any degree of certainty." (Luxemburg 2008: 140)

C de Rebecca,

I was meaning to get back to you earlier but I've been fighting a bout of Covid. The lethargy, the malaise! I was in the depths of this thing. I've never felt so sick before. Once this terrible episode is firmly behind me, I am going to make it my life's mission to fight the vaccine apartheid that has denied millions in the Global South access to this life-saving jab.

I can't wait to get back to organizing. I feel like I've been away for such a long time. Being forced to isolate with not much to do has been excruciating but has also allowed me to sort of simmer down and just reflect on a lot of things. Like, how we are going to survive the inevitable pushback (in the form of sanctions or worse) from the U.S. if the Socialist evolution happens here in our lifetime?

At the Congress in Caracas I met amazing women from all over Venezuela and away from all the politicking, we got to hang out and over a bottle of rum, I got some really ingenious hacks on how to make scarce resources stretch. Like recycling soap bars and using crayons in lieu of lipstick! I kid you not. The blockade has made these women really resourceful. I hate that they have had to resort to this but on the flip side, they're sticking it up to mindless consumerism in a capitalist world. It felt great kicking back and sharing stories over *caraotas negras*, a black bean dish, and corn-husk *tamales*. They were delish!

So, about the takeaways from the congress. Many of the African delegates pledged to establish Bolívar-Chávez centres in their home countries. These centres will be the bridges connecting our homes and Venezuela as we work together to fight U.S. hegemony, which continues to wreak havoc in the Global South. Now that we are witnessing the increasing assault in Cuba, it's crucial that we get to work.

In her 1913 speech delivered in Leipzig, our good sis Rosa said, "Every proletarian man and woman must today say to him- or herself: everything that happens in foreign policy affects the proletariat's interests."[27] It is imperative that our comrades on the continent understand that what is happening in Venezuela and Cuba affects them too. And eventually, it will catch up with us.

Right now, I'm listening to Manu Chao's album on loop. It is a bop! I'm loving the reggae influence. Thank you so much for introducing me to him, comrade. This is the push I needed to finally start my *Español* lessons.

What else? Yesterday, I watched a documentary on the Bosnian genocide and thought of your friend Nela and how she overcame so much to become the formidable woman she is today and how she has applied herself to help others like her. Rosa would be proud! She embodies so much of her spirit. Please pass on my regards to her and let her know she has a comrade in Kenya. The rundown you gave

---

27 See Luxemburg 1913.

85

of the political situation in Sweden has me going down a rabbit hole. Now I'm liking and retweeting expletives directed towards Jimmie Åkesson on Twitter! That's how invested I am. I really want Nooshi Dadgostar and the Left party to get their act together and do what's right for the people and not make silly concessions to the enemy.

The political situation in Sweden right now might seem chaotic and all over the place but if you ask me, it's benign compared to what is currently happening in Kenya. Now that the state and the predatory International Monetary Fund (IMF) have reached an agreement on (negative) economic policies, we are witnessing in real time the negative impact of Structural Adjustment Programs: Fees at public universities have skyrocketed, public hospitals might as well ask for vital organs in lieu of payment, and many Kenyans can barely afford to eat. All the while, our lame-duck president and his Deputy are engaged in a stupid battle for supremacy. Mainstream politicking here has become unbearably banal and I would take an adventurist, anarchy uprising over this nonsense at this point. But I've got to stay focused and look at the bigger picture. Mobilize, Educate and Organize.

I'd like to say yes. A thousand times yes to your Rosa Luxemburg International proposal. Let's do it comrade. Where do we start? I'm ready!

I do hope you're having a great time with your family this summer, comrade. How are the kids loving it so far? I can't wait to come visiting next summer. You, Nela and I will have so much fun dancing to Manu Chao and reading letters from this book. A girl can dream!

Always in solidarity,
Mo

References

Brecht, Bertolt (2021), "We hear." Translation for this book by Tom Kuhn.

Brecht, Bertolt (2018), *The Collected Poems of Bertolt Brecht*. Eds. Tom Kuhn and David Constantine. Harrisonburg: LSC Communications.

Brie, Michael (2019), "Show Us the Wonder! Where is Your Wonder?" *Rosa Luxemburg Stiftung*. Accessed on 18.08.21, at https://www.rosalux.de/en/publication/id/39794/show-us-the-wonder-where-is-your-wonder.

Harvey, David (2010), "Crises of Capitalism." RSA Animate. *You Tube*. Accessed on 08.08.2021, at https://www.youtube.com/watch?v=qOP2V_np2c0.

Luxemburg, Rosa (1913), "Another view at things." *GHDI*. Accessed on 14.06.2021, at https://ghdi.ghi-dc.org/sub_document.cfm?document_id=781.

Luxemburg, Rosa (1918), "Letter to Sophie Liebknecht," *Marxist Internet Archive*. Accessed on 27.07.21, at https://www.marxists.org/archive/luxemburg/1918/03/24.htm.

Luxemburg, Rosa (1982), *Gesammelte Briefe. Band 2*. Institut für Marxismus-Leninismus beim ZK der SED. Berlin: Dietz Verlag.

Luxemburg, Rosa (1987), *Gesammelte Briefe. Band 5*. Institut für Marxismus-Leninismus beim ZK der SED. Berlin: Dietz Verlag.

Luxemburg, Rosa (2004), *The Rosa Luxemburg Reader*. Eds. Peter Hudis and Kevin B. Anderson. New York: Monthly Review Press.

Luxemburg, Rosa (2008), *The Essential Rosa Luxemburg: Reform or Revolution & The Mass Strike*. Ed. Helen Scott. Chicago: Haymarket Books.

Luxemburg, Rosa (2013), *The Letters of Rosa Luxemburg*. Eds. Georg Adler, Peter Hudis, and Annelies Laschitza. London and New York: Verso Books.

Wasi'o jitahudi kusonga
hawatambui minyororo zao. [28]

---

28 "Those who do not move, do not notice their chains." (No reference)

Rosa Luxemburg

Philatelistenverband der DDR im DKB, Bezirksverband Potsdam

4. Sevgi Doğan

&

Paul Mason

Dear Paul,

Even though in the past I used to write letters with a pen and paper, today it seems somewhat strange to exchange letters with a person when there are such simpler and speedier ways to communicate. Some time back, during our graduate education at Istanbul University (one of the most politically active universities at the time), I and one of my friends with whom I still, sometimes, exchange letters, had this strange, romantic and nostalgic idea of keeping the tradition of handwritten correspondence alive. I remember that in the first year of university, I wrote a letter to a political prisoner whose address I'd found in *Leman*, a political humour magazine. Thinking how it was important for a prisoner to receive a letter from the *outside*, I decided to write to him so we could speak of life and perhaps even some political issues. I soon received a letter from him, full of philosophical and political thoughts, but my family became worried about our correspondence as they feared it may lead to some problems for my education. So unfortunately, I stopped writing, and I also stopped sharing my political activities with my parents so as not to worry them again.

This idea of correspondence reminds us of the idea of digitalization, which is high on our agenda nowadays due to the Covid pandemic. I suppose that one of the most important things that we realize at this time when we are locked in at home and communication is largely limited to digital tools is how valuable 'dialogue and conversation,' that is 'relation,' as well as 'nature' and 'freedom' are. Sitting at the table under the window of my attic room, looking out at the sky, I try to meditate upon the concepts of 'freedom,' 'correspondence' and 'imprisonment/deprivation' together. In Turkish, the latter, *'mahkûmiyet/mahrumiyet,'* seem almost the same word; just one letter separates them from each other. This similarity tempts me to view imprisonment as a kind of deprivation, that is the deprivation of *freedom* and *right*, which is something that can immediately be applied to Rosa Luxemburg who was so often deprived of her freedom by being imprisoned.

I am reflecting on these concepts while the sun appears and disappears among the clouds and there is a smell of sadness in the air that accompanies light rain and wind. Yet just yesterday the warmth of the sun carried a mood of optimism to the people who are sentenced to remain at their homes under the blue sky. As I walked along the ancient aqueduct active between the seventeenth and twentieth centuries that crosses the countryside from Asciano Pisano to Pisa, seeing the yellow and purple flowers lying along the road, I enjoyed this view and thought that the inhabitants of a few large and small houses on the very green mountains of Pisa had completed the day with this magnificent view.

Thanks to her literary ability, Luxemburg would, of course, describe my short nature walk much better than me. We can see this ability in one of her letters to Leo Jogiches (dated March 20, 1893), for instance, in which she portrays a walk in nature near her house, leading us to imagine a grey sky "covered with clouds of different sizes and different shadings" and having "the look of a deep, stormy sea;" and then she continues to make us enjoy a landscape beautified with the descriptions of Lake

Geneva, the mountains of Switzerland, the nature abounding with flowers around which "bees are buzzing."[1]

While I am thinking about Luxemburg's interest in nature, occasionally the darkening sky makes almost harmonious sounds on the window, with small raindrops adding pessimism to the romance created by the idea of correspondence. In this case, with you, Paul. Of course, the pessimism that creeps over the 21st century is not the fault of the weather. Rather, the dark sky is like a reminder of the dark times we're living in, times in which Luxemburg's question of "Socialism or Barbarism" is once more of crucial importance, as the pandemic and its consequences have again revealed the barbarity of capitalism.

This leads me to ask myself: how did Rosa Luxemburg remain so luminous and clear about her principles considering the dark times she lived in? In one of her letters from prison to Mathilde Wurm, while trying to encourage her friend to be stronger in these dark times, Luxemburg expresses her feelings for life and confesses that despite "all its horrors" she continues to love it. Her clarity of mind is noticeable by the flow and naturalness of words sliding from her pen:

> To be a human being is the main thing, above all else. And that means: to be firm and clear and cheerful, yes, cheerful in spite of everything and anything, because howling is the business of the weak. To be a human being means to joyfully toss your entire life 'on the giant scales of fate' if it must be so, and at the same time to rejoice in the brightness of every day and the beauty of every cloud. Oh, I do not know any recipe that can be written down on how to be a human being, I only know when a person is one, and you too always used to know when we walked together through the fields of Südende for hours at a time and the red glow of evening lay upon the stalks of grain. The world is so beautiful, with all its horrors, and would be even more beautiful if there were no weaklings or cowards in it.[2]

At this stage, I would like to tell you a little bit about my own dark times and then I shall come back to Luxemburg's letter. I come from a Kurdish-Alawite family that lives in Turkey. Because of the political and religious conflicts between the minority Alawite and the majority Sunni Muslims in the 1990s, my family tried to hide their being Alawite for fear of discrimination. At the same time, due to the Kurdish conflict, my family rejected being Kurdish as they did not agree with the armed struggle waged by the PKK. So, from an early age, I grew up with this refusal and concealing of our ethnic and religious identities, and I was told by my parents many times not to tell anyone about our background. For me, however, it seemed so absurd to conceal this identity and so I continued to express who I was, even though I am not a believer. But of course, the discrimination was real, and I experienced it frequently. In terms of my being Kurdish, while studying at Istanbul University in 2001, I signed a petition demanding education in the Kurdish language, as a result of which I was suspended. Coming from a low-income family, we were very concerned that I would lose my right to education and that I might even be imprisoned, but fortunately, in those days, we still had a somewhat functional justice system, and I

1 Luxemburg 2013a: 3.
2 Ibid: 363-364.

was able to continue my studies having lost only one semester. Then, there were the dark times, because of my ethnical background *and* my ideological convictions. For example, after finishing my PhD in Italy, I returned to Turkey with great expectations of finding a job at a university. However, when I applied for a position in one of the public universities, due to my published political writings I was judged as being a sympathizer of the Kurdish party HDP and consequently denied the position. And while I was lucky never to have spent time in jail, I know of many people, some of whom are my friends, who were repeatedly imprisoned for their allegedly subversive political activities.

Considering all these personal dark times, Luxemburg's words bring to mind the issue of *the right to life*: I mean, how can a person/human being simply take away another person's ability to see the changes that the sun creates in nature, the opening of flowers, the breathing of leaves, the snow melting in the mountains and the floating of small currents?

In Turkey, anyone can be simply investigated, arrested, convicted, detained, and imprisoned. Following the failed coup in 2016, more than 41,000 people were arrested and more than 100,000 were suspended or dismissed from the public service, including professors, teachers and judges. Many journalists, in addition to the loss of their jobs, were and are still being imprisoned. The political regime takes people's lives away just like that. But I ask myself why this is happening again when we have witnessed so many dramatic and *catastrophic* examples in history just a few decades ago, in Germany and here in Italy? I guess one explanation is that wo/man is a being who finds it hard to learn from human history, and that a lack and/or denial of historical memory leads to many other catastrophes. A retrospective reading and analysis of past events will demonstrate how similar processes happened throughout human history. This is obvious in the work of Luxemburg and Antonio Gramsci, especially in their thoughts about the rise of authoritarian and fascist regimes. In his *Prison Notebooks*, Gramsci defined the Italian political crisis as *catastrofica*, which can also be applied to today's political crisis in Turkey. Gramsci writes:

> [...] the historical events which have culminated in a great 'heroic' personality. Caesarism can be said to express a situation in which the forces in conflict balance each other in a *catastrophic* [italics mine] manner; that is to say, they balance each other in such a way that a continuation of the conflict can only terminate in their reciprocal destruction.[3]

In other words, in the battle between forces, in which there are neither losers nor victors, the new cannot be born, and the balance between them turns out to be *catastrophic*, dramatic and *aggressive*. We can see this aggressive, Ceasarian attitude from the Turkish regime's attack on academics (e.g. the recent 'top-down' appointment of the rector of Boğaziçi University), the incessant demands for the closure of HDP, and the withdrawal from an international treaty, the *Istanbul Convention*, protecting women's rights, again through a 'top-down' decision by the president of the republic. Before Gramsci ended up in prison and at a time when fascism was slowly beginning to emerge, in his 1921 article "Legalità" (legality), he talks about how the bourgeois class came to power by defending and exercising

3 Gramsci 1992: 219.

the right to vote and free organization first, but by opposing these rights when they became threatening to themselves. Similarly, Luxemburg, in reflecting on "The Nationalities Question" in her 1918 booklet *The Russian Revolution*, warned that the bourgeoisie will do whatever it takes to turn the popular vote in their favour,

> Even without German military occupation, the famous "popular plebiscite," supposing that it had come to that in the border states, would have yielded a result, in all probability, which would have given the Bolsheviks little cause for rejoicing; for we must take into consideration the psychology of the peasant masses and of great sections of the petty bourgeoisie, and the thousand ways in which the bourgeoisie could have influenced the vote. Indeed, it can be taken as an unbreakable rule in these matters of plebiscites on the national question that the ruling class will either know how to prevent them where it doesn't suit their purpose, or where they somehow occur, will know how to influence their results by all sorts of means, big and little, the same means which make it impossible to introduce socialism by a popular vote.[4]

Gramsci's and Luxemburg's statements on the right to vote and the influencing of plebiscites are directly relevant to the situation of today's democracy in Turkey. For example, the ruling class and authoritarian regime lost the election for the Istanbul Metropolitan Municipality in 2019, only to subsequently cancel the results with the help of the Supreme Election Committee (note: they lost the repeat election as well). In fact, when it came to power in 2002, thanks to free and fair elections, the government of Erdoğan described itself as one of the people and against the political elites (sounds familiar?). However, over the years he has done nothing but humiliate and disdain people when criticism and public dissatisfaction are expressed and directed against him. Just three examples: Erdoğan did not hesitate to say the following words about the 2009 strike of the Tekel workers after their state company was sold to British American Tobacco: "feet will be heads!"; in the same vein, during the Gezi resistance in 2013, he used the word "çapulcu" (marauder) to describe the protesters; finally, in 2016, he defined intellectuals as "so-called intellectuals," "terrorists" and "traitors" for signing a petition defending human rights.

In sum, I wonder whether, as Luxemburg points out, we can come up with a "recipe" for how to be a human being? I do not know if we can say dialectically that the crisis of capitalism – or as Gramsci puts it, the catastrophe of capitalism – will inevitably turn itself into a new humanity or a resurrection of a new humanism. Perhaps we need to redefine what humanism means in light of the 21st century?

I am aware that these are huge questions but at least we may try to reflect on them. As Luxemburg says: "but when the whole world is out of joint, then I merely seek to understand what is going on and why, and then I have done my duty, and I am calm and in good spirits from then on. *Ultra posse nemo obligatur*."[5]

---

4 Luxemburg 2004: 296.
5 Luxemburg 2013a: 366.

I look forward to receiving your letter very soon.

I am sending my very joyful greetings from Pisa...

Sevgi...

PS: I am sending you a Turkish song called *"Insan Insan"* (Human Human) asking what it is to be human.[6]

Pisa Aqueduct

---

6 Listen at: https://www.youtube.com/watch?v=fEzpsVi1Qd0. Lyrics at https://lyricstranslate.com/en/insan-insan-human-human.html.

Dear Sergi

Thank you for your letter. My reply is late because I was on a deadline trying to copy-edit the proofs of my forthcoming book, *How To Stop Fascism*. And also because I am, temporarily and in a limited sense, 'free.' Last week the prohibition on cross-border travel within the UK ended, and I was able to drive five and a half hours to my caravan on the Welsh coast, and walk at last along the cliffs and woodlands.

It's still bitterly cold here but every day the sky has been clear blue. The sea is sparkling and suddenly all food tastes good again. The English winter is always dark and cold, but the lockdown and the social tensions it has increased – which are evident every day too in the anger expressed against me on Twitter, both by the far right and the Stalinist Left – made it one of the bleakest winters I can remember.

The passage you quote from Luxemburg's letters, where she defines being human as the capacity "to joyfully toss your entire life 'on the giant scales of fate' if it must be so, and at the same time to rejoice in the brightness of every day and the beauty of every cloud" is a great starting point for our exchange. At the age of 61 I can at least say I've tried to do that – although not enough.

Let me start by telling you how I first encountered Rosa Luxemburg. I was sent to a Catholic grammar school – a free but elitist school designed to train future priests, administrators, police officers, etc. I knew before I went there that I was an atheist, but only at the age of 16 did I get to read *The Communist Manifesto*, which was in the school library, complete with an introduction explaining why Marxism was wrong.

I understood there and then the basic principles of historical materialism: that history is driven by class antagonism, that capitalism – with its unique and relentless technological change – logically prepares the conditions for a classless society, that the bourgeoisie are a bunch of hypocritical assholes, and that the general working class culture around me – at this time, moulded around racist, sexist 'comedy' on state-run TV – was only an 'ideology,' and could be blown away through the experience of struggle.

I decided I would wait until going to university to become a political activist, as my small town – Leigh in Lancashire, England – had absolutely zero political life or culture beyond the heavily bureaucratic trade union movement. On arrival at Sheffield University in September 1978 I went up to the socialist students' stall and demanded to know why all the Left groups were obsessed with Leon Trotsky, and not with Antonio Gramsci. To prepare for my sudden liberation from home and school, I had been reading *Gramsci For Beginners*, and agreed with the idea of a long, slow, cultural and ideological project to prepare the revolution (this was the era of Punk Rock).

The person who answered became my lifelong friend – Matthew Cobb, now professor of zoology at Manchester, and a historian of the French Resistance. He explained that a massive class battle was coming, that Gramsci was the icon of the Eurocommunists who had abandoned the trade union struggle, and that Leninism was the only way forward. There would be no time for a long, slow cultural struggle – and the Eurocommunists were actually arguing that industrial battles were pointless.

University life became one giant and endless political meeting. All around us were undefeated and well-organised workers, a Labour Party that was suddenly swinging to the left, and the intellectual ferment of post-structuralism: everyone was either a Trotskyist, a Maoist or a self-proclaimed Althusserian. In the midst of all this, I became aware that everyone was, in one way or another, involved in a "break with Luxemburgism." In short, I knew about the British Left's "break with Luxemburg" before I knew about Luxemburg!

Here's the background. After May 1968, and the massive demo against the Vietnam War in October that year, two parallel things happened: the rank and file workers took a turn to spontaneous action, independent of the union officials, creating grassroots networks around 'shop stewards' – what Rosa would have known as *Obleute*. And in parallel, a non-Stalinist Left appeared.

Anarchism was weak in Britain because it was highly libertarian and detached from the working class. As the communist movement splintered, after the Prague Spring, the 68 generation began looking for a form of socially liberal revolutionary politics – distinct from Leninism, because they hated the idea of democratic centralism. The most dynamic group, the International Socialists (later the SWP) never exactly described themselves as Luxemburgists, but for a time they propagated the idea that (a) workers could be spontaneously revolutionary, and (b) the party has to be the creation of, and the servant of, the mass movement – not the other way around.

This, to my certain knowledge, was the only form of Leftism ever actually accepted by the shop stewards of my father's generation. They were miners, printers, engineering workers, factory workers, dockers... they knew instinctively that they did not need a vanguard cadre party to achieve what they were trying to achieve. They believed in their own, spontaneously generated, political culture. They didn't need to read Luxemburg's *The Mass Strike*, because in February 1974 they had actually brought down the Conservative government through a mass strike. But then, around 1975-76, the union bureaucrats took back control, signed collaboration deals with the Labour government, and there began what the SWP leader Tony Cliff called "the downturn" in the class struggle. The first time I heard the term, I assumed it would be temporary; so did everyone else. Instead, it was the first stage of the permanent defeat and dissolution of the working-class movement I grew up in.

The British Left's response to the downturn was actually intelligent, and drew from the experience of educated worker activists. They reasoned: a massive showdown is coming – either we defeat the capitalists, or they smash us. It can't go on like this. So, the politics of the post-68 Left are not enough. We need something stronger. This was the time when most of the New Left swung firmly towards Trotskyism – a more acceptable and revolutionary form of Leninism, still distinct from the 'tankies' of the CP, and still wedded to rank-and-file action. The workers were demanding something stronger than 'Luxemburgism' and the Left now supplied it.

I remember going to a meeting with Tony Cliff, where he would say, "Lenin and Trotsky were right on the party question, Rosa was wrong." These were big meetings, not just students but factory workers attending, and at the back were always feminists, who had rejected Leninism, and every time Cliff said the word "Rosa" they would shout "Luxemburg!"

That was my introduction to Luxemburg: as someone wrong on the question of spontaneity, wrong on the National Question, who had inexplicably flipped into participation in the doomed Spartakist insurrection, and whose book *The Accumulation of Capital* had given Stalinism the ammunition for the underconsumptionist thesis.

Luxemburg, for those who came into politics this way, was used as a kind of 'bad example.' But because, despite all my Leninist indoctrination, I continued to believe in the spontaneity of the masses, and liked her writing, and there were few other female revolutionary role models, I was, and have remained, determined to "do her justice," even if only – as in the final article "Order Reigns In Berlin" – as a chronicler of defeat.

Well, over the next five years we were defeated. The last great mass strike in British history – the one-year long miners' strike from 1984-85 – demonstrated the weakness of both the syndicalist spontaneity of the workers and the book-learned Leninism of the Left. If we are talking about 'dark times,' for me the immediate aftermath of the defeat of the working class was the darkest. I was moved by your account of growing up as an Alawite-Kurd: people like me have never had to hide who we are, because we are part of the white, European, Christian imperialist horde brought up to believe, as WEB Du Bois put it, that we have "ownership of the earth forever." Nevertheless, to be any kind of Marxist in the era when much of the working class was rejecting solidarity, community and co-operation in favour of the dictatorship of the market and the individual was a great education in ostracism! Then neoliberal globalisation took off, leaving those of us who remained revolutionary Marxists looking to the Global South for inspiration: to Nicaragua, the struggle in Chiapas and of course the anti-apartheid revolt in South Africa.

Attempting to innovate within historical materialism at this time was difficult but possible. The differences between humanist Marxists and the dominant anti-humanism of the structuralists seemed secondary. As a new historical subject emerged – the more networked, educated, individualistic city-dwelling generation, which I think is a kind of sublated proletariat – they were highly attracted to anti-capitalism, but saw Marxism like a 'pick and mix' stall in the supermarket: they would take from it what they needed and discard the rest.

It was only during the upsurge that began in December 2010 – with the Tunisian revolt and the London student occupations – that I began to realise that, huddled within this single beleaguered tradition of Marxism were actually 'two Marxisms' and that they were incompatible: the anti-humanism shared by the Stalinists and post-structuralists, and the democratic humanism of the horizontalist and environmental Left. By now, most young Leftists and demonstrators were thoroughly imbued with the thought-patterns of postmodernism. Though they might reject as absurd Baudrillard on the Iraq war, and few had read Deleuze and Guattari, the Leftism that emerged spontaneously during the 2011 uprisings was implicitly anti-humanist.

I am still grappling with the question of why that happened. I think it is, first, because the anti-humanist interpretation of Marx begun (arguably) by Engels, Plekhanov, Labriola etc. solidified into a common doctrine shared not just by the Communist parties but by a generation of academics who had also been Trotskyists. Trotsky, like Luxemburg, was a personally humanistic Marxist who never theorised, and indeed could not theorise, his humanism *within* Marxism. Luxemburg could not have even known about the existence of the 1844 writings or the *Grundrisse*; Trotsky, who could have known about the former, makes no reference to them.

So for the 'heterodox' saints in the pantheon of Marxism as I learned it – Trotsky, Luxemburg, Gramsci – the questions you and I study: Marx as a much more "Hegelian" figure than most will admit, Marx as a radical humanist, Marxism as a philosophy of human freedom – were untheorised. There is then a straight line via Althusser and Foucault to the default ideology of many young protesters today: that human beings are just really machines; that history is a process without a subject (i.e. a machine); that cause and effect are disjointed, with 'power' – that nebulous concept borrowed from Nietzsche and Bergson by Foucault and the postmodernists – now more important than class, gender and ethnicity in the understanding of unfreedom.

What I saw in the squares of Greece and Spain in 2011, in the mass riots triggered by the student protests in London, and then in Gezi Park in 2013 were, I believe, the '1905' of the revolution that is coming. I saw young people determined to use the network technologies designed to enslave them as tools for self-liberation. I saw them create their own definitions of freedom and try to create – in the here and now, just as Luxemburg taught – the advance forms of the society they wished to build. (In the case of Gezi Park, it involved drinking beer openly, wearing leotards, doing yoga, showing your midriff and for the school students, doing their homework together on the grass, or collecting food and handing it out for free, or dancing arm in arm in defiance of Erdogan and his elderly rhetoric).

But the Marxism they reached for was not good enough. It has been over-academicised. It has become tolerant of side-by-side interpretations – so that no matter how clearly you or I might show that Marxism is a form of humanism, and has profound continuities with Hegelian and Aristotelian philosophy, that is "just your opinion." Postmodernism robbed academia of its common standards of truth and logic, while the defeat of the working class robbed us of that ultimate test: does it make sense to them, can they live by it, can they co-create Marxism through their struggles.

Having lived through the 1905 stage, we are now (in Russian parallel) in the Stolypin Reaction phase. Trump, Erdogan, Bolsonaro, Modi, Putin, Duterte – large parts of the world are run by populist ethno-nationalist gargoyles, while in the wings the new version of the Black Hundreds, the alt-right, propagate the myth of a coming global ethnic civil war. In the face of it, not only is social-democracy paralysed and in retreat, but all the new 'isms' – horizontalism, radical leftism, the left nationalisms and the ecological protest movement – are in crisis.

I experienced two defeats between 2015 and 2019: of Syriza in Greece and of Corbyn's Labour Party in Britain. Thousands of young protesters flooded to Syriza between 2011 and 2015. They transformed its character. Even lifelong anarchists became cadres of what was still, essentially, a Eurocommunist party. I didn't realise until I got on the inside that, when they hold central committee meetings, the meetings fill a small cinema and the front ten rows are grey haired men, who have "learned nothing and forgotten nothing" from the era of Togliatti. It was they who, despite all the rhetoric of Tsipras and the hope generated by the activists, just wanted a chance to govern Greece as reformists. They never took seriously preparing the masses for revolt; they didn't know what to do; they never in my experience actually appeared on the streets. They expected the Althusserian history machine – the "process without a subject" – to do the job.

I was amazed, but should not have been, to find that within the Corbyn movement the dominant form of Marxism was this same, ossified, anti-humanist thought. The remnants of British communism never bothered to explain the collapse of the Soviet Union, or engage with the revelations of inhumanity that emerged afterwards, or – and this proved important in the collapse of Corbynism – to accept the vast anti-Semitism perpetrated by Stalinism during its coverup of the specifically Jewish aspects of the Holocaust. New faces appeared, young academics who knew all about Nietzsche, Althusser, Foucault and Judith Butler but regarded early Marxism as "Hegelian rubbish;" the same ones believed Stalinist brutalism in architecture was actually beautiful, or did uncritical PhDs on socialist realism in art. Weirdly, it turns out that anti-humanist Marxism is like the tardigrade – a tiny creature that can withstand any hostile conditions. It has become a form of eternal fatalism.

So, the same kind of people that sabotaged the Syriza government sabotaged the Corbyn movement in Britain. I could devote a whole letter to what Rosa Luxemburg might have said about them! People who only wanted a job in the bureaucracy. People with a pet theory who only wanted the chance to give lectures about that theory, unchallenged by their peers. Corbyn operated the same kind of bureaucracy as the Labour right wing did; he refused to democratise the party selection processes; and under the influence of the economic nationalism of revived Stalinism, he tried to enact a 'left Brexit' – alienating wide sections of the progressive, urban, ethnic minority vote.

Basically, because the revolutionary generation – Luxemburg, Trotsky and Gramsci – never fully engaged with the theoretical and philosophical crisis of Marxism, we are left with a self-replicating anti-humanism. The experience of Corbyn and Syriza convinced me of what EP Thompson famously wrote in his 1978 book *The Poverty of Theory*: there are two Marxisms and they are not compatible. In the work of Luxemburg, they exist separately in the public and private spheres. In private she is a thorough and complete humanist. In public, she bridges the chasm with the famous phrase: history will do its work, see that you do your work.

I remain, like Luxemburg, philosophically cheerful. Capitalism is producing clowns like Erdogan, Putin, Bolsonaro etc. because it cannot produce anything better. It is alive only because of the oxygen tent of central bank money and state support. The planet is signalling its rejection of this 250-year-old system based on waste and carbon. At some point the reactionary phase will end. The sources of hope are everywhere – from Kurdistan, to the women's demonstrations over the Istanbul conventions, to the big demo I hope will happen here in the UK over COP26.

The point now is to make sure that in this phase there is a real and thorough philosophical revival and modernization of Marxism. Not because Marxism alone has all the answers, but because in its blurred, anti-humanist form it is guiding people towards the wrong ones. As Rosa said: "True Marxism fights also against those who seek to falsify it."[7]

In Solidarity

Paul

---

7 Luxemburg 2004: 363.

The leadership has failed. Even so, the leadership can and must be recreated from the masses, and out of the masses.[8]

8 "The leadership has failed. Even so, the leadership can and must be recreated for the masses, and out of the masses." (Luxemburg 2004: 378)

Dear Paul,

I am glad to receive your deep and intense letter. It is a strange coincidence that when I am writing to you the sky is overcast and coloured with grey. Sometimes early in the morning you find yourself "in a completely lousy mood" as Luxemburg said in one of her letters and this weather does not help you to collect yourself. On the other hand, yesterday a lockdown was concluded for some of the regions including Tuscany. It is good news, at least you can now see more people out in the streets, visiting bars and restaurants, which is really helpful to overcome this "lousy mood."[9]

Your story about how you encountered Rosa Luxemburg describes clearly the general historical panorama of the British Left and the perception of Marxism and Marx's ideas at that period after the 1970s. But your description also explains its relation to Luxemburg and the humanist aspect of Marxism. I always think that *The Communist Manifesto* should be read in schools, in order to teach students how capitalism is harmful; but your experience demonstrates that quite the contrary happened.

Your words about Stalinism (or Stalinist 'tankies') remind me of a book by Gustaw Herling, *Il pellegrino della libertà* (The Pilgrim of Freedom). Herling was a Jewish-Polish dissident and writer during WW II. In one of his accounts, he talks about his experiences in the forced labour camp of Kargopol in Arkhangelsk in Russia between 1941-1942. In another account, he explains that when Hitler occupied Poland in September 1939, he started to organize one of the first underground newspapers to fight for the independence of Poland through the pen. Finally, Herling also described the anti-democratic referendum carried out by the Soviet Union after WWII, which tried to align Poland to the USSR, and the terrifying political atmosphere during those years. He expounded that those who considered themselves to be "true" communists were actually those individuals blindly loyal to everything that Stalin said and who hence did not dare to criticize any decisions of the regime. Regarding that, he wrote that "every free word, the slightest criticism by a more open-minded communist, if expressed in such circumstances as to be heard by the most faithful comrades, was sufficient for the NKVD to justify a ten-year sentence."[10]

Given accounts such as these, I ask myself how the Stalinists can justify and/or deny such historical experiences, evidences or testimonies? And this is still going on today. I once told a Kurdish communist friend of mine about my Ukrainian friend's family's experience during the Stalinist period, and he told me flat out that they were telling lies aimed at discrediting the Soviet heritage. So I wonder, if it so easy to deny people's concrete experiences, why should we not believe the Turkish nationalists when they claim that there is no Kurdish question or that there was no Armenian genocide, stating that Kurdish and Armenian people want to denigrate

---

9 Luxemburg 2013a: 371.
10 Herling 2006: 28.

102

the Republic of Turkey, which is what Erdoğan is saying again these days? I can only assume that this behaviour of the traditional Left implies that they ignore the subjects and their history, or rather that they divide them into two camps: those who believe(d) in Stalin and those who criticize(d) him; moreover, they appear to try to keep the "reality of history" hidden in order to escape from having to face the facts.

I presume that when Luxemburg criticizes the centralism of the party, she seeks to reflect her concern about the emergence of authoritarianism and of restrictions on all forms of liberty/freedom. History, unfortunately, proved her foresight. The history of Marxism shows us that the role of the subject in the revolutionary transformation of society and how to structure a relationship between subjects and objects, or between subjectivity and objectivity, is one of the key recurring problems that must constantly be addressed. Of course, Luxemburg and Gramsci also dealt with this question of subjects in both practice and theory. As to the role of the historic subject, Luxemburg puts consciousness as a way to freedom at the centre of the question. In 1908, in one of her speeches she said that "what the masses lack is general enlightenment, the theory which gives us the possibility of systematizing the hard facts and forging them into a deadly weapon to use against our opponents." And in another text, she maintains that "[n]o, it is not the organization that comes before everything else, but it is above all the revolutionary *spirit of enlightenment!*"[11] In other words, theory, consciousness, and philosophy are crucial elements of Luxemburg's understanding of revolutionary struggle. Her outlook echoes that of Gramsci's approach to Marxism as ideology. Gramsci's analysis of the changes created by fascist ideology and culture within Italian society displays that the ruling class established its hegemony by ideological apparatus and so by passive revolution. Therefore, the working class must use its own ideology, i.e. Marxism, as a means to fight against bourgeois ideology. Marxism can and must be an ideological apparatus to struggle against capitalism, it is not only an end in itself!

Your letter clearly reveals the practical and theoretical problems of Marxism through historical uprisings and rebellions in different parts of the world, and the incapacity of leftist parties to carry the mass movements to a revolutionary and transformative moment. So, it seems that the problem is still about how Marxism and Marxists combine theory and practice in the light of ongoing cultural and technological changes and new forms of social struggles. In fact, there have been so many uprisings, riots, and mass movements throughout history, but what often appears to happen is that we get so excited by these events that we fall into the delusion that the '1905 revolution' that you talk about has finally come again. We have seen this most recently in the Black Lives Matter protests, in Rojava and, if we go a little further back, as you said, in 2011 Spain and London, in the 2013 Gezi Park protests, and during the Arab Spring in 2010. As I personally experienced the Gezi Park protests, at the time we were extremely convinced that a revolutionary transformation could definitely come out of it. But it did not happen! Quite the contrary, the regime has tightened its grip, as I described in my first letter. And though I was disappointed about the outcomes, I learned a lot from it, especially that the diversity and multiplicity of this movement established the possibility of a 'dialogue.' I really felt free among this dialogue and diversity; I learned through

---

11 Luxemburg 2019: 213.

experiences of a real historical event that led different groups to intersect with one another. I saw that people needed to be listened to, to speak and to make their voices heard. In other words, I witnessed how people demanded to be(come) an agent, that is a subject, a conscious-individual, which the authoritarian regime had hitherto ignored.

Being a part of this movement and having the experience of collectivity and responsibility led us to become hopeful, feel confident in ourselves and to have the feeling of being strong enough to change something in our lives. On the other hand, I hold that these movements deprived of *permanency* demonstrate that a political *leadership* and a strong revolutionary motivation is necessary to construct an *integral movement* and unite the different political demands around a transformative revolutionary demand. In almost all her writings, Luxemburg underlines that the masses are the leadership of the movement and not the organizations, i.e. the Social Democratic Party, which does not mean that the masses do not have any organization but that "step-by step they built and strengthened their organizations in the course of the struggle. The point is that this is a totally mechanical and non-dialectical conception, that strong organizations must always precede the struggle. The opposite is true: organizations are born out of struggle, together with class enlightenment."[12] If we evaluate the recent uprisings in light of this passage from Luxemburg, we could conclude that the mass movements did not transform into a revolutionary organization because of the absence of class enlightenment. That is to say, I believe things may have turned out differently if they had put Marx's *Capital* at the centre of their demands, not for reforms but for revolutionary transformation.

In 20th century Turkey, although the Turkish Left was extremely visible in the streets and squares, it did not make any substantial gains because it was divided into thousands of pieces. In contrast, I think that in today's Turkey the Kurdish, Feminist and LGBT movements are stronger than ever. The Turkish Left did not reconcile with the Kurdish Left for a long time because for the former the class struggle came first. However, in particular during the Gezi Protest, after they personally experienced brutal attacks by the police and the government, they began to understand how the Kurdish people had suffered. Maybe the Turkish Left were simply not able to contemplate the question through a humanist aspect. As you say, the anti-humanist character of capitalism has spread over every fabric of society, from academia to politics, to political parties and to all public and private institutions etc. The results are evident. On the one hand, anti-humanism leads to moral and ethical corruption because of the disappearance of the individual/subject equipped with dialectical and collective values; on the other hand, the disappearance of a dialectical relationship between objectivity and subjectivity is the result of an anti-humanist perspective in which human beings are alienated, isolated from their nature and where humanistic relationships are reduced to material ones. So, the traditional Left and the social democratic segment have an ossified aspect, which never understood this dialectical relationship, and what's worse they are not open to innovation, closed to (self-) criticism, and unwilling to face the reality of their past.

---

12 Ibid.

Contrary to the weakness of Social Democracy and the left, if we take the recent increase in strength of the feminist movement into consideration, we can say that women are currently making a great contribution to the transformation of society across the world. From my experiences in Turkey and Italy, I can say that in Turkey this movement is even stronger than in Italy. Despite state repression and Covid-19 prohibitions, the feminists are the only movement that still fights on the streets of Turkey. Though I have struggled all my life with a male-dominant society and family, I had a class-struggle perspective to the woman question. In fact, in my view feminist movements and my collaborations with them have demonstrated how their/ our contributions are incalculable in terms of theory *and* practices, and how they make changes to women, men, and all society. In sum, criticisms and deficiencies aside, I am certainly convinced that women can bring extremely significant changes and different/new perspectives if they have a chance. It is time to give the stage to women!

What else? In your letter, you say that "basically, because the revolutionary generation – Luxemburg, Trotsky and Gramsci – never fully engaged with the theoretical and philosophical crisis of Marxism, we are left with a self-replicating anti-humanism." I guess that Luxemburg could not do it due to her murder at an early age and we will never know whether she would have done it if she had lived longer. In the case of Gramsci, I am not sure if it is correct to claim that he did not engage *enough* with it. In fact, I would say that Gramsci contributed quite a lot to the debates about the crisis of Marxism, for example with his theory of hegemony or his criticism of Marx's understanding of ideology, etc. Concerning the latter, while Marx regards ideology as an unfair, one-sided or partial idea and illusion that creates mystifications, Gramsci does not only consider ideology as false consciousness but also as a vision or understanding of a world; in other words, in the *Prison Notebooks* he mentions Marx's theory and Marxism as *Weltanschauung*. So, Marxism is also an ideology for him: "Marx laughs at ideologies but, as a current politician, as a revolutionary, he is an ideologue. [...] as a revolutionary, that is, as a current man of action, he cannot disregard ideologies and practical schemes, which are potential historical entities, in formation."[13] Actually, Lenin was the first who placed socialist ideology against all other bourgeois ideologies. This indicates a break with the orthodox understanding of Marxism, which relied on a reductionist economic and materialist approach and offers a dialectical relationship between the materialist and idealist elements, which means a return to Hegel's *Science of Logic*.

Finally, I agree with you when you say that "capitalism is producing clowns like Erdoğan, Putin, Bolsonaro etc., because it cannot produce anything better." In Turkey since 2000, Erdoğan has won "democratically" in four national elections – 2002, 2007, 2011, and 2015. This means that the subject that we talked about before decided four times to put Erdoğan into power, despite the fact that since 2011, the AKP increased the pressure against opposition parties and against general society and is currently trying to close the HDP, which has grown in recent years as a result of the freedom allowed in the first period of AKP between 2002-2011. As a matter of fact, there is a long list of prohibited and banned parties since the foundation of the Republic. But as you said, "at some point the reactionary phase will end." I strongly

---

13 Gramsci 1984: 17 (Translation by the author, with the support of Daria Davitti).

believe this, and we can see it in Turkey today: every day Erdoğan grows weaker, and his demand to close the HDP is one of the indications of this. The government is aware that the HDP is trying to bring peace to the people of Turkey after a decades-long conflict; the AKP realizes that its power is in danger, and this leads to increasing political instability in the country.

The conflict is now between secular forces – liberals, non-conservative parties like the CHP and the Left – and religious forces like some radical religious groups and those religious-conservatives who support AKP. Who will win? We do not know! But we cannot separate people into secular and religious as political parties do. The true way is to reconcile them based on a humanist aspect. Having said that, it is extremely difficult to predict the future of my country and I am so worried about the overall situation, especially that people may become demoralized. The whole society feels depressed because of the pervasive political and human corruption ruling Turkey today. But we must not get too demoralized. I know that if I turn my back on Turkey, it will be difficult to continue to work on the topics that I want to research. While after completing my PhD in Italy, I was happy to go back to my country, now I am not sure about it anymore. But then I have always had this idea of return in my mind and I have not abandoned it. Also, to be honest, Turkey might be bad, but this does not mean that in Europe everything is perfect. Neoliberal policies, fascism, authoritarianism, and capitalism do not exist only in third-world countries like Turkey, so in different ways our situations intersect. Hence, our struggle does not recognize any borders: everywhere you find capitalism in cooperation with fascism and authoritarianism. Maybe your book, *How to Stop Fascism*, which seems very timely, speaks to this struggle. I will be more than happy to read it.

All the best,

Sevgi

Da questo punto di vista, la ballerina di varietà le cui gambe portano profitto nelle tasche dell'impresario è un lavoratore produttivo, metre tutta la fatica delle donne e madri proletarie fra quattro mura domestiche è considerata improduttiva. Ciò suona brutale e folle, ma corrisponde esattamente alla brutalità e alla insensatezza della nostra attuale economia capitalistica.[14]

---

14 "From this point of view, the music-hall dancer whose legs sweep profit into her employer's pocket is a productive worker, whereas all the toil of the proletarian women and mothers in the four walls of their homes is considered unproductive. This sounds brutal and insane, but corresponds exactly to the brutality and insanity of our present capitalist economy." (Luxemburg 2004: 241)

Dear Sergi

I'm sorry for my late reply. We had elections on 6 May – only local, city and regional elections but they were bad for the Labour Party and precipitated a minor national crisis. Then the Israelis attacked Gaza.

Yesterday I went on the huge pro-Palestinian demo in London – I can't tell you how big it was, but it was maybe 50,000, maybe even bigger. The absolute militancy of the youth – Arab, Somali, Nigerian or just British Muslim kids born to families from India, Bangladesh, Turkey and Pakistan – reminded me of Black Lives Matter last summer. And it contrasts with the depressed and bitter mood of the so-called 'traditional working class' of elderly, white, home-owning people who are currently in thrall to Johnson's xenophobic project.

Your letter made me think simultaneously about the crisis of Marxism and the crisis of social democracy. The first is solvable, the second is not. Let me expand on why I think the 'crisis of Marxism' has spiralled out of control. At its outbreak, in the Bernstein debates, it concerned the failure of the working class to behave as the theory predicted: Bernstein pointed out that the proletariat was becoming stratified; that white collar proletarians had a different consciousness to manufacturing and mine workers; and this was the rationale for learning to live with capitalism as it inevitably but slowly 'grew over' into socialism.

By the time Korsch returns to the crisis, in 1923, the dysfunctions of the theory are even greater. Marxism no longer describes the state accurately, he writes; it over-emphasises economic development; and by grafting itself onto peasant and semi-Jacobin revolutions in Russia and Asia, it has become, he alleges "an ideology." Then, in the 1960s, when again the crisis is evident in the work of people like Marcuse, it is the alleged 'failure' of the proletariat that means the historic subject – in the destruction of capitalism – has to be understood as the urban underclass, black people, youth, women, peasant insurrectionaries in the Third World.

Finally, after the brief flurry of rank-and-file militancy at the end of the Keynesian era, the crisis returns. All the same forces – feminism, anti-racism, the LGBT movements, the urban underclass – are now understood as central, but it is only for a process of reforming capitalism, not transcending it. Into the ideological vacuum moved what I want to call 'postmodernism' but which should actually be called neo-Nietzscheanism, because it includes above all thinkers like Foucault (whose supporters insist is not really PoMo).

Neo-Nietzscheanism is opposed to the scientific method, proletarian morality and the idea of lawfulness in history. It moved into the space vacated by Marxism because it was a thorough 'slave ideology' for neoliberalism. It justified passivity, fragmentation and hopelessness. As a response, I wrote *Postcapitalism* because I thought it possible – indeed urgent – to show that the contradictions within the mode of production were acute, and could lead logically to a post-market, post-scarcity economy. I wrote the sequel, *Clear Bright Future*, after rethinking the problem of proletarian agency in Marx. It seems to me, in the early Marx, there is a teleological view of the human being which does not need 'the proletariat' – in the sense historically constituted between 1800 and 1980 – to be a) the sole agent of capitalism's destruction, or b) to 'bear' (*tragen*) the future property relations of communism within its daily life.

Instead, capitalism will be overthrown – as Brecht says in the final scene of the film *Kuhle Wampe* (1932) – by "those who do not like it." And the transition will not take the form of systematic scarcity, but as a struggle over distributional justice as digital technologies rapidly reduce the production cost of goods, services and ideas (and therefore labour power). These two ideas – the postcapitalist transition arising from the destruction of the law of value by zero-cost goods, and the revolution arising from the everyday lives of people exploited in multiple ways, seeking individual human freedom in the face of corporate and financial power – form the basis of my political project.

But is it Marxism? It's become common to reply: there is a Marxist method, which has to be applied to new phenomena, rejecting old conclusions as capitalism and society morph in response to their contradictions. But it seems to me that if Marxism were to follow faithfully the scientific method, it must also be prepared to abandon its premises. For example, Engels wrote:

> All historical struggles, whether they proceed in the political, religious, philosophical or some other ideological domain, are in fact only the more or less clear expression of struggles of social classes, and that the existence and thereby the collisions, too, between these classes are in turn conditioned by the degree of development of their economic position, by the mode of their production and of their exchange determined by it.[15]

This "great law of motion of history," Engels claimed, had the same status for history as the first law of thermodynamics does in science. Here, in a nutshell, lies the problem. In 1885, when Engels wrote these words, the third law of thermodynamics had not even been discovered. Physics was actually in crisis, because the 'law' Engels referred to conflicted with other laws. Out of this crisis came the theory of relativity, quantum theory and eventually chaos theory.

If Marxism is supposed to be a science – which was the claim accepted by all the writers considered here – it has not only to accept that some of its conclusions might be disproved but that the basic principles of the method themselves can be called into question. This can happen for the same reason that 19th century physics disintegrated: because the world is complex and our tools for grasping that complexity get better over time. If a thing starts behaving in violently different ways to what the theory predicts, the response of the scientist should be to attack the theory with all the tools – mental and practical – available.

---

15 See Engels 1885.

I now think the 1844 manuscripts contain two, parallel, theories of history. A humanist-teleological one, whereby the whole of humanity owns the *telos* of classlessness, and an instrumentalist one, where only the proletariat does so, and only by virtue of its long-forgotten propertyless lifestyle.

Failure to deal with that contradiction is the root of every recurrent crisis of Marxism. But I am optimistic that it can be overcome. The collapse of proletarian solidarity – as evidenced in our May elections, where the small-town, elderly, white, ex-industrial workers moved even further, and more vociferously away from the 'woke' Labour-supporting workers of the big cities – is not a disaster provided you can construct a new, broader alliance of producers, consumers and financially exploited people in its place.

The crisis of social democracy stems from its inability to do just that. Especially in Britain, where the Labour Party – as it says on the label – was built by trade unions to represent all workers in a project to reform capitalism. As politics have become driven by culture, values and identity, it is almost impossible to construct an offer representing 'all workers.' An example: Labour is denounced as 'politically correct' for wanting shorter sentences for criminals. This is a complete fiction. But when Labour (today) proposes longer sentences for those perpetrating rape, stalking and domestic violence against women, this too is denounced as 'woke' by the misogynist right. It's a no-win situation.

So there is now an argument, which I am at the centre of, about which way to move. The Labour Party has lost its base in Scotland to progressive nationalists and is losing support in the cities to the Greens, who are left, anti-imperialist and quite anti-capitalist. It has lost an entire layer of pro-Brexit xenophobic workers, who want to celebrate the imperialist past even as the country slides into post-imperial decay. But it is solid, and advancing, among the workers of the big cities.

It can try to recreate the party as an alliance of the left and centre – moving the centre of gravity towards liberalism, as suggested by Blair. Or it can become part of a wider, progressive alliance with the Scottish Nationalists, Greens, Liberals and smaller parties, as I argue. To the extent that Plan A does not work, or doesn't happen, it has to do plan B. The problem is, the people we are dealing with here have no theories. When I think of Rosa Luxemburg, in the famous picture of the SPD Party School – her scowl as she stands almost the lone female in the room, and the only young person on the staff – she is at least trying to download a basic theoretical framework into the heads of her future killers (Ebert is in the room).

Today that has become impossible. The Labour Party used to 'weigh' – metaphorically – its votes, not count them. There was no need for theory, strategy, a transition plan. Even its electoral agitation – ten years into the decline of party loyalty – is entirely configured around 'getting out' a vote that is no longer there. Few in the party even understand the problem. Or they are in revolt against the new conditions, asking "how do we get back to the way things were?" Until 6 May I thought this problem was retrievable, by refocusing the party on a radical economic offer, but conceding 'traditional' social democratic politics to the elderly workers, on policing, crime, defence etc. – as Tsipras did in Greece. Now I am not so sure.

And in the middle of it, the Gaza war has intensified the culture war here. Last night some Islamists carrying Palestinian flags drove through the Jewish areas of London shouting vile antisemitic slogans. Labour's anti-imperialist left, on the platform of one regional demonstration, was shouted down by Islamists. From here, to France under Macron, to Italy in the dying days of Draghi's centrism, it looks like the right will get their 'civil war' – against modernity, 'wokeness,' refugees and Islam. So the forces acting to disintegrate social democracy look – in this one moment I am describing – stronger than the forces trying to renew it. Luxemburg would have understood this. She understood the disintegration of the SPD as an opportunity, not a tragedy. But her focus was – and would have been if she had survived – on creating a pathway from something old and something new. In the conditions you describe in Turkey, with the HDP, CHP, the networked movements, feminism and the Kurds, you already have the 'new' – the old forms of the Left clearly have barely survived. I would be interested to know what your advice is, for those of us stepping newly into this world of political jeopardy and fragmentation.

As I am writing, the temperature is cool across the whole of Western Europe, while in the Russian north it is 20 degrees above its May average! A reminder that climate change places a ticking clock to the side of the chessboard of the class struggle, which was not there before. I am attaching a shot of the Palestinian demo I just went on.

Once again sorry for my late reply!

In solidarity
Paul

Pro-Palestine Demo

Dear Paul,

These last days – like many people – I have been watching and following a series of videos posted by the ultranationalist mafia leader Sedat Peker about deep state relations and secrets in Turkey. Some of the things he mentions were already known but there are many serious claims that would not be known without this sort of confession; and they have not been refuted yet by the government (AKP) or president Erdoğan. Peker's claims and confessions of the crimes he committed make it difficult to differentiate the mafia from the state (the new formation of political power resulting from the 2017/8 transition to the presidential or single-man system may help people to see how the identity of the state and the mafia are linked). The number of views shows that for many people his videos are more attractive and intriguing than *The Godfather* or other movies on Netflix. But why? What is so attractive about them?

I think the tragic situation of the Turkish population and their incredible interest (including my own) in these videos is not only about the general crisis of *politics* and therefore of *democracy* in Turkey, but it is also a result of that other crisis you were talking about in your letter: the crisis of *Marxism* from Bernstein to today; the crisis of our ability to unite the 'old' theory with a new one; and our being unable to convince people to make a choice between "barbarism or socialism." In my view, the crisis of Marxism can be evaluated by different elements. One of them is related to the historical subject or the subject of history that you described very well in your letter. As you said, Marcuse puts a new historical subject against the established subject of the working class in his *One-Dimensional Man*. These subjects or individuals have dissolved from the masses, and they liberated themselves from "all propaganda, indoctrination, and manipulation" and therefore, they are capable of "knowing and comprehending the facts and of evaluating the alternatives." Marcuse writes that "society would be rational and free to the extent to which it is organized, sustained, and reproduced by an essentially *new historical Subject*."[16] But the question remains: how can these different, today largely fragmented subjects – feminists, workers, ecologists, human rights defenders, students, anti-racist activists, etc. – struggle 'together' and not only for reforms but to 'transcend' society as you put it? On this point, we have to think these subjects, *again*, in relation to capital/the capitalist mode of production with the final aim of overcoming capitalist society.

From your political project based on two ideas – post-capitalist transition and revolution arising from everyday lives of people – I wonder how we can relate "those who do not like it [capitalism]" to the capitalist mode of production. If they do not like it, it means that they are in some way in connection with it; probably most people do not even have a direct relation with capitalism but, in some way, they are related to it. If we think about housewives, the homeless and those who are marginalized or excluded from society and do not work and hence do not produce any surplus value: they do not produce surplus value, but they are the result of this

---

16 Marcuse 2007: 256.

value; they do not possess the means of production as the working class, but they are the result of the capitalist mode of production. So they are still part of the same class: the oppressed class, which could be the point of departure to unite different subjects for fighting against what makes them oppressed.

I think that your second idea, revolution arising from the everyday lives of people, is very important, but I am not sure if you are referring only to post-capitalist lives. I also read it as *before* and *during* the post-capitalist transition and, as I understood it, contains both theory and praxis for a forward movement. So, I guess this is where social movements are/can be crucial for everyday changes and to question the political situation in any country. As we know, authoritarian political leaders are afraid of the masses and of mass movements, leading them to be(come) more aggressive, more dominating and controlling, including working together with criminal elements if needed. The ruling class and its apparatus, that is the STATE, can try to defeat any sort of revolutionary movements through their criminal activities. Luxemburg in some way refers to the ruling class' efforts to maintain its power when she underlines that even when some demands are successfully gained through struggles and battles, like during the 1905/6 revolution, "the enemy is not yet overthrown, we have not yet struck the weapons from his hands, and the fighters for freedom may not yet dream of a respite, because the enemy is making a renewed effort to gather up his remaining strength."[17] In Turkey, after the Gezi Park protests, Erdoğan's fear of the masses became especially obvious when his government strengthened its authority and power by negotiating with radical terrorist organizations and by creating a climate of fear through triggering conflicts within society with the help of the mafia.

The growth of this relation of the state with the mafia(s) in Turkey, although it has always existed, demonstrates that the state exists only to hide and protect criminals, as the Peker confessions reveal. As a result, the whole political philosophy about the existence of the Hobbesian liberal state based on protection collapses! The State = mafia! Turkey is now like a boiling cauldron, which may explode at any moment! Moral and political corruption dominates the entire Turkish system and institutions, forcing us to think once again about what the state is or what the *essence* of the state is.

This briefly brings me to Lenin's *Philosophical Notebooks on Hegel's Science of Logic*, in which he discusses Hegelian concepts such as appearance and essence. After his analysis of Hegel's "Doctrine of Being," Lenin does not make a firm distinction between these two concepts as he had in his previous works. Instead, he affirms that essence and appearance can be both subjective and objective. Hegel, on the other hand, talks about the identity of essence and appearance. Against the Kantian understanding of essence which does not allow us to know the essence of things (the thing-in-itself), Hegel suggests his theory of identity which is a method of overcoming contradictions through the identity of opposites, for instance, the identity of theory and practice, essence and appearance, subjective and objective, etc. Therefore, in contrast to Kant, Hegel highlights that the thing-in-itself, or essence, can be known through its experiences and relation with appearance. Hegel's theory of identity includes non-identity, which means that he associated this law of identity

---

17 Luxemburg 2019: 512.

with differences. In other words, Hegel talks about a dialectical relationship between essence and appearance: without appearance, we cannot know what essence is.

When we evaluate the Turkish case through Hegel's saying that "essence must appear," we can say that in this particular historical moment essence has appeared one way or another! And this essence is that the state has become a theatre of war for obtaining or maintaining political power by any means necessary. While in a democratic political environment, there is a distinct separation between the state and the parties, in the Turkish case, the ruling party and the state have become identical. In her famous 1899 pamphlet, *Social Reform or Revolution?*, in which she criticizes Bernstein's understanding of "the evolution of the State in society," Luxemburg refers to the relationship between capitalism and the State. She writes that "capitalist development modifies essentially the nature of the State, widening its sphere of action, constantly imposing on it new functions (especially those affecting economic life), making more and more necessary its intervention and control in society."[18] She continues by mentioning another transformation in the nature of the state resulting from the same capitalist development:

> The present State is, first of all, an organisation of the ruling class. It assumes functions favouring social developments specifically because, and in the measure that, these interests and social developments coincide, in a general fashion, with the interests of the dominant class. [...] When capitalist development has reached a certain level, the interests of the bourgeoisie, as a class, and the needs of economic progress begin to clash even in the capitalist sense. We believe that this phase has already begun.[19]

When we think about the Turkish case, it seems that the clash has begun and the State is no longer the representative of a dominant class, but it has become a dysfunctional set of institutions – at least for the whole of society – where a small group of people hold (on to) power to protect themselves and run the country as a family business. That is to say, it is *oligarchic* in nature.

In one of his videos, Peker claims that within the state there are some who do not want the conflict between Turks and Kurds to stop because both sides benefit from cocaine and gun sales. Regarding this, Rosa Luxemburg's analysis about the relationship between the state, militarism and capitalism continues to be pertinent. According to Luxemburg, for the capitalist class, militarism is indispensable for three reasons: "First, as a means of struggle for the defence of 'national' interests in competition against other 'national' groups. Second, as a method of placement for financial and industrial capital. Third, as an instrument of class domination over the labouring population inside the country."[20] For the latter we can give an example of controlling other ethnic (for example, Turkey) or religious groups (for example, Israel). Plus, we can add a fourth one, namely that militarism helps to keep the patriarchal system alive.

---

18 Luxemburg 2008: 61.
19 Luxemburg 2008: 62.
20 Ibid: 63.

But I have gotten side-tracked a little. You ask me what I suggest about the crisis of Marxism. I will try to answer but it will be just an attempt. You speak of the need for theory by referring to the importance of Luxemburg's party school and how the British Labour Party ignores or underestimates theory. I agree with you about the importance of theory or philosophy for revolutionary subjects and movements. But I also believe in struggling for rights and freedom through democratic instruments, in order to facilitate revolutionary transformation. Moreover, these types of struggles can enrich theory through practical activities, such as the demand for human rights and the education of women, thereby protecting women and girls from violence, or the demand for the protection of nature or the environment. In addition to having a strong ideology or theory and philosophy, I also think the leader of a powerful party is crucial, along with the active participation of civil society, such as non-governmental organizations and associations which are important for propagating theory or philosophy about equality, peace, society, humanism, conflict, and cultural, religious, ethnic diversity, gender, etc. These organizations and parties can concentrate on particular issues at the local, regional or national level.

I think we can/should think about, even if in a utopic manner, the content of a future humanist or post-capitalist society. We can begin to envision how this society could function, through debates at the local level in which everyone can participate and take responsibility for their political or organizational issues. I consider Hegel's *Philosophy of Right* as an example, in which he talks about corporations in which every individual finds their identity, and we can think it in the form of a commune – both the historic examples and current ones found in various parts of the world. For example, in Turkey, the communist mayor of Dersim (Tunceli), Fatih Maçoğlu, has been trying to achieve a type of communal or collective living since 2019. There are three different organizations: political, economic and social, which are interrelated. For example, the economic one can be developed through collaboration with peasants and workers, and with those who are experts in communal economy. I am aware that these claims are very simple and need more detail. I am thinking while writing to you. I hope this make sense. What do you think?

So, I suppose that this will be my last letter to you. I have enjoyed writing these letters and arguing with you about theory and praxis through the experiences of two countries, and in the company of Rosa Luxemburg's great intelligence and brilliant thoughts. I would like to conclude my letter with a verse by the Turkish poet Cemal Süreya's (1931-1990), "*Karacaoğlan*," about the 17th-century Ottoman folk poet of the same name: "*Umut'un içinde mut varsa umutsuzluğun da içinde umut.*" In Turkish, '*umut*' means 'hope' and '*mut*' means happiness whereas '*umutsuzluk*' signifies hopelessness, so the verse can be translated as "if there is '*mut*' (happiness) in '*umut*' (hope), there is also '*umut*' (hope) in '*umutsuzluk*' (hopelessness)." Doesn't this remind us once again of Hegelian dialectics, that "the negative is just as much positive": i.e., the togetherness of opposites?

In his *Hegel Notebooks*, Lenin also highlights this statement, and following it he notes that negation is something definite, and that through negation and inner contradictions, the *new one* takes the place of the old one. This is affirmed by what Luxemburg says in "New Year, New Struggle": "everything flows and only change endures."[21] As to change, although Luxemburg agrees with Hegel's point that "the History of the World is not the theatre of happiness,"[22] she understands that the way to happiness is through the difficulty of struggle, as she writes: "a year of struggle is behind us; years of struggle lie ahead."[23] However, this realism of Luxemburg never prevents her from believing in class-consciousness, i.e. the subjects of revolution who will eventually overcome this difficulty. In her 1905 "The Revolution in Russia," she confirms this confidence as follows: "In Russia, as everywhere in the world, the cause of freedom and of social progress now lies with the class-conscious proletariat. And it is in good hands!"[24] So, in spite of our difficulties and dark times, "*umut*/hope" always exists in the history of the world.

Greeting from the library in Pisa.

In solidarity
Sevgi

---

21 Luxemburg 2019: 507.
22 Hegel 2001: 41.
23 Luxemburg 2019: 512.
24 Luxemburg 2019: 63.

Rosa Luxemburg

Dear Sergi

What a brilliant letter. I learned a lot from it and it made me once again dig out Lenin on Hegel, which I will read this week! It will take me some time, but I might write a reply to it, though we are supposed to stop. It would be great to go on communicating and to meet if you ever come to London, or I go to Italy (if the Internazionale festival ever resumes!).

I think the whole process of renewing Marxism comes down to rediscovering its origins in Hegel, and then adapting the results to a very different reality – including the revolution towards indeterminacy and complexity and science! I do not have any drawing materials with me in my caravan on the edge of Wales, so I will not send a drawing... yours was very eloquent about Rosa. Instead, I send you a screen grab from *R is for Rosa*... I sat down with the animator and asked: what would imperialism look like if it was a character in the film? She produced this. The caption could easily be "State = Mafia". But also, State = Machine and State = Death.

I also send you a selfie from the Palestine solidarity demo in London. The keffiyeh I was wearing was given to me in Gaza in 2014 – and the instant I took the photo I sent it straight to the man who gave it to me, who was under bombardment at that moment. That's a form of international communications the Bolsheviks never had!

If I were to summarise what I learned from Luxemburg, over these many years, it is this: either the masses "own" Marxism or it is not Marxism. Either it arises out of the experience of opposing capitalism, or it is just a doctrine, to wither away as its 19th century logical premises are eroded.

In Solidarity — The struggle is ultimately one for life, liberty and humanity!

Paul

PS: We'll meet in person one day, hopefully in Taksim as the youth, the women, the LGBT people and the Kurds party on the ruins of Erdogan's dictatorship!

Imperialism

May 29, Pisa

Dear Paul,

I am really very happy to hear that you enjoyed my letter, which I thought was not good enough after sending it to you. It would be my pleasure to keep communicating and hopefully we can do something together again. I hope we can meet in person somewhere in Italy or in London (it is like a dream for me to be there), of course, I will be more than happy to meet you in Taksim, although my situation is very complicated and unstable.

I like your imperialism picture. It tells everything about the capitalist system. In London, you had a huge demonstration, in Italy it was not so crowded. But still, people got out to protest and express their solidarity.

I have nothing to say but to confirm your conclusion. Each time I talk with my left-liberal friends about capitalism, the justice-system and equality, it becomes clearer that a Marxism created by the masses themselves would be a unique solution, in line with what was suggested by Marx and Engels in *The Communist Manifesto*: "The emancipation of the working class must be the work of the working class itself." Following them, in 1905, Luxemburg holds that "[…] the broad mass of the proletariat *itself* must really understand the needs, conditions, and methods of its own liberation, and at the right moment, according to *its own will as a class*, must step up to begin to fight."[25] Luxemburg's courage and keen intelligence teaches me to be brave and ready to fight against injustice even if nobody believes in you and what you fight for.

We have to continue to smile at life even in dark times, in this sense I hope that Luxemburg's joyful spirit will always guide us: "in the dark I smile at life, as if I knew a magical secret that shows all evil and sad things to be untrue and changes them into pure lightness and happiness. And all the while I'm searching for some reason for this joy, but I find nothing, and have to laugh at myself again. I believe that the secret is nothing less than life itself."[26]

Struggle for a collective and free life forever! Smiling at life audaciously!

In solidarity and all the best,

Sevgi…

25 Ibid: 154.
26 Luxemburg 2013a: 455.

Ciwak o hemden, tiştên hewce û pêvîst
çênake: Qriz!
Car caran tiştên aborî yê cêdike lê
nikarî hemu bikar bîne, gelek dikanan
de tijî tistên nefiruti hene lê gel xela
yê da ye. Hewcedarî û têrbun, armanca
kedkarî û encama wî ê dî bihevdû nagire,
tistek tarî û razdar ketîye navber o
wan û ewan ji hevdu qetandî ye.[27]

---

27 "Present-day society however produces what it neither wants nor can use: crises. It periodically produces means of subsistence that it cannot consume; it suffers periodic hunger alongside tremendous stocks of unsold products. Need and satisfaction, the purpose and the result of labour, no longer match; between them stands something unclear and puzzling." (Luxemburg 2013b: 129)

July 15, London

Dear Sevgi

I will finish with a story about Luxemburg, and how you can always find something 'new' in her work. This year I had to make a documentary series about Rosa, and we decided to get an actress to read her words to the camera. Josephine Rogers is a classically trained English actress, but in the rehearsal we both struggled with the delivery. Rosa's paragraphs are long, and typically contain phrases and ideas, 'nested' within each other, so that the payoff for one idea comes after an idea that is introduced later. Here's an example from the *Junius Pamphlet*:

> For the first time, the ravening beasts set loose upon all quarters of the globe by capitalist Europe have broken into Europe itself. A cry of horror went through the world when Belgium, that precious jewel of European civilization, fell into shards under the impact of the blind forces of destruction. This same "civilized world" looked on passively as the same imperialism ordained the cruel destruction of ten thousand Herero tribesmen and filled the sands of the Kalahari with the mad shrieks and death rattles of men dying of thirst; [...] None the less, the imperialist bestiality raging in Europe's fields has one effect about which the "civilized world" is not horrified and for which it has no breaking heart: that is *the mass destruction of the European proletariat*.[28]

It was only when we thought about it like this that Rosa's words made sense as speeches. She is looking, metaphorically, at two cameras: in one camera is the masses, whom she addresses with simple, clear language; and in the other camera are Kautsky, Bernstein and Ebert, to whom she throws comic asides, in an idiom that almost feels Yiddish (which her biographer says she only used for insults and self-irony).

If you read Luxemburg aloud, you have to use these two voices, official social-democratic prose and 'shtick' – or dramatic irony. I had spent nearly 40 years engaged with these texts, and it took the act of directing someone to perform them, to really understand them.

Yours is an amazing story, Sevgi. I am heading back to Wales trying to prepare for my book launch!

Solidarity and good luck!
Ben

---

28 See Luxemburg 1915.

References

Engels, Frederick (1885), "Preface to the Third German Edition of The Eigthteenth Brumaire of Louis Bonaparte." *Marxist Internet Archive*. Accessed on 22.08.21, at https://www.marxists.org/archive/marx/works/1885/prefaces/18th-brumaire.htm.

Gramsci, Antonio (1984), "Astrattismo e intransigenza", in *Il nostro Marx: 1918-1919*. Ed. Sergio Caprioglio. Torino: Nuova Universale Einaudi.

Herling, Gustaw (2006), *Il Pellegrino della libertà: saggi e racconti*. Napoli: L'Ancora del Mediterraneo.

Luxemburg, Rosa (1915), The Junius Pamphlet. *Marxist Internet Archive*. Accessed on 22.08.21, at https://www.marxists.org/archive/luxemburg/1915/junius/ch08.htm.

Luxemburg, Rosa (2004), *The Rosa Luxemburg Reader*. Eds. Peter Hudis and Kevin B. Anderson. New York: Monthly Review Press.

Luxemburg, Rosa (2008), *The Essential Rosa Luxemburg*. Ed. Helen Scott. Chicago:Haymarket Books.

Luxemburg, Rosa (2013a), *The Letters of Rosa Luxemburg*. Eds. Georg Adler, Peter Hudis, and Annelies Laschitza. London and New York: Verso Books.

Luxemburg, Rosa (2013b), *The Complete Works of Rosa Luxemburg, Vol. I: Economic Writings 1*. Ed. Peter Hudis. London and New York: Verso Books.

Luxemburg, Rosa (2019), "Remarks at the Jena Congress on Relations Between the Party and the Trade Unions, with Reference to the 1905 Revolution in Russia [September 1905]," in *The Complete Works of Rosa Luxemburg III: Political Writings 1: On Revolution 1897-1905*. Eds. Peter Hudis, Axel Fair-Schulz and William A. Pelz. London and New York: Verso.

Marcuse, Herbert (2007), *One-Dimensional Man: Studies in the Ideology of Advanced Industrial Society*. London and New York: Routledge & Kegan Paul.

Order reigns in Berlin — you stupid lackey! Your 'order' is built on sand.[29]

29 "Order reigns in Berlin – you stupid lackey. Your 'order' is built on sand." (Luxemburg 2004: 378)

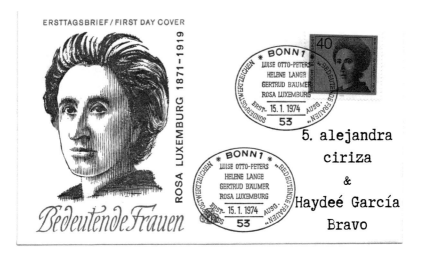

ERSTTAGSBRIEF / FIRST DAY COVER

ROSA LUXEMBURG 1871–1919

Bedeutende Frauen

BONN 1
LUISE OTTO-PETERS
HELENE LANGE
GERTRUD BÄUMER
ROSA LUXEMBURG
ERST. 15. 1. 1974 AUSG.
53
SONDERPOSTWERTZEICHEN BEDEUTENDE FRAUEN

BONN 1
LUISE OTTO-PETERS
HELENE LANGE
GERTRUD BÄUMER
ROSA LUXEMBURG
ERST. 15. 1. 1974 AUSG.
53
SONDERPOSTWERTZEICHEN BEDEUTENDE FRAUEN

40

5. alejandra
ciriza
&
Haydeé García
Bravo

Shamed, dishonored, wading in blood and dripping with filth, thus capitalist society stands. Not as we usually see it, playing the roles of peace and righteousness, of order, of philosophy, of ethics-but as a roaring beast, as an orgy of anarchy, as a pestilential breath, devastating culture and humanity-so it appears in all its hideous nakedness.

Rosa Luxemburg[1]

Querida Haydée

I have been thinking a lot about Rosa these days, like someone who thinks of a beloved and close friend, *una amiga* I often turn to and consult when current affairs remind me of past events, and when I need someone with whom to think in ways simultaneously loving and unwavering, the way she used to think, agitate and write to her friends.

The horrifying news from Colombia, the open war waged against the *Guardia Indígena*, the violence and grief that President Duque and his henchmen are unleashing on those who dare to openly defy them or even just resist, remind me of Rosa's very relevant observations about the politics of the bourgeoisie, and the incompatibility between the most basic forms of democratic tolerance and the movement towards barbarism as represented by the capitalist economy.

We here on South American soil, from the Rio Bravo southwards, know all too well what this entails, thanks not only to the colonial experience – if that were not enough already – but also to the variety of forms and attempts at recolonizing the continent, both in the past and present. Down here in the *Cono Sur*, the savage wounds inflicted upon us by the military dictatorships of the 1960s and 70s are still wide open, whether in Brazil, Chile, Uruguay, Argentina, Bolivia or Paraguay. As it were, our republican era is a vivid example of this bourgeois tendency to ride roughshod over the very same institutions it extols: in the past military coup d'états, today legal coups like those in Bolivia (2019), Honduras (2009) and Brazil (2016). Then there are the brutalities resulting from the reign of narcopolitics in Mexico and Colombia, as well as a pillaging neoliberalism burning the entrails of the people of Ecuador and blinding the eyes of hundreds of protestors in Chile.

The list is interminable, but the above examples alone leave no doubt that we urgently need to read and analyse our continental vicissitudes, our politics as feminists included, *en clave de Rosa*, that is to say, with and through Rosa Luxemburg. For instance, I am thinking about *"El violador eres tú"* ("The Rapist is You"), the wonderful resistance performance created by the feminist collective *Las Tesis* in Chile in response to the widespread use of sexual violence by the Chilean police in order to repress political dissent.[2] The song immediately resonated across the continent and then the rest of the world, spreading like a tidal wave of protest, performing a strategy of internationalism that we feminists have begun in the most diverse ways,

1 Luxemburg 2004: 313.
2 Listen at https://www.youtube.com/watch?v=hZN_QaIUJj.

not just with songs, but also with marches and the international feminist strike. Who other than Rosa Luxemburg as our guest of honour in all these feminist debates and actions? Rosa and the general strike. So much for us to (still) think about.

As a matter of fact, Rosa and her reflections come up for me time and again when thinking about all that is happening on our unfortunate continent, what is happening with us women, subject to the most brutal violence. Her brilliant diagnosis: Capitalism cannot but advance over all land, relations and human beings by means of the most diverse types of violence and barbarism, including this most recent version of the extermination of women: the privatization of their bodies, their transformation into commodities and into new territories for the valorisation of Capital. How can we understand the ongoing *terricida* and femicide without the help of Rosa, my dear Haydeé?

I cannot stop pondering how she was able to combine her sound education as an economist and her sharp capacity to consider the political consequences of the capitalist economy, for example when realizing what would be the result of the necessity of the European countries and their economies to expand in space. One is reminded of her observations in *The Junius Pamphlet*:

> Capitalist desire for imperialist expansion, as the expression of its highest maturity in the last period of its life, has the economic tendency to change the whole world into capitalistically producing nations, to sweep away all super-annuated, precapitalistic methods of production and society, to subjugate all the riches of the earth and all means of production to capital, to turn the labouring masses of the peoples of all zones into wage slaves. In Africa and in Asia, from the most northern regions to the southernmost point of South America and in the South Seas, the remnants of old communistic social groups, of feudal society, of patriarchal systems, and of ancient handicraft production are destroyed and stamped out by capitalism. Whole peoples are destroyed, ancient civilizations are levelled to the ground, and in their place profiteering in its most modern forms is being established.[3]

I am also thinking about her articulating the advancement of capitalism and the destruction of existing social relations and of nature, exactly as it has been happening here on our continent. In Argentina, ongoing, multiple extractivist interventions are penetrating into areas hitherto peripheral, like the remaining jungles of Salta, Chaco and Formosa; the search for lithium in Puna, or the ongoing fracking activities in the Patagonian Plateau. The overall devastation and misery, the destruction of all forms of community relations, of nature and bodies, confirm in our everyday lives the connection Rosa saw between capitalism, the destruction of pre-existing social relations and the most extreme forms of violence.

What she calls "capitalist desire" continues to expand everywhere, and even more so in these pandemic times. The brutal consequences of a system in which people produce what they don't need while lacking the most basic means for the reproduction of their own existence, are ever more crudely visible for anyone who wants to see them. It is just like Rosa said. We have become wage-earning slaves,

---

3 Luxemburg 2004: 338.

prisoners of multiple crises, from the overaccumulation of commodities to the massive laying-off of workers. This capitalist desire is such that it penetrates the very depths of our bodies, the very last corners of nature and even those spaces that the bourgeoisie once venerated under the pretext of privacy. Nothing is sacred in this predatory frenzy that destroys the old, impoverishes and makes precarious ever larger number of people and appropriates ever bigger chunks of free labour. Rosa points out precisely this in her lectures on political economy, given at the School of the German Social-Democratic Party (SPD) from 1907 onward when saying:

> In this way, one continent after another comes inextricably under the rule of capital, and on every continent one territory after another, one race after another, with ever new and uncounted millions succumbing to proletarianization, enslavement, insecurity of existence, in short, immiseration. The establishment of the capitalist world economy brings in its wake the spread of ever greater misery, an unbearable burden of labour and a growing insecurity of existence across the whole globe, corresponding to the accumulation of capital in a few hands.[4]

This reflection of Rosa strikes me as absolutely key in understanding the current capitalist crisis, the impacts of the pandemic, but also those things that happen to us as women, i.e. the different ways capitalism affects us in our often proletarianized and/or un(der)employed existences, the unbearable and unsustainable quantities of free female labour that capital devours in the most diverse forms, among others, as a readily available workforce that becomes employable only if and when capital demands it, or for the free reproduction of human life wrapped in sugar-coated notions of love, care, etc. In other words, depredation and privatization are real, but they are made invisible once again by plain old mystification.

How accurately Rosa saw that capitalism advances by way of the cannibalization of other forms of social organization – devouring, incorporating and subordinating them – and the use of free labour made available thanks to the social, racial and sexual division of labour. Thus, the tight relation between capitalism and colonialism, obscured from view back then and still today. Thus, the intimate relation between capitalism and patriarchy, which continues to be so frequently sidestepped even among battle-hardened feminists. In short, this rapacious, profit-seeking machinery excretes and denies our human bodies, the very material nature of life and our connection with the most elemental and social needs of nourishment, rest, affect and relations with others.

This is what looking at the world *en clave de Rosa* allows us to see and comprehend: the logic of the accumulation of capital and its articulation through politics, the logic of capital and the exploitation of women and racialized people, the logic of capital and the devouring of free labour, the logic of capital and the long, never-ending, exhausting, unsustainable and un(der)paid working days of countless human beings. It is these growing levels of exploitation and extortion we face day after day – of course since long before the pandemic – but nowadays with an even greater loss of life and basic rights.

---

4 Luxemburg 2013a: 297.

Hence this deepest of affinities I feel in relation to Rosa: not only did she provide me and so many other feminists with the necessary tools to interpret the ties that bind together economics and politics, but she has gifted us with the wonderful example of her own life: her sharp sensitivity vis-à-vis the pulse of the times, her rigorous political ethics in times of defeat, her precious words of encouragement and gratitude towards other women, her deep sense of solidarity with nature, and her knowledge of those secret bonds of kinship we humans have with buffalos, birds, and yes, the numerous, precious wild plants she cultivated and encountered in many a prison courtyard.

It is Rosa's exemplary life, dearest Haydeé, that has instilled in me a deep desire to learn from her the key personal and political lessons that allow us to develop feminist friendships and appreciate their enormous importance for the sustenance of life, for making more liveable our ever so uncertain lives. To learn from her about the vibrant internationalism that resulted in strikes, marches, debates and incarcerations, and which recently found expression in our own feminist internationalism vibrating to the beat of *"Canción sin Miedo,"*[5] the beautiful song by Vivir Quintana, so personal, so political, so mobilizing in these difficult times.

Te abrazo (I embrace you)

alejandra

5 Listen at https://www.youtube.com/watch?v=-UgyLRjz3Oc.

Avergonzada, deshonrada, chorreando
mugre: así vermos a la sociedad
capitalista.[6]

---

6 "Shamed, dishonoured, wading in the blood and dripping with guilt, the capitalist society stands." (Luxemburg 2004: 313)

alejandra querida,

After many work-related delays I am now finally able to write back to you. *Gracias,* first of all, for your beautiful letter. I should start off by recognizing that you are the expert in Rosa, or *Rosita,* as I lovingly call her, a name of which I am sure she would have approved since she herself so often used the diminutive in her communication with friends and comrades, from Sonja (Sophie Liebknecht), Tilde (Mathilde Wurm), Lulu (Luise Kautsky), Diudiu (Kostja Zetkin), Hänschen (Hans Diefenbach) and Mitek (Mieczyslaw Hartman) to Julek (Julian Marchlewski), Wlad (Władysław Henrich), and her *gatita,* her beloved little cat, Mimi.

Similar to you, I feel *Rosita* very close to me, almost like a contemporary, in spite of our being a little over a century removed from her life. But really, what is time for an important figure like her? In fact, if we think of time as a vast, immeasurable entity, then Rosa's short life – just like other important historical events such as the Paris Commune; the Haitian, Mexican, Russian and Cuban revolutions; or the successful anti-colonial uprisings on the African continent (which others can you think of, ale?) – was of such intensity that it continues to illuminate our path like fireflies in the dark or like those kaleidoscopes through which one can always discern new and rich possibilities.

Wasn't Red Rosa admirable in every dimension of her life? A Marxist and inexhaustible fighter, *una luchadora incansable,* who was committed to the struggles of working-class women, a woman full of love and a polyglot educated in a variety of fields, because when in Zurich not only did she study philosophy, but also botany, zoology, mathematics and economics, and – this continues to amaze me – she obtained her PhD at only 27 years of age, at a time when very few women had the opportunity to do so!

The same Rosa who since early childhood confronted adversity with integrity and who, when she was 4-5 years old, was forced to spend all her time in bed without being able to move. The same Rosa who at age 15 was already politically active in the Polish socialist party "Proletariat," and who at age 18 began her nomadic existence, having to leave her native Poland for Zurich – apparently hiding in a cart full of straw – in order to avoid being caught by the police who would continue to hound her throughout her life, whether in Poland or Germany.

What's more, Rosita was not afraid of intimacy like many of the politicians-cum-marble statues far removed from all the human things that happen around them. On the contrary, her life, her work and her political commitment can be regarded as an early embodiment of what would soon become the flagship of the international feminist movement, i.e. "the personal is political," which Rosita would probably have expressed dialectically: and the political is personal as well. No doubt, her

133

capacity for tenderness was revolutionary, as was the great passion she brought to every task, leaving no one who ever met her indifferent: neither women, nor men and surely no other living beings either.

For me, Rosa's life, from beginning to end, was like a solar flare, which continues to burn brightly despite the more than hundred years that have passed since her assassination a few weeks before her 48th birthday. And even though we do not know with absolute certainty the date on which she opened her eyes for the first time, I want to believe that Rosa was indeed born in March, at the beginning of spring in the northern hemisphere, coming (in)to life with the same revolutionary fervour so palpably expressed by the people of the Paris Commune that very same March of 1871. Because spring is not only "Le Temps des Cerises,"[7] the season of flowering cherry trees, but also the time of the year when life itself undergoes a process of renewal and rejuvenation. In Mexico City, for example, it is the time when the Jacaranda trees explode in all their violet beauty, thereby playing an indispensable part in our annual feminist marches on International Women's Day. How I would love you to join us one day – as soon as the pandemic allows – for one of our marches against femicide and all other forms of violence against women. Wouldn't it be great if we could march arm-in-arm, together with the other women of my collective from the South of Mexico City, "Las Sureñas Insurrectas," just like Rosa and Clara Zetkin did in that emblematic 1910 image? That gesture has always fascinated me, as it expresses in such a dignified manner something that you mentioned in your letter: friendship between women, walking side-by-side, supporting one another, talking and sharing.

In April you told me by e-mail that you were going to the city of Rosario to finally meet one of your grandchildren, Emiliano, who you said received his name "because of Zapata." It made me very happy to learn that he was named in honour of our great Mexican revolutionary. Later I realized that both Luxemburg and Zapata were murdered in the same year, 1919. Rosa on January 15 and Emiliano on April 10. Zapata and Luxemburg, both with piercing dark eyes, an unyielding personality and hailing from the margins of the world-system – from the so-called forgotten people, the "pueblos perdidos": Anenecuilco in the state of Morelos, Mexico and Zamość, in the state of Lublin, Poland – can today be considered as among the world's most important historical figures, symbolizing "la revolución del pueblo" ("the people's revolution") against the power of the bourgeoisie and against capital, which, just as you emphasize in your letter, continues to devour everything in its way: land, bodies, relationships.

In his 1911 "Plan de Ayala," Zapata – "el general" or "calpuleque" (meaning "chief" in Náhuatl) – outlined something that I am sure Rosa would have approved of: the indispensable people's struggle for democracy, justice and freedom, denouncing the usurpation and monopoly of the "land, hills and waters," and decreeing the expropriation of all large estates and the restitution of the land to ejidos[8] and comunidades, i.e. collective land distribution. In a recent text published in the journal Memoria. Revista de Crítica Militante, which I am a part of, one of the great Zapata scholars, Francisco Pineda (1955-2019), describes how the ruling oligarchy first

---

7 Editor's Note: "Le Temps de Cerises" is a famous song closely associated with the days of the Paris Commune.
8 Ejido is a communal form of landownership derived from indigenous communities in Mexico.

tried to kill Zapata and when that didn't work, attempted to denigrate him with various farcical accusations, resulting in "the leader of the Liberation Army thus identif[ying] the main forces of social confrontation: on one side, the honourable Mexican people, and on the other, the self-enrichment and ridiculous farce of the worthless and despicable [oligarchs]."[9] In this sense, it appears almost certain that Rosa would have supported Zapata's radical and irrevocable perspective, possibly with certain criticisms, but undoubtedly denouncing the reformist positions of people like Francisco I. Madero. In short, both Rosa and Emiliano remain highly emblematic figures, reborn with every insurrection and revolt.

So please tell me about Emiliano and the rest of your family. How was it to finally see him? And how was it to meet your children Martina, Valentín and Andrés after such a long break due to the pandemic? You know, I have not seen my own family – my mother, father, my niece Sofía, my nephew Tadeo and others – in more than six months. They all live in the place where I was born: in Matehuala, San Luis Potosí, in the middle of a semidesert, very close to Wirikuta. Have you heard of Wirikuta, *mi querida amiga*? It is one of the sacred places of the *wixárika* people, also known as *huicholes*, and the site where it is said that the sun rose for the very first time, thereby destabilizing the colonial cartography imposed on us for so long by the West.

Today, Wirikuta is being besieged by the voracity of international mining capital, with the support of successive neoliberal national governments who have generously granted concessions in over 40% of the national territory, up to a period of fifty years. One company in particular, Canadian *First Majestic*, is contaminating our waterways and territories through open-pit mining, in the process destroying the delicate social fabric, because they operate precisely in an area with an ever higher number of people passing through, trying to reach the United States with the goal of increasing their chances of physical survival and perhaps even obtaining a scrap of the so-called American Dream, which is fast becoming more and more of a nightmare. And so naturally some people say to themselves that "if the company gives me a few cents to do some weeding or to look after the scrub, well, then I prefer to stay." The problem is that this work is done merely to prepare the terrain for future mining operations, and recent history suggests that these companies bring nothing but further poverty, with an attendant increase in (organized) crime, which together have become one of the most hideous developments in the current phase of capitalism. In short, the communities increasingly begin to confront each other, and the result is not only a highly complex, explosive overall scenario but a situation in which both the present and future are at stake. To me, this appears to be very similar to what you describe in your letter about the different regions of Argentina, followed by your very pertinent suggestion to understand what is happening *en clave de Rosa*. Perhaps in your next letter you could give me some advice on which texts of hers to read in more detail? Do you see a connection with what Rosa called capitalist and non-capitalist strata, or the struggle of capital against the natural economy?

What else? Oh yes, you mentioned the composer and singer-songwriter Vivir Quintana, who by the way was born near the very same trail northwards frequented today by so many migrants from all over Central America. "*Canción sin miedo*," her powerful feminist song you shared, is one of my favourites and I continue to choke

9 See Pineda 2019.

up every time I listen to it, though eventually, thanks to the power I feel from the *compañeras* next to me, my chest opens up and I begin to sing. The version you sent is one of the first, from March 2020, performed with Chilean artist Mon Laferte and the El Palomar Choir at Zócalo square, in the heart of Mexico City-Tenochtitlan, just before the first Covid-related confinement began. Since then, countless women of all ages have made the song their own and there are now multiple versions out there, all of them extremely moving. Of course, the other song you mention, by *Las Tesis*, is also very popular within our movement and I have even performed it on various occasions. You are so right when you say that the feminism we are a part of is a direct descendent of Rosa and her "vibrant internationalism."

Something else that caught my attention is the paragraph you cite about the advance of capital and how Rosa taught this at the SPD Party School. May 15 is Teachers' Day here in Mexico and a little earlier today my partner Pepe Gandarilla, whom you know, reminded me of this crucial aspect of Rosa's life, i.e. the absolutely essential work she did as a political educator for a number of years. Can you believe that even to be able to do this work she had to overcome all kinds of obstacles, because her colleagues, almost all of them men, wanted to give the job to Rudolf Hilferding?[10] But just like on so many other occasions Rosa fought (back) and achieved what she set out to do.

If there is one thing about Rosa, however, that has really left a lasting impression on me it is her straightforward and open commitment to living a full and dignified life, in which not a single detail is ever lost or disregarded, and where everything is joined and woven together. As you know, she was one of a kind in articulating the most complex concepts in any given situation, political or otherwise, thereby raising to the highest level of expression the Marxian method of relating the abstract to the concrete, all the while living out with such intensity her capacity to love – free of any type of puritanism – and constantly re-affirming her willingness to be fully involved, to understand and acknowledge what she was doing and feeling, and to grant her passions the necessary space to express themselves. As, for example, when she writes to her partner Leo Jogiches in March 1894 and criticizes him for never speaking about anything but the greater cause:

> It really annoys me – the fact that whenever I take a letter in hand, whether from someone else or from you – everywhere it's the same – it's either the next issue, or it's the pamphlet, or it's this article or that one. That would all be fine if at least in addition to that, alongside of that, there was a bit of the human person, the soul, the individual to be seen. But from you there's nothing, absolutely nothing. During this time have you had no impressions, have no thoughts occurred to you, have you read nothing, had no perceptions that you could share with me?[11]

---

10 Editor's note: Rudolf Hilferding (1877-1941) was an Austrian-German Marxist economist and one of the chief theoreticians of German Social-Democracy.
11 Luxemburg 2013b: 10.

In this and so many other letters of hers – it really is astonishing how tireless she was; I wonder how she had time for everything – Rosa gives an early account of how capitalism gradually manages to invade all aspects of life, something we women understand all too well, now that this has in fact become one of its most potent mechanisms, as you so aptly describe.

Another facet I'd like to mention is what I believe to be the deep links between Rosa and one of the heroines of the Paris Commune, Louise Michel, a connection similar to that between trees and forests that happens underground: through, between and among the roots. Rosita's admiration for the Commune is of course well known, and I think what characterized both these revolutionary women was what we may call today an "ecological" understanding of the world, that is to say, that nature and culture must not be separated and that there exists an interdependent co-existence between humans and non-humans. Furthermore, both of them, in their very own ways, but nourished by the same organic, living humus, managed to sustain their sensibility in even the most difficult conditions, whether in prison or exile, as evidenced by their many beautiful drawings of plants and flowers. I am sending you a type of postcard that I made from these images.

What's more, neither of them would allow herself to be victimized in any way. Quite the opposite, how much resonance and similarities do we find between the "We will come back by all possible ways" spoken by Louise facing her persecutors before being sent into exile in New Caledonia, and those final published words of Rosa's just before her life was cut short:

> "Order prevails in Berlin!" You foolish lackeys! Your "order" is built on sand. Tomorrow the revolution will "rise up again, clashing its weapons," and to your horror it will proclaim with trumpets blazing: I was, I am, I shall be![12]

Finally, both of them developed and sustained a strong anticolonial perspective. Louise due to her time spent in exile and her support for the Kanak-led 1878 anti-imperial insurrection, and in the case of Rosa we can find this stance in her both terrifying and beautiful letter to her Jewish friend and party comrade Mathilde Wurm, written from Wronke Prison on February 16, 1917:

> [...] above all one must at all times live as a complete human being. What do you want with this theme of the "special suffering of the Jews"? I am just as much concerned with the poor victims on the rubber plantations of Putumayo, the Blacks in Africa with whose corpses the Europeans play catch.[13]

Rosa continues with a quote by German General von Trotha who led the 1904-07 extermination campaign against the indigenous Herero and Nama people in the former *Deutsch-Südwestafrika*, today's Namibia: "And the death rattles of the dying, the demented cries of those driven mad by thirst faded away in the sublime stillness of eternity," to which Rosa responds emphatically:

---

12 Luxemburg 2004: 378.
13 Luxemburg 2013b: 375.

Oh that "sublime stillness of eternity," in which so many cries of anguish have faded away unheard, they resound within me so strongly that I have no special place in my heart for the [Jewish] ghetto. I feel at home in the entire world, wherever there are clouds and birds and human tears.[14]

Don't you think that Rosa would be on the side of the Palestinian people today, as they are once again under cruel and inhumane attack by the Israeli government?

…

To finish, you will not believe this, but perhaps due to the delay in writing my letter to you, I have even begun to dream of you and Rosa. Possibly it also had to do with the fact that these days, before going to bed – dead tired after so many e-meetings, classes and seminars, and having spent the whole day in front of the computer – I give myself the gift of reading a few pages of literature, such as the extraordinary sci-fi novel I just finished, *Women at the Edge of Time* by the US-American writer and critic Marge Piercy. Intriguingly, in the novel, one of the characters or "per", short for person, is called Luxemburg. Other "pers" that appear in the book are Louise Michel and Simón Bolívar, as well as many other important beings and organic processes such as Dawn, Hawk, Bee and Luciente, the latter being the one who takes the novel's protagonist, Connie, a Mexican-American woman subjected to all kinds of injustices and misfortunes, into a future society free of all forms of oppression. In other words, Rosa is just one of many "pers" engaged in this time-travel, but still, what I love about the book is that she forms part of this imagined future, in which every "per" chooses their own name and where some of the most terrible and pain-inducing inventions humankind has come up with, such as the notion of "race" and "sex-gender assignment," have finally ceased to exist.

And then I woke up at dawn that very same day of the dream, and the first thing I heard were the trills of the birds outside the window, as even here in the big city there exist a few spaces of revitalizing joy, just like Rosita always managed to find or, if necessary, create in even the most unlikely places. I have attached the audio for you, and I invite you to just close your eyes and imagine you are here, listening to their music.

Well, it is time to bring this first letter to a close. What an endless spring of inspiration our Rosa is. A tumultuous torrent from which to constantly drink and refresh ourselves. ale, there are still so many important issues in your letter I could respond to, and I hope to do so in our future correspondence, but for now

(I embrace you and wait for your next letter with great excitement),

Te abrazo y espero ya con ilusión
tu próxima carta,
Haydée

---

14 Ibid: 376.

Reconocer que el caos es el elemento
vital del capitalismo, es pronunciar
su sentencia de muerte [15]

---

15 "To discover and confess that anarchy is the life element of the rule of capital means in the same breath to
pronounce a death sentence." (Luxemburg 2013a: 134)

Querida Haydée:

Just now I am managing to sit down and respond to your beautiful letter. I sometimes catch myself thinking, especially when feeling overwhelmed by tiredness and bad news, that the times we live in are not propitious for writing, at least for this type of writing, more personal yet still deeply political in nature.

But then I think of Rosa and realize how endlessly small I am. I recall her capacity to enjoy every second and I remember those many powerful letters she wrote in conditions so much worse than mine, the university professor who spends endless hours in front of a computer, but in a pleasant and warm place, next to the marvellous red of the Santa Rita vine that adorns the window of the *casita* I live in, which used to belong to my mother. Outside, the little orange tree I planted only five years ago is beginning to bear fruit. It looks like this winter – in a few weeks' time – I will be eating my own oranges. I have become quite the lay gardener. Later I will send you some photos of my flowers and cacti, which I look after with great care.

But before I let myself be carried away too much, I am sending you the fragment of a letter Rosa wrote to Hanna-Elsbeth Stühmer on March 10, 1917. Rosa invites her interlocutor "to take a turn with me in this tiny realm of nature [the yard of Wronke prison]" and to "observe and read along with me – observe – and read along with me! […] what abundance when you take a closer look!" Then she says:

> Just here in the dewy grass, if you will bend down, dear lady! Do you see these masses of green clover leaves? Observe how strangely and faintly iridescent they are bluish, rosy and mother-of-pearl. What causes it? Each little leaf is bedecked with tiny dewdrops in which the slanting morning light is refracted, giving the leaves their iridescent rainbow shimmer. Have you ever tried to tie together a little bouquet of such simple three-leaved clover stems? They look delightful in a small vase or glass. All seemingly the same, but when you look more closely, each little leaf is slightly different, just as a tree does not really have two leaves the same. Larger and smaller, lighter and darker, the little clover leaves with their elegant oval shape are a varied and lively sight. When I first sent a small bouquet of these clover leaves to the superintendent as a morning greeting, she asked afterwards with interest where I had picked it. The ladies have no idea what grows and flourishes in their own yard and every time I produced an attractive bouquet using the most modest means and a little skill, they asked in astonishment where it came from. Since then, the little clover bouquets have in fact become very fashionable and I was delighted to see on several mornings one or other of the ladies stooping in the yard and hurriedly collecting a handful of the three-leaved stems.[16]

I understand that this quote is rather long, but I just did not want to take anything

---

16 See Luxemburg 1917a.

away from Rosa's capacity for language, this really taking her time in expressing her thoughts and ideas, and the sense of solace these minute descriptions provide, all of which is encroached upon today by our ever more accelerated lives in pursuit of who knows what ephemeral illusion. Rosa wrote with such palpable joy and that is why I believe it is crucial that we not only take seriously her economic texts, but that we engage with her letters, her affects, her different loves and passions, her relationships with (female) friends, and also the subtleness of her writing, the sort of grounded patience her words express and which her more urgent texts sometimes lack. But then, how could they not be urgent since Rosa lived her life with such deep sense of urgency?

You asked me about my favourite revolutions, well, today is May 25, the anniversary of the 1810 May Revolution that took place in present-day Argentina. This uprising by *criollos, pardos and mestizos*, that is to say, racialized subjects, unleashed the revolutionary storms that swept across *Nuestramérica*[17] at the beginning of the 19th century. While this revolution has been interpreted by bourgeois historiography as a mere change of authority that benefitted the merchants of Buenos Aires, thereby following Tocqueville in erasing the capacity for subversion of the subaltern sectors, I do believe that what happened was a genuine revolution from below that shook the ruling classes and that nobody can take away from us. I suggest that next time you come to Argentina we go and look for the book by Andrés Rivera, *La Revolución es un sueño eterno* ("The Revolution is an eternal dream"), in which he tells the story of the revolution through the eyes of one of its protagonists, Juan José Castelli, aka the Orator of the Revolution, who belonged to the Jacobin wing of the revolutionary forces.

In more general terms, I am still passionately in love with what might be called the upward cycle of the early 19th century revolutions, up to 1824, and including the great Haitian revolution, which continues to be largely absent from our indo-afro-latino-american history as Afro-Brazilian historian Lélia González (1934-1994) liked to call it. 1824 really did mark a point of inflection. All we need to do is follow in the steps of Bolívar in order to realize when and how the downward cycle begins and the dominant classes return to order, in sync with a reinforced colonial logic, which had never been successfully expelled from inside ourselves. All of this is so complex, isn't it? How do we know if and when a revolution really manages to subvert the established order? How does it unfold from conditions not of our own choosing? What really is the relative weight of these conditions as opposed to the weight of the subjectivities constructed in the heat of class struggle? Subjectivities such as those of Toussaint L'Ouverture, Mariano Moreno, Juan José Castelli, Juana Azurduy, Remedios del Valle and later Emiliano Zapata, *el* Che Guevara and his *compañera* in Bolivia, Haydée Tamara Bunke (better known as Tania), of Camillo Torres and Salvador Allende, who is once again being championed today by the many young people at the forefront of the Chilean insurrection. And not to forget the protagonists of the struggles of the 1960s and 70s here in Argentina. So many people to name, so many powerful revolutionary subjectivities.

---

17 Editor's note: *Nuestra América*, Our America, is an important text written by Cuban poet and politician José Martí in 1891. His eloquent insistence on the need for a genuinely independent and sovereign Latin American subcontinent, free of colonial and imperialist interference, has since become a rallying call of the Latin American Left.

In your letter you mention this final text of Rosa's "Order prevails in Berlin," which never ceases to resonate with us, especially in times of defeat. Just like Rosa I really believe that the current order "is built on sand" and that "tomorrow the revolution will rise up again, [… and] proclaim with trumpets blazing: I was, I am, I shall be!" In fact, isn't this happening again these days, right here on our continent, in such unexpected places as Chile and Colombia? You know, I was very young when the Allende-led *Unidad Popular* triumphed in Chile in the early 1970s and so I spent my youth in the company of the music of bands like Quilapayún, which once again today accompanies the struggle of the people of Chile, the *rotxs* and *pibas* as well as the indigenous Mapuches trying to regain their land and dignity. *El pueblo unido, jamás será vencido!* The people united will never be defeated! Which is precisely what so many young Colombians in Medellín are also singing these days, those who have nothing to lose but their chains: *El pueblo unido, jamás será vencido!*[18]

As someone whose political socialization began in those revolutionary 1970s, I cannot but think that the defeats of the emancipatory processes of the time have left us with a debt to pay. And in this sense, just as you affirmed, Rosa is indeed like a solar flare, which continues to illuminate our path more than a hundred years after her assassination and 150 years since her birth. Because she was a revolutionary and an internationalist. Because she knew and understood that even when we are defeated that does not change the fact that the bourgeois order is built on sand and that it will eventually be overthrown, or rather that we will demolish it stone by stone from its very foundations, which is really the only way to demolish anything. We will demolish it in its capitalist character, but also in its colonialism and racism, in its patriarchal horrors and in its heterosexism. And we will do so by cultivating the capacity for waiting that Rosa so masterfully achieved, a type of waiting that, mind you, is not the same as passivity. We will do so by devoting ourselves to transmitting her legacy, by learning from her, by finding and exploring our affinities, like the love for plants and music, and like the stubborn expectation and desire for a time of revolution and the transformation of *everything*.

Just now I re-read one of the letters she wrote to Diefenbach from jail. Rosa had just been transferred from Wronke to Breslau and found herself in a quite inhospitable place. So once again she looked out for the birds, from whom she learned the rare capacity to search for the inexhaustible sources of hope around her/us. She wrote:

Hänschen, do you know that in their autumnal flights to the south, large birds like cranes often carry on their backs an entire load of smaller birds, such as larks, swallows, gold crests, etc.?! This is not just some fairy story for children, but a scientifically verified observation. And the little ones cheerfully twitter and converse in their "seats on the bus"! ... Do you know that in these autumnal migrations it often happens that birds of prey – sparrow hawks, falcons, harrier hawks – will make the journey in a single flock together with little songbirds, which they normally feed upon, in other circumstances, but during this journey a kind of God's truce [*treuga Dei*], a general armistice, is in force? When I read something like this I am so thrilled and it puts me in such a mood of joie de vivre that I begin to consider even Breslau a place fit for humans to live in. I myself don't know why this affects me so; perhaps

18 Listen at https://www.youtube.com/watch?v=4imww8Ejs20.

it's because I'm reminded again that life is indeed a beautiful story. Here at first I came close to forgetting that, but now it's coming back to me. I will not let things get me down.[19]

Isn't that It, *mi querida*?

Autumn is now fast advancing here in the South. The Liquidambar tree at the back of the house is turning all hues of red and yellow and the days are getting shorter. Yet, I am not losing hope that both the season and the generally stormy times we live in will soon change again and that we can meet on March 8 next year – whether in your beautiful Mexico full of flowers or here on my humble soil – in order to "march arm-in-arm, supporting one another, talking and sharing." I would really like that.

Hopefully, if you manage to come, you can finally meet my grandchildren Amparo and Emiliano, both of whom are delightful. Perhaps you could even tell them stories about his namesake, Emiliano Zapata. I also wish that you can at long last return to your hometown of Matehuala, where I have never been, even though I did come across it many years ago when I studied the economic history of *Nuestramérica*. It was then that I learned about this other Potosí[20] and its relevance for the colonial system, but that was all really. Why don't you tell me a little bit more? I have seen a number of beautiful images, but I lack more concrete knowledge.

Speaking of economics and the colonial system, you asked me whether I think

19 Luxemburg 2013b: 439.
20 Editor's note: In Latin America/Abya Yala there are two well-known cities named Potosí, one in Mexico, the other in modern-day Bolivia. The former was named after the latter, but both are historically important for their role in the colonial economy and the beginning of capitalism in Europe.

that what is currently happening in Mexico with the imperialist open-pit mining activities has something to do with the encroachment of capitalism over other economic relations. My short answer is a resounding yes, it certainly does. Rosa explains this meticulously in her economic writings, for example in her *Introduction to Political Economy* and in her magnum opus *The Accumulation of Capital*, both of which you can find online in Spanish at the Marxists Internet Archives. Flicking through the *Introduction to Political Economy* just now, I found the following, very illuminating quote:

> We thus discover that one "commodity" is exported and imported today that was unknown in the time of King Nebuchadnezzar as well as in the whole of the antique and medieval periods: capital. And this commodity does not serve to fill "certain gaps" in other countries' "national economies," but quite the reverse – opening up gaps, rifts and splits in the edifice of traditional "national economies," and acting like gunpowder to transform these "national economies" sooner or later into heaps of rubble. In this way, the "commodity" capital spreads still more remarkable "commodities" on an ever more massive scale from various old countries to the whole world: modern means of transport and the destruction of whole indigenous populations, money economy and an indebted peasantry, riches and poverty, proletariat and exploitation, insecurity of existence and crises, anarchy and revolutions. The European "national economies" extend their polyp-like tentacles to all countries and people of the earth, strangling them in a great net of capitalist exploitation.[21]

Substitute "Canadian" for "European" and you'll find a very adequate explanation for what is happening: contamination, destruction of the social fabric, extreme impoverishment, the expansion and interiorization of capitalist values…You know, people think from where they stand, and the common ground for all of us are the many years of neoliberal politics and capitalist depredation, reinforced by highly efficient pedagogies of cruelty and individualism. And what they destroy is not only nature, our lands and the social relations we have created, but also our sense of community and our capacities for solidarity and the collective, *lo colectivo*.

I suppose this is why this dialogue with you and Rosa is so stimulating for me. It feels like we are wagering on our capacity to weave *lo colectivo*. It also feels like a commitment to our evolving friendship, which so far has been marked by a very few brief meetings, like for example when we met in Buenos Aires for the activities to commemorate the 100 years of Rosa's murder. Unfortunately, due to family commitments – I have a very intense relationship to my children, perhaps because I am an intense person myself – I was unable to attend what you told me was a wonderful play dedicated to Rosa, *La conducta de los pájaros*, performed by Eliana Wassermann, but at least we managed to stroll around aimlessly a little, sharing food and drinking coffee.

Well, as I said, I will be waiting for your visit as soon as the pandemic allows. My partner Gustavo will do the cooking and then we can all go for a walk around the city together. It may not be as beautiful as your Mexico, but I am confident you

---

21 Luxemburg 2013: 115-116.

will enjoy the nearby mountains of the *cordillera*. I also promise that we shall drink a good local *vino*, produced right here by the sun-trapped, dry lands of Mendoza.

Last question, just out of curiosity: is there a nickname by which people call you, a diminutive?

Te abrazo a la espera de tu respuesta
(I embrace you awaiting your next letter)

alejandro

Fue sólo porque analizó el capitalismo desde un punto de vista socialista... que Marx pudo descifrar los jeroglíficos de la economía capitalista. [22]

22 "It is only because Marx looked at capitalism from the socialist's viewpoint, that is, from the historic viewpoint, that he was enabled to decipher the hieroglyphics of capitalist economy." (Luxemburg 2008: 79)

June 26
Tlalpan, in the vicinity of the Ajusco[23] mountain range,
South of Mexico City, at 2480m of altitude

$\mathcal{A}le\ querida,$

I am so sorry it's taken me exactly a month to write back to you. Believe me, I was really hoping to do so earlier, but I was snowed under with endless work and so many events around me and hence the month simply passed in the blink of an eye.

I would like to start off by expressing my gratitude for your beautiful, rich and profound letter. I am not sure I will be able to do justice to all the different issues you raise, but I shall try anyway and at the very least our correspondence, from which I am learning so much, will continue. As a matter of fact, I feel that the two of us really resonate with each other and as a result this whole exchange has been for me like a fresh summer rain that makes one blossom, just like your oranges and the Santa Rita, or Bougainvillea as we call it here (by its colonial name), which excites and embellishes its surroundings when- and wherever it grows, in our case in spring. I have attached a photo for you from our communal garden in the housing unit where we live. What fascinates me about this plant is its history of travel, from Brazil to Europe and then across the planet, with all kinds of variations and adaptations emerging, such is the story of so many other plants. Here in Mexico, we drink its flowers as part of a tea with lemon and honey to cure coughs and colds and it works wonders.

Santa Rita o Buganvilia

Unfortunately, even though plants are such good companions, the fact that Pepe and I live in a flat means we have mostly ornamental plants like the "over-refined and decadent" orchids that Rosa admired with such "great resistance."[24] How I wish I could transform our apartment into a jungle! But it delights me to know that you have a garden and that you have even planted your own fruit trees. Hopefully I can take you up on your invitation to visit you soon. The way you described it, it just

---

23 Ajusco is originally a Náhuatl word and can be translated as "source of waters" or "watered grove".
24 See Luxemburg 1917b.

exudes hominess. In terms of you saying that Mendoza may not be as beautiful as Mexico, isn't it true that every place has its own beauty, its own *encanto*? Ideally, we can even visit each other, so we could talk and enjoy ourselves and I could show you around different places that I believe you might appreciate and then, every once in a while, we could take a break and watch the sky and "be good" together:

> Just now the sun – I took a little break from writing, to observe the heavens – has dropped much lower behind the [men's prison] building, and high up in the sky, myriads of little clouds have silently assembled-God knows from where-their edges have a silvery sheen, but in the middle they are a soft grey, and with all their ragged outlines they are heading north. In this procession of clouds there is so much smiling unconcern that I have to smile along with them, just as I always go along with the rhythm of life around me. With the presence of a sky like this, how could one possibly be "bad" or petty? As long as you never forget to look around you, you will always be "good" without fail.[25]

In this sense and looking into the distance from the window of my study not far from the Ajusco mountain range, I agree with you about our smallness, because like yours, my general living conditions are infinitely better than Rosa's. Then again, I know that you are a woman of many battles, perhaps the main one being against the historical amnesia that the henchman of the military dictatorships and their descendants have been forever trying to impose on the people of Argentina. What greatness of heart you and Rosita have.

And it's in her letters, like some of the ones you shared, where one can really feel it. What moves me particularly is her sensitivity, which allowed her to find growing, pulsating life even in the most desolate prison yard, her love of life through all of her senses, and her need to share this love with others. I get emotional when I read how Rosa was able to communicate lovingly and full of hope with plants and flowers and how she kept spreading seeds of joy among other prisoners and even the female wardens; and what to say about her capacity to really see the smallest details, the most minimal changes of colour and form and how this became the basis of her understanding and weaving of interdependent friend- and comradeships, and even interdependent interspecies relations like when she talks so beautifully about the birds that at certain times carry other, smaller birds in order *to fly together* (!!!). What a great lesson for us humans to learn. Hers was a genuine *Aesthetics of Liberation*, to say it in the words of Enrique Dussel's 2018 text.

Querida amiga, you show great gentleness in your writing when you point out that Rosa was a female militant, a revolutionary, a loving thinker, a powerful theoretician and a woman of both patience and urgency all at once. I believe that what you mention is one of her biggest legacies: to learn how to slow down in order to extend the time of joy without losing sight of the utopian horizon of transformation, but rather nourishing it with these seemingly small but foundational moments.

Speaking of which, it was very meaningful for me that you wrote your letter on May 25, that you called my attention to the importance of the revolution, and the

---

25 Luxemburg 2013b: 432.

emphasis you gave to the many other uprisings that ignited the Independence Revolutions across the continent. In fact, what you invite us to do is to reclaim the very idea of Revolution itself, which is something I subscribe to, because I have been coming across more and more people with an historical revisionist attitude that denies the importance of the revolutions and who claim, as you say, that these were but mere changes of authority, or who evaluate them and their corollaries with the exclusive benefit of hindsight, all of which appear to me very unjust positions to take in relation to history and the people who made these revolutions with their dreams and ideals. By the way, in our library we have the book by Andrés Rivera you mention. My partner has spent quite a bit of time in Argentina, particularly in Buenos Aires, and since he is a great bibliophile, he once bought a copy, and thanks to your recommendation I now finally have the incentive to read it. In return, I recommend another book that attempts to connect the multiple uprisings, *En el espejo haitiano. Los indios del Bajío y el colapso del orden colonial en América Latina*, by the eminent Mexican historian Luis Fernando Granados.[26] Here is a quote from the book:

> After the fuse was lit in May at the Río de la Plata, in September 1810, it was the turn of the *"indios, mestizos* and *castas, campesinos, mineros* and *artesanos pueblerinos* [...] to gather on the outskirts of the world's capital of silver," Guanajuato, to start the Independence revolution in Mexico.

Regarding your reference to Lélia Gonzalez, let me tell you that we literally just translated a short but very powerful texts of hers, *"Mujer negra, esa quilombola,"* originally published in November 1981, for the commemoration of the death of Zumbi dos Palmares, the great revolutionary leader of the first Slave resistance movement in Brazil in the 17th century.[27] As you well know, Zumbi was decapitated, just like Tupac Amaru a century later in Peru, and both of them were accompanied in life and struggle – which are always one and the same thing, just as they were for Rosa – by important women: Dandara, mentioned by Lélia, and Micaela Bastidas. Today, Zumbi and Tupac Amaru form part of the deep roots of emancipation that continue to ground our struggles, and the mythical idea of their eventual return, which has been passed on from generation to generation, still serves as the insurgent seed that inspires multiple movements today.

In short, thanks to your letter, which gave me the feeling that we were on a journey together rediscovering the history of our continental uprisings and insurrections, I feel a renewed sense of confidence and courage in relation to our current struggles. And as I re-read your letter, I am listening to different versions of *El pueblo unido jamás será vencido*, which really was/is one of the official anthems of all the political and social movements in which I have participated, whether in the struggles for the democratization of the political system in my home state of San Luis Potosí, the support for the (Neo)Zapatistas in 1994, the many rallies against the privatization of our national oil resources, the defence of Wirikuta, the 2004/5 protests against the attempt to prevent current president Andrés Manuel López Obrador from running in the presidential elections, the protests against the fraudulent 2006 general elections,

---

26 Editor's note: Unfortunately, on July 10 of this year, Luis Fernando Granados passed away from cancer at the age of 52. Rest in Power, Luis.
27 November 20 has since become *El Día de la Conciencia Negra*, Black Consciousness Day, in Brazil.

or the countless Feminist marches over the years, among many other actions. I still get goosebumps every time I hear the song or when I witness other collective bodies singing it, everyone vibrating in unison, just as is happening now with the Colombian people in revolt. The repression is always the same: violent, sinister, irresponsible. In contrast, our protests are multi-coloured, kaleidoscopic, full of dancing, discussions, hugs, shared work ("*la minga*") and an immense rebellious energy, a joyful courage, again reminding us of Rosita who always gave her all in everything she did and who knew how to emerge stronger even from misfortune.

In one of her many letters to Luise Kautsky, this one from January 26, 1917, from Wronke Prison, Rosa demonstrates this strength of character, but also the value she gave to their friendship:

> Now I am bright and lively again and in a good mood, and the only way you're failing me is that you're not here chitchatting and laughing as only the two of us understand how to do. I would very soon get you laughing again, even though your last few letters sounded disturbingly gloomy. You know, once when we were coming home from an evening at Bebel's and around midnight in the middle of the street three of us were putting on a regular frog's concert, you said that when we two were together you always felt a little tipsy, as though we had been drinking bubbly. That's exactly what I love about you, that I can always put you in a champagne mood, with life making our fingers tingle and us ready for any kind of foolishness. We can go without seeing each other for three years, and then within half an hour it's as though we'd seen each other only yesterday [...][28]

Doesn't this type of profound connection over many years merit highlighting, particularly in light of what you said about capitalist values undermining our capacity for solidarity and maintaining social relations? A little further down she adds:

> I can grieve or feel bad if Mimi is sick, or if you are not well. But when the whole world is out of joint, then I merely seek to understand what is going on and why, and then I have done my duty, and I am calm and in good spirits from then on. *Ultra posse nemo obligatur.* And then for me there still remains everything else that makes me happy: music and painting and clouds and doing botany in the spring and good books and Mimi and you and much more. In short, I am "stinking rich" and I'm thinking of staying that way to the end. This giving oneself up completely to the headaches and miseries of the day is completely incomprehensible and intolerable to me. See, for example, how Goethe stood above things with cool composure. [...] I don't ask that you be a poet like Goethe, but everyone can adopt for themselves his outlook on life-the universalism of interests, the inner harmony-or at least strive toward that. And if you say something like: but Goethe was not a political fighter, my opinion is this: a fighter is precisely a person who must strive to rise above things, otherwise one's nose will get stuck in every bit of nonsense.[29]

28 Luxemburg 2013b: 365-366.
29 Ibid: 366-367.

So every time I get sad because of something that happens around me, like for example the surprising right-turn in the recent Mexican midterms – especially here in Mexico City, which since I arrived more than 25 years ago has always felt to me like a very libertarian, left and emancipatory city – I try to remind myself that history is full of reversals and setbacks and that we have to stay alert and find ways to confront things "with cool composure," or perhaps with something akin to Rosa's and Sonja Liebknecht's inspiring "boisterous gales of laughter [...] – in spite of everything." In that letter, Rosa tries to cheer up Sonja after the arrest of her husband Karl and she continues by saying:

> [...] everything is part of life: sorrow and parting and longing. One must always take it as a whole, including everything, and find all of it beautiful and good. At least that is what I do. Not through some elaborately worked out form of wisdom, but simply "just so," because of my very nature. I feel instinctively that this is the only correct way to take life, and therefore I really do feel happy in every situation. I also would not want to exclude anything from my life, nor have it be any way other than it was and is. If I could only bring you to this conception of life![30]

To read Rosa really does give one strength - her words are like little dewdrops that splash vitality, imbue new life and restore one's composure. Perhaps we should prescribe collective readings of Rosita whenever our goings get tough. You must already be doing this as part of your Rosa reading groups with the *Mujeres del Sur*?

As your days shorten, here they get longer. We just had the summer solstice, the longest day of the year and despite the usual rains and very little sun, Mexico City was illuminated until late in the day. This reminds me of a summer solstice I witnessed in Ushuaia, the so-called end of the world. I still have the stamp in my passport saying *"Las Malvinas son Argentinas"* ("The Falkland Islands belong to Argentina"). For sure, Rosita would be on the side of the Argentine people, that is to say, on our side. She who had the gaze of an eagle, as Lenin said of her (not without a certain masculine aftertaste). She, the perennial internationalist who paid attention to the struggles of so many people and places around the world.

You asked me about San Luis Potosí, the second Potosí. Well, together with Guanajuato (the cradle of independence) and Zacatecas, it was one of the three sites with the highest gold and silver production in colonial times, making Mexico (Nueva España) the biggest silver producer in the world in the 18th century (according to Humboldt). In fact, Rosa hints at this in her dissertation when she speaks of the "sudden influx of precious metals from the New World."[31] San Luis was founded at the end of the 16th century, in 1592, in the region that is historically known as Gran Tunal, bordering on Gran Chichimeca, a territory originally inhabited by numerous nomad people who put up great resistance against the Spanish *conquistadores*. Generally speaking, today's state of San Luis Potosí is very rich in cultural terms and with regards to its wide variety of landscapes. Oh how I wish to eventually show you its four very distinct regions: the *altiplano*, the high plateau, where I was born, with its spectacular night sky in the desert; the *región centro*, with the state

---

30 Ibid: 399-400.
31 Muiña 2019: 158.

capital and one of the most important baroque churches in the country; the *zona media*, home to a series of incredible sites like the Media Luna Lagoon, and what to say of *La Huasteca region*, the rich intercultural area with its exuberance of tastes and colours. As you can imagine all these treasures have over the centuries provoked the voracity of Capital, but our people have put up stern resistance and therefore we continue to live our lives, day by day, with great integrity.

Thanks to your recommendation, I have (re-)read Rosa's posthumously published book *Introduction to Political Economy*, which addresses a series of important issues you raise in your letter. Rosa was very clear that colonialism was/is a necessary condition for capitalism and not, as has been claimed many times, an unfortunate anomaly. She also argues convincingly that the "non-capitalist strata" as she calls them in *The Accumulation of Capital* are fundamental for the dynamics of capital accumulation, that the unpaid (forced) labour extracted from its people fuels production and that it is precisely in these non-capitalist regions of the world that new markets are forced open and from which new resources are constantly appropriated.

I am sure you agree with me that the way she presents the issues is often astonishing in its clarity and sense of conviction, like when she chooses a title for the opening chapter in the form of a question – "What is Political Economy?" – and then immediately follows this with a great truth: "Political economy is a curious science. Difficulties and conflicting opinions arise at the very first step on its terrain [...]"[32] Next, she introduces the main ideas of some of the most renowned bourgeois scholars of the time and remarks bitingly: "What we're offered is precisely nothing but echoing phrases, hollow words screwed together [...] for ordinary mortals, this has the same numbing effect as a millwheel turning in the brain."[33] And then Rosa makes a remark that I believe we must collectively recover for our times, to make our analyses accessible:

> [...] anyone who thinks clearly, and has a genuine mastery of his subject matter, also expresses himself clearly and understandably. [...] We shall go on to show that the obscure and confusing language of bourgeois scholars as to the nature of political economy is not accidental, but actually expresses two things: both the unclearness of these gentlemen themselves, and their tendentious, stubborn rejection of a real explanation of the question.[34]

For Rosa the Theoretician, the science of political economy implied the challenge of complexity, diagnosis and transformation, and "if it is the task and object of political economy to explain the laws of the origin, development and spread of the capitalist mode of production, it is an unavoidable consequence that it must as a further consequence also discover the laws of the decline of capitalism [...][35] For Rosita these laws are those of dialectical materialism, with the working class as its protagonist, female proletarians included, because "[t]he workshop of the future requires many hands and hearts. [... so let's] hurry to join the struggle for the emancipation of women and of humankind from the horrors of capitalist domination!"[36]

---

32 Luxemburg 2013a: 89.
33 Ibid: 91.
34 Ibid.
35 Ibid: 141.
36 Luxemburg 2004: 244-245.

To conclude, ale, *camarada querida e intensa*, as you describe yourself and as I perceive you to be, I assume that you enjoy cooking, so I have an idea. Why don't we invent a dish in honour of Rosa, *una receta-homenaje*, and we can invite her to our table next to the stove just like she used to invite Sophie Liebknecht:

> the cosy hours in my kitchen, where you and Mimi waited patiently at the little table with the white tablecloth to receive proof of my culinary skill. (Do you still remember the superb green beans in the Parisian style [haricots verts a la Parisienne]?) […] I have the vivid memory that it was invariably hot sunny weather, and only in such weather does one have the proper joyous feeling of spring.[37]

Why not even invent a new slogan to chant during one of our future Feminist marches, inspired by the multiple *feminismos comunitarios* that understand that the cauldron is not only a place for cooking, but for many other things:

Juntémonos en torno al fogón, que ahí también puede iniciar una revolución![38]

Finally, you asked me whether I had a nickname or diminutive, and the answer is yes, I have one. At home, people have called me Yeye since I was a child, which I sometimes spell in even shorter form: YY. Very close *amigas* and my partner Pepe call me by this name occasionally and what surprises me is how hearing them pronounce it feels like a caress, a tactility of the soul, playful and sweet. Please feel free to call me this and please tell me what you are called, or which affectionate nickname you prefer.

Muchos cariños y un abrazo apretado,

YY

---

37 Luxemburg 2013b: 400.
38 Editor's note: Translated literally, "Let's gather around the stove, because it is (also) a place from which to start a revolution." In the Spanish original, the final words of each phrase (*fogón* and *revolución*) rhyme.

*El taller del futuro
necesita de muchas
manos y corazones* [39]

---

39 "The workshop of the future requires many hands and hearts." (Luxemburg 2004: 244)

154

Mi muy querida Yeye :

I just read your long and splendid letter, but since for the purpose of this book project, we are meant to bring an end to our exchange, it will not be possible for me to do justice to everything you wrote. Hence, I will only pick up on a few ideas in relation to the legacy that Rosa has bequeathed us, her unforeseen heiresses, the pariahs and daughters of this beautiful and torn continent. Rosa, sower of revolutionary desire that fuses economy, politics, the body, nature, music and the delicate weft of affects and friendships, just like in those letters of hers you sent, to Luise Kautsky and Sophie Liebknecht, in which shared experiences, collective "champagne laughter" and intimate memories of time spent together in the kitchen blend. One can almost see and touch the white tablecloth, the *haricots verts* and Mimi waiting expectingly.

For those of us who come from a Marxist tradition, it is so important to establish this connection with Rosa in time and space, bringing together past and present, and exploring across the terrain of history the conditions of possibility for political transformation even when it does not seem to be very close on the horizon. I look to Rosa for this inspiration, this desire for kinship with the whole universe, this capacity to listen to the fluttering of plants, birds and other species, including the human one, even when what she has to hear is at times brutally cruel. I admire in her this mix of determination and gentleness, which I believe is so necessary in the current "moment(s) of danger," as Walter Benjamin may have called the times we live in.

Yeye, this may disappoint you, but at home the person responsible for cooking every day is my partner Gustavo, who loves to cook. He comes from an Italian tradition and both his mother and grandmother were great *cocineras*. Of course, in my family there has been a lot of cooking as well. My grandmother, the fairy of sweets; my mother with her sophisticated and exquisite cuisine; my sister whose almond cake regularly produces expressions of collective delight; and even my sons and my granddaughter Amparo enjoy cooking. As I said, I do not frequently cook, but I enjoy making salads and I occasionally make sweets such as crystallized oranges or what we call *mermelada inglesa*, with lemons, oranges and apples harvested from our own garden. I also prepare quite a delicious pudding with lemon and poppy seeds, which I will make for you when you visit me one day.

My dear, you told me by mail that you and Pepe will soon be going on vacation. Please enjoy your holiday. I hope you will be able to rest, go for walks, breathe, sit in the sun or perhaps watch the rain slowly dripping down the beautiful and intense summer green.

Un abrazo a/rre todo

arita/ aiusha /alex ,
como me decían en la infancia

Para la proletaria su casa es el mundo entero.[40]

40 "For the proletarian woman, the whole world is her house." (Luxemburg 2004: 243)

156

July 3,
Tlalpan, in the vicinity of the Ajusco mountain range, Mexico City

Our organizations, however,
they prove themselves in struggle,
they can only exist in struggle,
and they only grow in struggle.

Rosa Luxemburg[41]

Entrañable alita,

How I love it that they call(ed) you "little wing" and that I too can call you this. It sounds so warm and affectionate, and it connects wonderfully with Rosa's love for birds. It also alludes to the polysemy of the word "wings", the essential physical element that makes them able to fly. As you know, we here in Mexico use the diminutive quite a lot, for cultural reasons that have survived both the *Conquista* – the Spanish colonization of the Americas – and these moments of danger Benjamin refers to. By way of example, in the Náhuatl language the suffix "tzin" denotes respect and affection at the same time and therefore approximately corresponds to the Mexican Spanish ending "ita-ito."

What I also loved is that you called us Rosa's unforeseen heiresses, which makes me think of the vines Rosa kept in her herbarium,[42] those incredible plants that move from the ground up, that grow everywhere, unexpectedly, often unnoticed, but so persistently and tenaciously!

Other than that, I want you to know that nothing you say disappoints me, *alita querida*. On the contrary, I consider it an expression of great honesty when you acknowledge your division of labour with Gustavo. Thanks also for telling me about some of the great *cocineras* in your family. On my side, I have been very lucky to get to know my two great-grandmothers Mariquita and Esperanza and my grandmother, *mi abuelita*, Mama Nane, all three of whom were very good cooks. And then there was my great-grandfather José, who used to keep goats and whom as I child I witnessed preparing their meat in various ways.

So just like John Berger (2015) gifted Rosa a collection of matchboxes containing coloured engravings of different songbirds, I have been thinking a little bit more about the dish in homage to her, and I finally dreamed up a recipe with a combination of different flavours from my homeland. Here it is:

Given Rosa's connection to flowers, the main ingredient will be *cabuches*, which are the flowers of the Biznaga cactus. They usually bloom in our spring, i.e. in March/April, and the people who harvest them are the workers, both male and female, of the semi-desert. In fact, the *cabuches* are quite difficult to pick between the many thorns. The way we commonly eat them is as part of

---

41 Luxemburgo 1978: 491.
42 Editor's note: The Spanish word for heiresses, "*herederas*," is very similar to the word for vine, "*enredadera*."

157

different salads and, in our case, I suggest we accompany them with a *salsa de pitayas*, or pitaya sauce, made of what is known as dragon fruit in other parts of the world. What is special about pitayas is that their colours are red, like the cause Rosa fought for, and white, to symbolize her pronounced sense of pacifism. Besides, they usually have an amazingly shiny pink (in Spanish *"rosa"*) peel and they are, like her, firm and vigorous on the outside and sweet and tender on the inside. Additional ingredients could include black beans with *epazote*, a herb that will add special aroma and flavour, *aguacate* (avocado) and *nopalitos*, the stems of the prickly pear cactus, which we eat very frequently here in Mexico. Finally, I am thinking of adding *cabrito a las brasas*, or barbecued goat meat, a local delicacy from my home region. In fact, we have a popular saying that goes *"las cabras tiran pa'l monte,"* in the sense of goats being indomitable and often walking up the steepest paths, which for me links powerfully with the search and struggle for freedom of the fugitives from colonial slavery, the *cimarronaje*. To top it all off, we could finish our meal with your special dessert: lemon pudding with poppy seeds, which represents the rebellious joy Rosa so beautifully embodied. And that's it. *Listo nuestro menú luxemburguiano!* Bon appétit!

Speaking of sustenance, how much has Rosita nourished us with her life force, in which the personal and the political are one total, feminine experience in permanent revolutionary passion. What she bequeathed us with in her life and letters is an irrevocable dignity with which to continue weaving with red thread – no longer of blood and sacrifice, but of struggle and commitment – our own his- and herstory.

So, considering what's happening on a planetary level today, with the brutal violence of capital (extractive *and* criminal at the same time) bringing us ever closer to the abyss, it is now more essential than ever to redouble her prophetic "Socialism or Barbarism," and to inculcate ourselves with this Luxemburguian passion for emancipatory transformation, because passion and commitment to the truth are not forms of indoctrination, but something that is shared with others and passed on. In this sense, I send you the following speech Rosa gave in October 1910, in the German city of Hagen, at the General Assembly of the Union of Metalworkers:

Party comrades! Each lockout is one new nail in the coffin of the capitalist order, because it's precisely the lockout method currently preferred—which fails to conquer the proletariat—which provides the best proof that the current ordering of society is no longer possible, but has indeed become untenable, and that it has to make way for a new ordering. And is not every mass strike a step forward to overcoming this old order? Party comrades, the famous *Communist Manifesto* of Marx and Engels concludes with the words: "The proletarians have nothing to lose but their chains. They have a world to win." We will only be armed for the great battle – which we'll have to fight in the coming period – when every proletarian organized in a union has understood that their vocation is in the Social Democratic party, when every socialist proletarian has understood that they have a duty to internalize socialist educational literature, and when every worker active in and organized through a union is simultaneously a steadfast warrior for socialist liberation, conscious of their goals. It is only under this battle cry that we'll be able to prove victorious in the coming battles, when the last proletarian has understood that they have only their chains to lose, but a whole world to win.[43]

To conclude, I subscribe to the words of the Mexican-Ecuadorian critical thinker Bolívar Echeverría, who in the prologue to Rosa's Spanish-language *Selected Works* stressed that "after Marx and Engels, no one more than Rosa Luxemburg has managed to define the total character, that is to say, the unitarily objective and subjective character, of the revolutionary situation."[44]

Red Rosa was, is and will be like an ardent ember, and even though more than a century has passed since a group of vile men cut her life short, her political ideas continue to irradiate and illuminate us.

alita, let us not say good-bye, but rather see you very soon. We are here waiting for you with open arms and hearts.

y firmando como nuestra Rosita, tuya y de la causa socialista,

---

43 Editor's note: Translation by Henry Holland. The full translation of the entire article will be available in *The Complete Works of Rosa Luxemburg, Volume 5* (Verso, forthcoming).
44 Echeverría in Luxemburgo 1978: 15.

Receta-homenaje a
Rosa Luxemburgo

El semi desierto, en el altiplano potosino

Cabuches, la flor de la biznaga

pitayas

Cabuches en salsa de pitaya para
Rosita, acompañados con nopalitos y
frijolitos negros con epazote y
aguacate
Cabrito-chivito a las brasas

Cabrito-chivito

Receta-Homenaje a Rosa Luxemburgo

160

References

Dussel, Enrique (2018), "Siete hipótesis para una estética de la liberación." *Praxis. Revista de Filosofía* No. 77, 1-37.

Berger, John (2015), "A letter to Rosa Luxemburg." *New Statesman*. Accessed on 27.08.21, at https://www.newstatesman.com/2015/09/letter-rosa-luxemburg-0.

Echeverría, Bolívar (1978), "Prólogo," in *Rosa Luxemburgo – Obras escogidas 1*. Mexico City: Ediciones Era.

Granados, Luis Fernando (2016), *En el espejo haitiano. Los indios del Bajío y el colapso del orden colonial en América Latina*. Mexico City: Era.

Luxemburg, Rosa (1917a), "Letter to Hanna-Elsbeth Stühmer." *RS LXMBRG*. Accessed on 22.08.21, at https://rosaluxemburg.org/en/material/2686/.

Luxemburg, Rosa (1917b), "Letter to Sophie Liebknecht." *Marxist Internet Archive*. Accessed on 22.08.21, at https://rosaluxemburg.org/en/material/2686/.

Luxemburg, Rosa (2004), *The Rosa Luxemburg Reader*. Eds. Peter Hudis and Kevin B. Anderson. New York: Monthly Review Press.

Luxemburg, Rosa (2008), *The Essential Rosa Luxemburg*. Ed. Helen Scott. Chicago: Haymarket Books.

Luxemburg, Rosa (2013a), "Introduction to Political Economy," in *The Complete Works of Rosa Luxemburg. Volume 1. Economic Writings 1*. Eds. David Fernbach, Joseph Fracchia and George Shriver. London and New York: Verso Books.

Luxemburg, Rosa (2013b), *The Letters of Rosa Luxemburg*. Eds. Georg Adler, Peter Hudis, and Annelies Laschitza. London and New York: Verso Books.

Luxemburg, Rosa (forthcoming), *The Complete Works of Rosa Luxemburg. Volume 5. Political Writings 3*. Eds. David Fernbach, Joseph Fracchia and George Shriver. London and New York: Verso Books.

Muiña, Ana (2019), *Rosa Luxemburg en la tormenta*. Madrid: La linterna sorda.

Pineda, Francisco (2019), "Operaciones especiales para asesinar a Emiliano Zapata," *Memoria. Revista de Crítica Militante*. Accessed on 23.07.21, at http://revistamemoria.mx/?p=2565.

Piercy, Marge (2020), *Mujer al borde del tiempo*. Bilbao: consonni.

Rivera, Andrés (2008), *La Revolución es un sueño eterno*. Buenos Aires: Seix Barral.

Translation from the original Argentine and Mexican Spanish: Hjalmar Jorge Joffre-Eichhorn.

Y sonrío en la oscuridad a la vida
como si supiera un secreto
prodigioso que niega todo lo
malvado, todo lo triste, y lo
transforma en alegría y felicidad
(...) creo que el secreto no es
otra cosa que la vida misma [45]

45 "And in the dark I smile at life, as if I knew some sort of magical secret that gives the lie to everything evil and sad and changes it into pure light and happiness. And all the while I'm searching within myself for some reason for this joy, I find nothing and must smile to myself again-and laugh at myself I believe that the secret is nothing other than life itself." (Luxemburg 2013b: 455)

Foto Ullstein

Rosa Luxemburg

ERSTTAGSBRIEF   Folio-print

6. Jane Anna Gordon
&
Xiong Min

I lie there quietly, alone, wrapped in these many-layered black veils of darkness, boredom, lack of freedom, and winter – and at the same time my heart is racing with an incomprehensible, unfamiliar inner joy as though I were walking across a flowering meadow in radiant sunshine. And in the dark I smile at life, as if I knew some sort of magical secret that gives the lie to everything evil and sad and changes it into pure light and happiness. And all the while I'm searching within myself for some reason for this joy, I find nothing and must smile to myself again – and laugh at myself. I believe that the secret is nothing other than life itself; the deep darkness of night is so beautiful and as soft as velvet, if one only looks at it the right way; and in the crunching of the damp sand beneath the slow, heavy steps of the sentries a beautiful small song of life is being sung – if one only knows how to listen properly.

Rosa Luxemburg[1]

March 16, 2021
West Hartford, Connecticut, USA

Dear Viong Min,

Ours is an interesting assignment! While we have not met each other until now, we are engaging in a way that is usually shared by people who hope to continue existing relations under conditions interrupted by necessary or chosen travel, incarceration or other forms of forced confinement or separation. In these cases, the words of the letter reach out across the physical distance, hoping to bridge it. Still, there is something so welcome about the direct and unmediated contact of the written letter; to meet someone without the stilted fluff of awkward formalities or the overly casual and brief mode of the email. And there is a sense in which we are not total strangers: a shared love of the words and deeds of Rosa Luxemburg and commitment to their continued relevance as guide and inspiration makes us already kindred spirits, if kindred spirits who have much to learn about and from each other!

When the pandemic lockdown began, a friend who works for our faculty union shared the link to the Resistance Revival Chorus's version of Woodie Guthrie's song, "All You Fascists Bound to Lose!"[2] I listened to it over and over and sent it to anyone who I thought would receive it warmly. In addition to the wonderful world of images of the video that illustrated the melody, I was moved by the confidence of its message: that fascists – of the past and present – are *bound* to lose. As I sang along or hummed the chorus while moving through my day, it felt like a kind of meditation. The confidence of the message had an inherent logic – you can only fight reality so long; you cannot oppress the majority of humankind forever. I wanted this to be true, especially as we faced Donald J. Trump's possible reelection to the presidency of the United States. But I realized that the confidence is actually born of the commitment the song nurtures and rekindles. As we sing the song, we recommit to helping its message be and become true.

1 Luxemburg 2013: 455.
2 Listen at https://www.youtube.com/watch?v=dWUa7aAlfLE.

Curious about the other music recorded by this multiracial group of women singers that had formed in the wake of Trump's election, I looked for more and found another song, "This Joy."[3] A straightforward, repeated melody, the message is simple:

> This Joy that I have, the world didn't give it to me;
> this joy that I have, the world didn't give it to me;
> this joy that I have, the world didn't give it to me;
> the world didn't give it, the world can't take it away.

As with "All you fascists bound to lose!," I listened to it over and over again. The message was true and something we want to be true and something we need to be true and something we can try to make true. Much as we try, as is true with desire, we cannot make other people, or ourselves, feel joy. We can set the conditions for its likely emergence; we can commit to cultivating it; we can name and celebrate it when it appears hesitantly or in its full glory.

The song expressed the idea that, especially for the Black women singing, their joy existed despite the world they occupy – this joy that I have, the world didn't give it to me. They felt and celebrated joy that they and others disavowed by this world had nurtured and generated. Having done so, it was also protected; since the world hadn't given it, it also couldn't take it. Their joy was autonomously produced; it could not be violently seized. Their joy was outside of, exceeding the predictable terms and coordinates of the world we know. Rather than accounting for how it had emerged – so that it could be duplicated or reproduced – the song named and celebrated it; almost teasing and taunting the world that could not capture or domesticate it. I am thinking about the incalculable, the human resources that the world as we know it does not generate and maybe therefore also can't take.

When Rosa writes "and in the crunching of the damp sand beneath the slow, heavy steps of the sentries a beautiful small song of life is being sung – if one only knows how to listen properly," I think often of what actually enables us to listen properly. The capacity to do so is not narrowly technical; it isn't even about the sufficient galvanizing of the will. For me, at least, really hearing is not just about registering what is being said but what goes unspoken, grasping the world of references, hopes, and disappointments that ground the phrases being uttered. I think it requires what Max Weber called an inner plasticity, an interior feeling that is still supple and responsive, capable of being touched and touching. For me, joy describes when this inner plasticity remains intact, when the suppleness has not become sedimented in ways that constrain how we do and do not hear. When sedimented, we hear impatiently, waiting only to identify what is already familiar and well-known, what only affirms existing impasses and impossibilities.

Rosa's reflections on how we can try and then be thankful for the actual feeling of such *inner plasticity*, which we cannot simply call up or manufacture, resonate deeply. For me, they arise in instances that I experience as a gift: when, after long periods of arid cold, a beam of sunlight feels as if it is gently touching my cheek; when, even with daily care and attention, a gawkish new shoot of a plant uncurls itself, daring also to reach toward the sky; when the timing of a seemingly chance

---

3 Listen at https://www.youtube.com/watch?v=1TbDPwA09Bc.

encounter seems to bespeak a larger, orchestrated design for which we and our ways of understanding human life could not account; when something offered up and out in to the world returns embellished *just so*.

It's clear, through Rosa's reflections, that she marked when such a feeling suddenly returned because she knew that it could be lost, temporarily but perhaps for longer. Feeling it was never to be taken for granted. It was precious and fiercely delicate. It could be eroded. I think we need that song's chorus because while joy may be independently generated, it can be taken away or at least threatened and tested. And it cannot be rebuilt through deliberate, straightforward design. Fascism is of course an enemy of joy. The closest thing to joy in its orbit is manufactured, saccharine happiness in which no formulaic rules are bent or broken.

Rosa's attention to joy or *inner plasticity* or the inward porosity and openness that was indispensable to her thought and politics – an orientation of putting into deeper and broader and ever more meaningful relation – connected, I think, to the ways in which she broadened the dialectic at the core of the Marxist project. Just as she refused to consider capitalism as a closed system, even as an exercise in conceptual clarification, or insisted on the dependency of capitalist domains on non- or pre-capitalist ones, or broadened the category of worker beyond the conventional proletariat and considered the actual globe when referring to the global, this attention to the indispensability of *joy* always and especially when it was imperiled seemed not like a whimsical, feminine aside, but as essential – and essential in ways that are affirmed and echoed and expanded in contemporary movements like Black Lives Matter.

Just as "All you fascists bound to lose!" is a statement of fact and a call to make the statement factual, "This joy" is a meditation on a good that can't be mass produced or controlled or commodified – that exceeds the totalizing world of capitalism – but that can be endangered. The song is a call to think about how to assure that it is not taken, because that joy is indispensable to surviving this world by birthing a new one inside and beyond it.

Do these questions and reflections have any resonance with you?

Much looking forward to receiving your letter,

Jane

166

"in every article you must live through the thing again, you must feel your way through it, and then fresh words — coming from the heart, going to the heart — would occur to express the old familiar thing."[4]

4 "In every article you must live through the thing again, you must feel your way through it, and then fresh words – coming from the heart, going to the heart – would occur to express the old familiar thing." (Luxemburg 2013: 65)

I must admit that your letter and the two songs mentioned in it cheered me up quite a bit. I felt the determination and confidence that goodness will prevail, the deep understanding of the infinite possibilities of the new world to come, which is the secret of the kind of magic that Rosa imparted in her letter to Sophie.

As you say, the love of Rosa has connected us in such an interesting and rewarding way. Even though we have never met, your letter gives me the impression that you are a passionate and righteous intellectual woman with an open mind and a love of life. Am I right? :)

Slightly different from what I imagined you to be, I think I am also an intellectual woman with a sense of justice, open-minded and good at finding beauty, but somehow I lack passion, and I have a mind of muddling along and worrying about gain and loss, and I often feel ashamed for it. I think the crux of my problem is a certain obsession with certainty, or rather, I am unintentionally following the kind of solidified thinking that you criticize in your letter. This is probably because I was born in the era of China's socialist planned economy. Although I was actually a beneficiary of the reform and opening up of China, the illusion of a carefree childhood always made me nostalgic for that era. Therefore, I was afraid of change and always saw the pessimistic side of the disruption of order. Even though in my teaching and in my life I have repeatedly found unexpected and surprising possibilities behind seemingly unchanging appearances, I still subconsciously seek the protection of certainty. Of course, when I say this, it also means that I am seeking change. Making changes is necessary. I can't help but think that if more Rosa-like people had stood with her in her time, history might have been rewritten, and the massacre of Jews by Hitler's regime might not have happened. In this sense, I couldn't agree more with you that "we need that song's chorus"!

This change is happening. Yesterday I had the last class of a course I am teaching. I used to despise the course because I resented its strong ideological color, and chose to play it safe by just reading from the book for fear that a thoughtless remark would be reported. Yet for the first time since the epidemic, I so genuinely wanted to share with my students the joy and method of thinking about issues, about Luxemburg, and about the essence of Marxism as I understood it. And once I started to do so, I not only felt more relaxed and happier than ever, but also received quite a few surprises from my students, like yesterday... A quarter of an hour before the end of class, I asked my students to draw a portrait of me as a souvenir. They were so excited about my request that they happily scribbled on the paper, handed me all kinds of exaggerated, realistic or imaginary drawings, and then said goodbye to me with smiles. The end of class soon arrived and there was only a chubby boy still drawing. I was both surprised and curious, what would he draw me as? Finally, I saw the drawing, in which several notes were floating in the air while I was listening with my eyes closed. What he drew was what I looked like during the break between classes! I have to admit that this is one of my favorite portraits, perhaps because through it I know he feels that inner plasticity you speak of, and what a delight that is!

治安学硕士
柏 澍
20201180095

Rosa once criticized her girlfriend Mathilde Wurm, "To me it is disastrous that you now have no time or mood for anything but 'item number one,' namely the miserable state of the party, because such one-sidedness also clouds one's political judgment, and above all one must at all times live as a complete human being."[5] Yes, one must at all times live as a complete human being! Perhaps it was Rosa's words that struck me invisibly, and during the epidemic I began to look more intently at the flowers and trees around me, and to recognize the different calls of the birds and their specific names.

A few days ago I watched my daughters walk into the campus and headed back to college to teach my own classes. The sun was shining, the breeze was blowing, and it was a beautiful, pleasant spring morning. Walking on the road, I felt that everyone passing by was so kind and lovely, even if most people were wearing masks. Suddenly, a melodious song attracted me, and I looked up to see a titmouse standing on an air-conditioning bracket of a high-rise building, looking left and right, and sometimes singing for a while. I stood there, listening for minutes, and could not help but think of Rosa's passage,

---

5 Luxemburg 2013: 375.

On my grave, as in my life, there will be no pompous phrases. Only two syllables will be allowed to appear on my gravestone: "Tsvee-tsvee." That is the call made by the large blue titmouse, which I can imitate so well that they all immediately come running. And just think, in this call, which is usually quite clear and thin, sparkling like a steel needle, in the last few days there has been quite a low, little trill, a tiny chesty sound. And do you know what that means, Miss Jacob? That is the first soft stirring of the coming spring. In spite of the snow and frost and the loneliness, we believe – the titmice and I – in the coming of spring! And if out of impatience I don't live through it, then don't forget that on my gravestone nothing is to appear except that "Tsvee-tsvee."[6]

Spring is really here! And even if it's not, it's important for us to keep it in our hearts.

Dear Jane, have you ever been to China? What are your images of China? What do you imagine about the future of the world? Maybe we could talk about it in our next letter :)

祝 好 ! (Best,)

致

6 Ibid: 373.

"使我感到兴趣的只是这一切的总和，而不是割裂开来的某一部分。"[7]

---

7 "It is only the whole that interests me, rather than any detached detail." (Luxemburg 2013: 432)

May 16, West Hartford

Dear Min,

While I will not belabour it, I am very sorry that you were waiting to hear from me as I thought I was awaiting word from you.[8] It makes me wonder about how indispensable lucky timing is to the development of core human relations... As I said in one of my email messages, I have had several letters to you brewing inside me, but deliberately reduced them to a simmer to avoid being overbearing. Ah, the joys of being socialized as female!

Regarding your question, I have never traveled to China, but do have many meaningful, mediated connections to it. First, my husband's paternal grandmother was a Jamaican-born Chinese-Scottish woman, Gertrude, who coupled with my husband's paternal grandfather, Colwood, an Afro-Jamaican draftsman. They had four children together, including my husband's father, before Colwood found himself someone he considered a more fitting, African-American wife. When Gertrude struggled to secure a home for herself, the four boys were left to fend for themselves, living for a time on the street. Gertrude later became a concubine to a Chinese merchant working in Jamaica. They had three more children. Six of Gertrude's seven children are close as adults living in the United States. In fact, two lived together in Long Island City, New York until the younger sister, Thelma, died. My husband, Lewis Gordon, is very interested in all of the dimensions of who he is – Chinese, East African, Irish, Palestinian Jewish, Scottish, and Tamil. He knows that his Chinese relatives were from Guangdong and that he is able to hear sounds that many non-Chinese speakers struggle to grasp because Cantonese was spoken around him when he was a little boy. Our children, who have grown up in the United States with its racial history, find their non-Black-Chinese Jamaican relatives intriguing. Physically Chinese, they speak like Black Jamaicans and are similar in their political and social orientations.

My sister-in-law is the daughter of a Chinese mother from Burma and a Chinese father from Singapore. She and my brother first met as architecture students in Boston. She agreed to marry him on the condition that they moved closer to her home. First they settled in Shanghai, now they live with their children and her family in Singapore. This means that my parents have no grandchildren who are not connected, in some way, to China's global diaspora! This is especially interesting since, for a very long time, we joked that our family followed the contours of the British empire, as we connected South Africa, England, and the United States, Jamaica and Singapore, and, more recently, Ghana.

My other, meaningful connection to China is through the university. As is true of so many U.S. universities, University of Connecticut enrolls large numbers of

---

8 Editor's note: Just like in the days of Luxemburg when handwritten letters would sometimes be held up somewhere or even be lost forever, Min's first letter to Jane was sent by email on March 28, but only made it into Jane's inbox in early May. In the meantime, both had been anxiously waiting for each other's responses.

Chinese students. One graduate student whom I mentor grew up on the China-Russia border. He is wonderfully intellectually curious and mature and especially interested in African-American, African, and Chinese historical progressive intellectual and political exchanges. When he is explaining a point to me, I often need to ask several questions to secure sufficient context to begin to understand. The asking and answering is fascinating and enriching. One example was his anger at the way that the U.S. press covers the treatment of Muslims in China. (It is regularly and consistently repeated, as if in one voice, that the Chinese government systematically violates the rights of Uyghurs through their surveillance and mass detention in reeducation camps (or segregated, enclosed sites of political indoctrination) that are fracturing Uyghur families and communities.) This is a "cause" that quickly unites Muslim- and Chinese-American students. In response, my student began to post video after video of Muslim Chinese people in China assembled and dancing to Uyghur music with dignity and joy. He was using his Facebook to wage what he considered a counter-propaganda campaign. But I needed to ask him several questions to understand the nature and meaning of his intervention. He explained that he sought to use contemporary footage to counter the idea that Muslims were being incarcerated in dehumanizing camps that could be compared to European or U.S. concentration camps, suggesting that China was no more humane or less oppressive than the Western countries criticizing it. (In these comments, his reflections reminded me of Rosa's important essay, "Martinique," from 1902 where she identified the hypocrisy of European powers showing outpourings of grief and support for the way the volcanic eruption of Mt. Pelée wreaked havoc on the very same Caribbean people that they had used political means to mow down in their own colonies.) More generally, most progressive intellectuals in the U.S. want to understand contemporary China. Each seeks to develop an accurate diagnosis and prognosis. More mundanely, I increasingly feel, when mentoring Chinese students like the one I mentioned, that I am contributing to the generation of the intelligentsia of the rising world power; that Chinese students who come to the U.S. to study increasingly resemble certain U.S.-Americans who would travel to declining European empires to help to envision and construct their own. As was true with some among the previous generations of U.S. students who mined Europe for important lessons in trying to build a better U.S. future, some Chinese students are also trying to envision what would be a progressive use of emergent Chinese power, both domestically and in the world at large. My student was struck by the way that the experience of anti-Chinese racism while studying in the United States had turned many critics of the Chinese government into the most avid of Chinese nationalists.

I think that you are right to frame your desire for certainty as an obstacle to living with passion. When I first began to really talk with the man who would become my husband – of 22 years today! – he cautioned me against the widespread tendency, in others and myself, to want "the outcome before the performance;" to want to know the results that would transpire before undertaking the relevant endeavor. He was and is an existentialist *and* profoundly brave. The same was true of his mother, who came to the United States as a young, dark-skinned Jamaican woman with almost no money or the requisite papers. While remarkably talented and hard-working, they learned over and over that they could not assume that the rules of fair play would apply to them. I think often of the contrast with my own parents. When they moved to the United States in 1979 in their early thirties, it was their third emigration. Also unusually talented and hard-working, and certainly experiencing discriminations and unfairness of different kinds, the rules of fair play did apply to them with relatively more, if not complete, consistency. While also daring in many important ways, until quite recently, they could more readily expect established rules of merit to work roughly as they should.

While it is certainly an orientation at which I have had to work – it did not come readily or easily – I have found the most rewarding experiences of my life – marrying my husband and becoming a mother in my early twenties; serving as the president of the Caribbean Philosophical Association and creating and leading its Summer School; directing and building the graduate program at my current institution – are those where I committed fully to relationships and endeavors where I could not know the full shape and content of the commitments I was making. All involved profound challenges for which I had no existing answers. In the face of them, I could only try my very best, working tirelessly and drawing on analogous and not-so-comparable experiences. I certainly made mistakes, sometimes quite dire ones. I am thankful that most were repairable, even if the repair took considerable time. These undertakings demanded embracing uncertainty. Increasingly the most valuable projects seem to be precisely those that are as necessary as they are not entirely clear. The promise is in dwelling in and creating through what we do not yet know. Through it, new kinds of relationships develop as well as new ways of doing and being.

Over the last half decade, when advocating for creating new rules or programs, I found myself repeating to cautious colleagues that we cannot know and avoid everything that might go wrong in advance; that we will need to begin to know what we need to fix. And we will have to make amendments and adjustments. In making such arguments with some colleagues to others, we are living and exemplifying an alternative to a sedimentary conservatism that allows fear to outweigh emergent possibilities. But of course, rather than simply admitting to fear, all kinds of possible, smart-sounding problems are trotted out as reasons never to begin anew. In my own small way, in these moments I feel imbued with the spirit of Rosa as she repeatedly challenged the collapse of the SPD into party proceduralism in view of aiming to cultivate the revolutionary subjectivity of the proletariat masses. Unlike so many of the party's leadership, she was not simply applying already worked out principles but trying to figure out the concepts, strategies, and diagnoses of her own time.

I increasingly discuss the need to begin and to try even where the prospects are unclear with my students who are rightly eager and anxious about their shared futures. Speaking of students, I would love to see any or all of the portraits yours drew of you!

Would you be willing to share them? I am especially curious to see the one that you said captured your 'listening eyes'!

Jane

PS: Almost eight years ago, my family moved from Providence, Rhode Island to a small town in Connecticut. In Providence, which is a small post-industrial immigrant city, we lived in an urban park. At home, in large part due to the variety of work schedules of our many neighbors, we heard a rich cacophony of sounds through the day and night. Now we live in what was once a mountain orchard. Except for the sounds of passing cars, it is sufficiently quiet that, especially each early morning, we hear the sounds of various birds. At first we filled feeders with bird seed and enjoyed watching the shapes and patterns of their always purposeful flight. The trouble was that the small set of bears that live higher up the mountain were also drawn to the seeds! When you (and Rosa) comment on what it is to hear the voices of birds, I think of a story told to me by a deaf colleague. She explained that she planned to hike with some friends and inserted a hearing aide to prepare for the fullest possible experience. She found the sounds of birds to be so loud that she didn't understand how any hearing person could think when they were around! For her, their sounds were a resounding, deafening intrusion!

PPS: Since writing last, I read and reread the talk you presented at the Rosa 150 international conference, "Rosa Luxemburg at 150: Revisiting Her Radical Life and Legacy," organized by the Rosa Luxemburg Foundation on March 4/5 this year. *It was so rich.* I was struck by your reflections regarding suffering; what we can mourn when it is at a safe distance. And how moving between proximity and distance is at the core of the work of intellectuals. My husband had a very severe case of COVID. While he seems now to have permanently turned a positive corner, he has struggled with its multifaceted symptoms for almost a year. And, as the entire world knows, Donald Trump couldn't have mishandled the pandemic more mightily. As a result, the majority of U.S.-Americans know someone who has died directly or indirectly due to COVID. Its toll is proximate. What I have found particularly difficult is losing close family members – not due to COVID – who live at a distance and being unable to travel to bury and mourn them. While one writes to their immediate kin and receives photographs and messages, as my husband observed, it feels as if these now deceased family have simply disappeared. I reflected to my students one week, when I had been hit with two particularly difficult, far-away losses, that it was as if the social fabric of my life wasn't even unravelling. It was simply disappearing into thin air.

"What do you want with this particular
suffering of the Jews? ... the Africans with whose
bodies the Europeans play a game of catch are just as
near to me."[9]

9 "What do you want with this particular suffering of the Jews? [...] the Africans with whose bodies the Europeans play a game of catch are just as near to me." (Luxemburg 2013: 375)

May 30, Wuhan

This is really fantastic! Because of the misunderstanding, I personally feel that I am closer to you. To use a Chinese expression: "no discord, no concord." :)

First of all, I want to hug you tightly, and wish you and your husband health and happiness! In terms of physical distance, it is obviously a distant hug, but from the fact that we have shared this world-changing year, it is also an embrace that empathizes and speaks for itself. I can't help but think of a poem written by Brecht in 1940:

> This is the year people will talk about.
> This is the year people will keep quiet about.
> The old see the young dying.
> The foolish see the wise dying.
> The earth no longer bears fruit, but it swallows.
> Rain does not fall from the sky, only iron.[10]

I think that only by replacing one of the sentences with "the young people watched the old people die," it is extremely applicable to today's world. Seeing you describe the sudden disappearance of some important people in life, silently, the living never even having the opportunity to say goodbye to them, I could understand the pain, although my situation is slightly different from yours. In fact, it was these key moments in my life that shaped my outlook on the world and life today.

My brother, mother and father left me due to accidents or illness when I was 3, 26 and 35 years old respectively, and my family of origin thus disappeared. I must admit that this made me extraordinarily greedy for life and afraid of death. In a sense, it not only aggravated my anxiety during the epidemic, but also helped me to ignite the courage to live a new life now. So I feel fortunate that the early death of my dearest did not make me feel numb or even disgusted with life, but made me awed to all forms of life and sensitive to all forms of oppression. For me, life is precious because of its impermanence, and it is worth living well.

Referring to the impermanence of life, I think that maybe just to deal with this impermanence, I subconsciously seek some certainties, in order to obtain comfort and security. As I said in the first letter, and as you responded, too much pursuit of certainty will limit us, and it will also limit our imagination and creation of this world. However, as I continued thinking about this issue, I couldn't help but wonder what am I talking about when I say, "certainty". In other words, are there different "certainties," some of which stand in the way, and some of which serve as the background and motivation for us to be human? I think I do need

---

10 Brecht 2018: 772.

some inherent certainties, such as knowing exactly that there is a constant good side in human beings, that the pursuit of public ethics and conscience is always meaningful and valuable, that I have been given unconditional family love and that I am now giving it to my children... Only on this basis can I have the confidence and courage to face and challenge the external uncertainty, and even seek and enjoy the many possibilities contained in it. Here I'd like to recommend to you a poem titled "Possibilities" written by Wisława Szymborska. I love it when she says, "I prefer not to maintain that reason is to blame for everything." I love the rich possibilities of life and humanity presented in this poem so much!

Unlike your happy marriage, a few years I chose ago to end an increasingly estranged and unhappy marriage that lasted 15 years. Rosa was quite unsatisfied with Mrs. Stein's weakness when Goethe broke off with her, and she wrote, "I cleave to the idea that a woman's character doesn't show itself when love begins, but when it ends."[11] In that way, I suppose Rosa won't feel disappointed with me. It was a very painful process, but it was also a process that brought me back to myself. It was during that marriage that I felt first-hand that women's discursive and decision-making power is to a large degree influenced by their economic independence, and that even for Chinese men with higher education, the concept of patriarchy is often still an internal background. And when I looked back at that marriage, I was surprised to find that I was actually practicing self-numbness and self-discipline all the time, under the implicit influence of gender inequality. I finally realized that the failure of my marriage was, to a certain extent, the complicity of the two people in it. In that case, I should also take on my own responsibility.

Dear Jane, when I know that your family has so many Chinese elements, I feel so cordial and happy! On the one hand, it does make me more open to you emotionally and psychologically, and I really appreciate your family's openness and acceptance of different cultures; on the other hand, it also allows me to see the real possibilities of the interaction between Chinese culture and other cultures. I believe that this kind of blending not only empowers the respective cultures with greater resilience and vitality, but is also becoming an emerging realistic way to resolve many contradictions and disputes. In the face of this integration, concepts such as 'nation' and 'race' that nowadays emphasize external distinctions rather than connections may become suspicious. Recently, I have been deeply attracted by Yo-Yo Ma, a cellist. I'm certainly attracted to the music he plays, especially the "Bach Suite". But what makes me even more impressed is that he has been trying to show with his various musical practices that what he really loves is people, not abstract people, not specific Chinese, Jamaicans, Americans... but concrete, flesh-and-blood individuals. Szymborska says in her poem, "I prefer myself liking people to myself loving mankind." I think that your family and Yo-Yo Ma have undoubtedly interpreted this perfectly. Moreover, the project initiated by Hjalmar in which we two are participating is also dedicated to building beautiful connections between individuals who share a common human foundation but are different from each other. It is precisely because of these incentives that I have become less pessimistic about the world, more in love with it, and am willing and actually doing something to make it a better place.

---

11 Luxemburg 1978: 163.

The real world is a complex place. It is not only filled with joy, but also with pain, compromise and cruelty. Knowing this, experiencing it personally, but still maintaining warmth and purity, and using their actions to promote change, and even living themselves as an antidote to suffering, this is what I think the ideal state of life is for intellectuals. In addition, from a teacher's point of view, I think it is also possible to use this metaphor: the teacher's job is to lead students to see and embark on this long road, from the pure state of the initial ignorance to the pure state with the vicissitudes of life without regrets. This path must be taken by the students themselves, after all. The teachers can neither go down this path in their place, nor can they promise to reduce the difficulties and obstacles in the process. The only work that teachers can do is to step on the road first, lead or wait for them when necessary, and give methodological guidance and spiritual comfort. Thus, I really appreciate the asking and answering between you and your Chinese student. I think this is the real education process. And I'm sure that Rosa must also agree with this, otherwise she wouldn't have complained about the way the trade union school organized: "there can be no idea at all of discussion with the teacher, no thorough treatment of the material by allowing questions and talking things over from every angle."[12]

Imperceptibly we have gone from spring to summer together. At this moment in front of my window, swallows are flying up and down, white-headed bulbul, gray magpie, blackbird, cuckoo, and many other unknown birds are singing in the trees, and they are sometimes mixed with cars' engines, the conversation of neighbors as they walk by and the sound of a high-speed train running in the distance... I like the story you shared with me. I'm not sure how you understood that story. My understanding is that in ordinary people's daily lives, beautiful things and natural sounds are often overlooked or only act as background, because they are too familiar and common to those people, however, they are often easily captured and felt by those who are usually regarded as disabled. Of course, if extended from the other side, what might be bearable to the average person might be unbearable to them. And I wonder if there is such a situation for Rosa as well? In any case, this story seems to tell us what Michael Sandel says, "Once the familiar turns strange, it's never quite the same again," and that will provoke a new way of seeing.

祝一切都好！(Best wishes,)

殷文

PS: Just this morning, I received a sad call that one of my uncles died of cancer. He watched me grow up; losing him has a special meaning to me. As Rosa described at the loss of her beloved Hans, the pain "is like a word cut short in mid-sentence, like a musical chord broken off, although I still keep hearing it."[13] The only consolation is that I could go to the neighboring city to say my final goodbye to him. I'll set out early tomorrow morning.

---

12 Luxemburg 2011: 304.
13 Luxemburg 2013: 441.

"无论在我的墓碑上还是在我的生活中都不会有傲慢虚伪的空话。"[14]

---

14 "On my grave, as in my life, there will be no pompous phrases." (Luxemburg 2013: 373)

June 17, West Hartford

$\mathcal{D}ea\mathcal{R}\ \mathcal{M}in,$

I seem to have begun all my recent correspondences – not only to you – with apologies. While these are heartfelt and warranted, there is also an absurdity to them. They are heartfelt when, as in our case, there was a genuine misunderstanding to which I clearly contributed. And they are warranted when addressed to those shepherding important collective projects that require coordinating momentum. Having served as shepherd on many occasions, I am all too familiar with the frustration of the sheep that appear to march to their own drummers! At the same time, I know that I am apologizing for circumstances that I could do nothing to improve. In a moment when rare opportunities required accumulating leadership roles, piling up complex and demanding responsibilities, when honest, there is no way that I could have been more efficient. It does not make sense to apologize for trying to rise positively to one's circumstances. At the same time, one does wish that one could do the impossible, have ever sharper anticipatory powers to puzzle through the juggling of convening deadlines! As I write this, the counsel of an older African American philosopher runs through my head: it is inelegant and ungainly to detail being overwhelmed to members of communities defined by having to shoulder far more than their share.

A more profound apology is for the reverberating "word cut short in mid-sentence," the "musical chord broken off" in the loss of your beloved uncle. My father commented recently on the radically dwindling number of people who share actual memories of his early life, who can affirm or correct the truth of formative, orienting biographical stories. Increasingly it is only my mom, my father's wife of over fifty years, who shares as her own the record of major portions of their lives. It is consoling to know that you were able to travel to say a final goodbye.

I loved the Chinese expression with which you opened your most recent letter, Min. I loved it because of its sagacious insight and because it is wisdom that I find profoundly challenging. As an orientation, I often am relatively quick to identify lines of division that surface in ways adjacent to the actual source of conflict. In my workplace, I never hesitate to identify these. It is not that I seek out conflict or discord. Many consider me easy to work with because, in a way that I associate with mothering, I can keep afloat and not collapse important differences. But I resent the time wasted through trying to minimize important disagreements. This is a public face connected to the commitments that drive how I understand my role. In private, I am much more afraid of conflict. I know that such conflicts can lead to more meaningful ultimate resolutions, often following hurt, but sense in a preverbal way that they can also lead to abrupt endings – to writing people off; shutting down connections that have functioned like avenues. My more theoretical self knows that differences that lead to endings might in fact be welcome and necessary but there is a childlike sensitivity to the gaping possibility of conflict as the beginning of an end. It is not that I have not seen relationships continue despite eruptions or that are interwoven with conflict. Indeed there are intimacies punctuated just so. What deepens the concord is that it has been reconstituted, refashioned. I am just

181

also aware of a profound, fleshy fear of discord that leaves things tattered. But the expression you shared is sufficiently pithy that it might serve as a mantra, one that is in fact connected to the thinking in much of my work.

I can also imagine Rosa turning that phrase over. Someone who wishes to touch others "like a clap of thunder" was certainly not fearful of discord! And so much of her work was about using disagreements as the basis for clarifying crucial theoretical insights and advancements. Whether naming Bernstein's reformism for the opportunistic turn from revolutionary socialism that it was or claiming that the same Marx who she revered had misunderstood the nature of primitive accumulation. Although those who sought to diminish the seriousness of her challenges said otherwise, her most important disagreements were never personal; they really were about the clarification of a larger project of studiously, steadily engaging in the long, stubborn fight for total transformation.

The challenging wisdom in this opening expression made me wonder about others that you find personally, intellectually, and politically orienting. While I am from communities replete with them, I don't keep a set of wise refrains ready at hand. My husband has a few favorite African proverbs that made their way into European and North American literature. Among them are "Don't fight with a fool; from a distance an observer won't be able to tell you apart" and "If you are taking a bath, and a thief steals your clothes, put something on before chasing him!"

I am similarly eager to accept your offer of saying more about contemporary China. At one level I realize that this is unfair. I would have to breathe deeply before answering if you asked me how you should understand contemporary life in the United States. But you did offer! I ask because, in scholarly settings, it is often bad form to ask what is precisely the most intellectually necessary and valuable: how should I understand China's self-understanding today? Its sense of its purpose and role in the world? When it is self-critical, what are the grounds? How does it use the decadence of the United States as a foil or trajectory to be avoided?

I reflect often about how Rosa thought and lived her thorough internationalism. Not only did she speak the multiple languages necessary to build meaningful relations that surmounted national borders, but she also read so widely. She always put everything that was close – being Jewish, Russian-occupied Poland, the proletariat in Germany – into relationship. Even then she had to rely on others for their insights about Asia or Africa or 5th century Athens. She read with her own indomitable spirit and demanding taste for accuracy, but there were instances where she had to work with the word of others, even when it later turned out to be wrong. One could say, as many do, that her most important, central points were right. And even where they were wrong, they were historic and teeming with prescient insight. But for her, the details being wrong is not a small matter or an aside. One builds the fabric of an analysis through just such sources. This is a long way of saying that your offer of insight into contemporary China is a gift that I welcome!

You are absolutely right that there is a difference between seeking certainties in ways that shut down new possibilities and those forms of orienting stabilities that should be able to function as a backdrop, as the furniture of a life. Not because they go unnoticed or unappreciated but because their taken-for-grantedness enables other forms of openness and growth. It should be a certainty that one can eat and access clean water and have shelter to sleep safely. It should be a fixture of life that one can learn about the world that one shares. Those certainties open doors and counter potential numbness.

Min, I am so curious to ask if you have read the writings of He-Yin Zhen? I teach an undergraduate and graduate course devoted to historical women political thinkers. When I first began teaching, I realized that most of my students genuinely thought that women had not written important political theoretical work prior to the 1960s. They simply assumed that their life conditions had made it impossible. All of their schooling implicitly affirmed such an assessment. In response, I began to offer a course that stopped in 1960 and was devoted to women writers beginning in the 15th century. Because I had never been taught this material, I began crudely, looking through works in feminist historiography and through syllabi offered in Religious Studies. It is in that course that I first taught Rosa! My husband was very excited when he came across a new English translation of several Chinese feminist writers.

It began with He-Yin Zhen, who was framed as an early 20th-century anarchist. My students found her curious and fascinating. They were drawn to many aspects of her arguments: to her focus on women having to take the lead in seeking their own emancipation lest it be reduced to empty, legislative measures loaned them by opportunistic men; that poverty made many women enter sex work and that even adjacent forms of work that were not supposed to involve sex frequently involved sexual violation; that the aim of women's liberation should not be rule of men by women but the eradication of rule as a model of political organization. They applauded her insistence that everyone (or no one) be expected to be monogamous; that women keep their mother's as well as their father's surnames; that support for the raising of children be shared. They found curious her argument that, if a marriage ends, someone who has been married before must couple with another person who has been previously married while first-time husbands can only partner with first-time wives. When I taught He-Yin most recently in a class with the Chinese student I mentioned in my previous letter, he had all kinds of questions about the way that particular terms had been translated and framed but more significantly by the failure of the editors to explain how He-Yin is understood in the larger political history of contemporary China. In his explanation, as a dangerous and consequential opportunist, one could appreciate her ideas on their own terms, but it was very difficult to understand how they fit into a larger political vision or set of commitments since she seemed to trade these in with relative ease.

Have you encountered the writing or historical figure of He-Yin? While the translated essays I am referring to are explicitly framed as anarchist, He-Yin's ideas, as represented in them, share much with those of Rosa. Rosa would have applauded her later comrade's insistence that those seeking their liberation lead the fight for it. Indeed, in mass gatherings and in the SPD party school, Rosa demonstrated her commitment to cultivating just that revolutionary subjectivity. She might have bellowed out, "hear, hear!" to He-Yin's insistence that most women's exploitation, including their vulnerability to sexual exploitation in sites of paid work, had primarily economic causes and that their needs would not be actively or skillfully pursued by the small set of elite women that were likely to be most readily enfranchised through the vote. And He-Yin's desire to see the eradication of rule and ruling reminds me of Rosa's formulation in *Reform or Revolution?*, that democracy was indispensable not because it renders the conquest of political power by the proletariat superfluous, but because it rendered that conquest necessary and possible. Both Rosa and He-Yin were powerful women's voices, echoing the revolutionary impulse across the ages. It is reignited in much of the most important and transformative contemporary, global women's activism.

I know that our formal time to correspond has come to an end. I don't know about you but I am often uplifted by occurrences that have the shape of coincidences but that seem too coherent to reduce to chance. An example would be when one mentions a far-away person in conversation one morning and, after much time, hears suddenly from them later in the day. Or you hear of a figure whom you've meant to investigate and then receive an advertisement for a new journal and in its table of contents is a critical essay devoted to that person. You know that your mention or thought did not cause the consequence, but it has the feeling that you whispered a request, unknowingly, into a universe that somehow enabled you to receive a highly mediated answer. You cannot account for how the request led to its being met and that is part of the wonder. While Hjalmar invited us to participate in this project to which we were drawn by a shared appreciation of Rosa's life and work, I had no sense of what the agreement entailed beyond something adventurous and new. But I have experienced it as putting out an only semi-conscious ask that has been answered so very richly.

With thanks, stay well, my friend,

Jane

PS: During the lockdown, my son was evacuated from his university dorm (and from New York City) and so continued his studies from home. Each day, he and I would spend an hour walking at a reservoir. On the other side of one of the largish bodies of water was a small mountain with a seemingly parallel path. I was very curious about how to walk on that side of this pool. While he didn't mind walking a distance, my son liked to take a familiar path. When he had returned to New York and I was with a friend closer to my age, we tried that route. While beautiful it took us massively off course – so much so that it took two hours to find our way back. At one point we walked through a wide-open field of tall grasses. It looked as if the wind was combing through them with a massive brush. In front of us, a group of swallows dove and glided. My only worry at the time had been whether I would find our way home in time for a scheduled virtual discussion of Rosa at which a former student was presenting. When I saw the birds, I was sure it was Rosa! The birds looked as if they had come alive from one of Kate Evans' graphic images of the swallows above Wronke Prison! I would love to find my way back to that field to find and photograph the swallows, but I am not sure how. Honestly, they were so beautiful and clear in the midst of our unclear and uncertain walk, they seem almost unreal. Instead I am pasting below images of some of the plants growing at my home. They are a constant source of wonder and delight. Each seems to experience the same combination of light, heat, and moisture differently so that the same day will be a magnificent one of thriving for one and a trying day for another. As some are so ready to blossom, others begin to fade in a never predictable symphony!

The hanging Orange flowers

The Magnolia tree once its flowers have fallen.
It always seems to reach out for a gentle touch.

I love your description of your outdoor adventure, and it's so fascinating! When I wrote this letter to you at my desk, my two cats, Si Belle and Mangosteen, were also lying on both sides of the desk, accompanying me. Rosa once mentioned in her letter that her Mimi often lay on the desk watching her like this. Thinking of this, I feel even closer to Rosa. Actually, once we keep Rosa in mind, we can always find relationship with her ☺.

Maybe it was because I thought of sharing my observation of my motherland with you, writing this reply to you suddenly became less relaxed. This is not because of how heavy it is to talk about China, but because I am afraid that my observations are one-sided, not objective, and will mislead you. Now that I have told you that there may be all of the above possibilities, it seems that I can lay down some of the burdens. So let's talk about China as I understand it from my personal perspective. :)

Undoubtedly, China has made great achievements in economic development in recent decades, and it does make a growing number of Chinese people live a life of no worries. Most of my previous generation suffered from scarcity, and in contrast to the old with the new, they were quite satisfied with the status quo. I am also relatively content at the moment. The career of a university teacher makes my life safer, and I can also enjoy more flexible schedules and relative freedom. Of course, I also feel fortunate that my children were born in this era of material abundance, which allows them not to exhaust all their energy to seek basic survival, but to have the opportunity to expand themselves to a higher level. It is certainly a great achievement that a country with such a large population can continue to develop for decades and benefit its citizens in general. On the one hand, this fact proves that China has indeed chosen the right way, which proves the governance ability of the Chinese government; on the other hand, it also benefits from the opening up to and acceptance of the external world, which has been going on for a long time.

It may be due to my personality, or it may be because I have formed a stereotype about politics – that is, I think it is dangerous, dirty and boring –, or it may be because I have been in the academic ivory tower for a long time, that I know little about specific politics, and I had not much interest in understanding it before the outbreak of the epidemic. This sounds quite contradictory, right? As a university teacher who teaches Marxism, she doesn't even care to understand politics?! But things are so magical sometimes. I can talk about Marxism in class without discussing specific political aspects, because my students and I generally know that it is a sensitive word that is best not to be touched. However, in the past year, the various magical illusions in the real world have so clearly highlighted the importance of politics, highlighting the close correlation between politics and economy, the community, and each individual within the community. Thus, if I still adhere to my position of

Mangosteen

'don't care about politics,' it is no different from hiding the alarm clock, or rather, to use a Chinese idiom, "to plug one's ears while stealing a bell." Of course, as an ordinary Chinese citizen, I am not without channels for participating in and discussing politics. I also participate in grassroots democratic elections or deliberations once or twice a year. Maybe I should start by cherishing more the votes in my hands.

In a letter to Konstantin Zetkin on July 7, 1910, Rosa briefly but aptly recounts an understanding of Chinese art:

> The book about China represents something completely new for me, because I know nothing about China. Flipping through the pages, I found this very interesting: M[eyer] writes that Chinese art is totally different from European art, in that it is not separate from life, but forms a unified whole with it. This I found to be a total confirmation of Tolstoy's view and that of the primitive peoples.[15]

I think this generalization is correct and can be extended to the understanding of Chinese traditional culture. Generally speaking, Chinese people are rational in

---

15 Luxemburg 1982: 188-189 (Translation: Patrick Anderson).

practicality, surpassing in life, and life contains everything to us. Yu Hua, a living Chinese writer, has written a best-selling novel called *To Live*. It has been around for 30 years and has sold more than 1 million copies every year. I think the reason why this book is so popular is that it contains some core codes of Chinese culture, which hit the deepest part of the Chinese people. In fact, this book is also one of my favorite books, because it depicts the Chinese people's view of life and death with calm and even cruel strokes: it is not to live on in degradation, but to live with hope and restraint, to live strong and flexible. Its power is not from shouting, attacking, but from enduring. In this sense, I think that the "non-interference in other countries' internal affairs" often emphasized by Chinese official media is not purely ideological propaganda, but is very in line with the connotation of Chinese cultural tradition. Chinese culture is not extrovert, expansionary and aggressive. We just want to live our lives well. And the world should not be just presented as a zero-sum game.

Although most Chinese people share such cultural genes, it does not prevent us from distorting our perception of reality by the powerful force of sensibility and emotion in times of change and social turmoil. The current division and confrontation among social strata or even among the same stratum intensified by the epidemic has projected into and invaded everyone's core circle of relatives and friends. I have just experienced such an event recently. There are two friends I have always respected and liked. They are my fellows in life and witnesses of each other's growth. I have no doubt about their character and knowledge. But at a recent gathering, when we talked about Fang Fang and her diary of her life in the early days of Covid-19 in Wuhan, they immediately became emotional and despised her. Except expressing disgust, they did not provide any reliable arguments to support their criticism that she must have been involved in the conspiracy to subvert the government of China and is responsible for spreading of rumours. One even admitted that he had not read her diary at all, and he just lost interest in reading immediately after listening to other people's narrations. For me, this is really a problem! It's not just concerning in terms of how to think of Fang Fang, this particular person, but about how to deal with divergent or even unpleasant opinions. Frankly speaking, I'm not a fan of Fang Fang, and I don't agree with all of her opinions. However, disagreeing with someone on the basis of full understanding and demonizing someone without even getting to know anything about the person are totally different. Yes, I have no way to cut off the bonds of long-established friendship with them, but I also have no way to accept that when they get to know the world, the basic thought resources are still from the simple distinction between friend and foe under the isolated national narrative and without any other alternatives. And I have no way to accept that as a scholar who is engaged in academic research, he can ignore facts and make sweeping comments on the basis of complete lack of material... I need to find a solution. Maybe you can give me some suggestions?

Before you mentioned He-Yin Zhen, I didn't know anything about her. I searched for information related to her on the Internet with great interest, and found some detailed and in-depth research about her; one of the main researchers, Liu He, is a scholar I admire very much. Thank you for introducing me to this woman who is hidden in the depths of history. I can't help but want to learn more. As far as I know, this is a woman who has been neglected because of her original thoughts but not in the social trends of the time, and how similar her experience is to Rosa! Moreover, the mainstream view in China seems to regard her as a negative figure: a shrew, an adulterer, and a traitor to the Chinese bourgeois democratic revolution in collusion with her husband. And it makes me even more curious about what she really was!

Dear Jane, I am so grateful that we met in such a way! The project we are involved in seems to be coming to an end, but if you are willing to, I would also be very happy to continue the dialogue with you in this form. For me, communication between us is both easy and difficult. It is easy because we are pen pals who met by chance. We didn't know each other and never met before. This relaxes me and even allows me to 'speak freely' to a certain extent, without fear of being accused and attacked because of 'inconsistency' – after all, we are far apart :) But it is also difficult, as even though I know that I don't have to hide myself, due to my long-term thinking habits I still need to spend a lot of time pulling off the mask that I otherwise wear unconsciously and inadvertently, to try to show you my real face. If everyone is more or less in an information cocoon in today's world, then let's help each other, try to break it, try to get out of it, and see the whole picture of the world. I always remember the words of Rosa, which seem to express a similar meaning: "It surprises me a little that Karl wants a book specifically about bird calls. For me the voice of the birds is inseparable from their habitat and their life as a whole, it is only the whole that interests me, rather than any detached detail."[16]

致以无尽的谢意和拥抱） ! (With many thanks and hugs,)
殷

PS: This year is both the 100th anniversary of the founding of the Communist Party of China and the 150th anniversary of Rosa's birth. Maybe this is just a coincidence, but as a researcher of Rosa Luxemburg and a member of the Chinese Communist Party, I do hope that they are connected in a secret but positive way.

---

16 Ibid: 432.

References

Brecht, Bertolt (2018), *The Collected Poems of Bertolt Brecht*. Eds. Tom Kuhn and David Constantine. Harrisonburg: LSC Communications.

Luxemburg, Rosa (1978), *The Letters of Rosa Luxemburg*. Ed. Stephen Eric Bronner. Boulder: Westview Press.

Luxemburg, Rosa (1982), *Gesammelte Briefe. Band 3*. Institut für Marxismus-Leninismus beim ZK der SED. Berlin: Dietz Verlag.

Luxemburg, Rosa (2004), *The Rosa Luxemburg Reader*. Eds. Peter Hudis and Kevin B. Anderson. New York: Monthly Review Press.

Luxemburg, Rosa (2013), *The Letters of Rosa Luxemburg*. Eds. Georg Adler, Peter Hudis, and Annelies Laschitza. London and New York: Verso Books.

自由始终是持不同思想者的
自由。" [17]

---

17 "Freedom is always and exclusively freedom for the one who thinks differently." (Luxemburg 2004: 305)

FDC
Ersttag:
15. Januar 1974   23974

7. Julia Killet
&
Nguyen Hong Duc

Dear Nguyen Hong Duc,

I send you warm greetings from Munich. Yesterday I re-read your recently published text, "Rosa Luxemburg's stand on democracy and its lessons for the practice of grassroots democracy in Vietnam today" and I am thrilled by your clear writing style and thought processes. I still remember our brief encounter at the Rosa Luxemburg Conference in Berlin in early March 2020, I found your presentation on this topic very interesting and captivating. Unfortunately, as the conference programme was filled with so many excellent speakers, we had little time to get to know each other. Therefore, I am now even more pleased that we have become pen pals and I am looking forward to exchanging our ideas and experiences.

Unfortunately, I have never been to Vietnam and know very little about the country. I also cannot imagine what it is like to live in a Socialist Republic. I currently live in the heart of capitalism in the southern German city of Munich in the state of Bavaria. Bavaria is one of the richest states in Germany. The strongest industries here include the car industry, the arms industry, the IT sector and mechanical engineering.

However, if you look at the state from a left-wing perspective, you quickly notice the far-reaching social differences: unemployment is comparatively low, but many people work in underpaid jobs. The natural landscape of the state is beautiful, with its mountains and lakes, and is a magnet for tourists from all over the world. At the same time, concrete, power lines and motorways are destroying the idyll, car exhaust fumes pollute the cities, and climate change is causing glaciers to melt and rocks to break away from the mountains. Rental prices in the cities are skyrocketing, while depopulation in rural areas is becoming more and more serious. The gap between rich and poor is widening. A few have so much money that their families will never have to work again. At the same time, there are many people who can no longer afford their rent despite having several jobs. Old people look for bottle deposits in rubbish bins because they cannot live on their pensions. Studies show that many families in Bavaria lack the money for a daily lunch, school equipment and excursions. On the one hand, Bavaria is considered cosmopolitan, on the other hand, refugees who put all their hopes on a future in Germany are locked up in mass accommodation in undignified conditions and deported to unsafe countries every day. Homeless people live under the bridges at the *Theresienwiese*, where socialist revolutionaries proclaimed the revolution 100 years ago and where the Oktoberfest is celebrated today. Poverty is not accidental, poverty is made by people and has a fundamental cause: capitalism.

It is really sad that today we still have to continue the struggle that Rosa Luxemburg led more than 100 years ago. By the way, do you know the left-wing writer Bertolt Brecht? He wrote the following poem in 1934, which I think is exemplary for the political work of Rosa Luxemburg and the Left movement worldwide:

Whosoever stays at home when the struggle begins
And lets others fight on his behalf
Must look out; for
He who does not share in the struggle
Will nonetheless share in the defeat.
He who seeks to evade the struggle
Cannot evade this struggle; for
He who has not fought for his own cause
Will fight for the cause of his enemy.[1]

When I started researching the life and work of the revolutionary Rosa Luxemburg, I was impressed by her courage, determination and unwillingness to compromise. Throughout her life, she fought to smash capitalism and build a classless society. I was inspired by how she attacked the ossified foundations of the ruling order in the German Empire with her radical and persistent demands for freedom, socialism and democracy. So today, whenever I lose myself in her writings and letters, when I read her delightful descriptions of animals and plants, her clever political conclusions, when I amuse myself with her bite and irony against political opponents or admire her universal scholarship, I draw strength for my own political work in Bavaria. You may remember that I told you that I have been running the Rosa Luxemburg Foundation in Bavaria since 2011. In the spirit of our namesake, we organise 200 political education projects a year and work with voluntary cooperation partners from the Left movement throughout the state. With our events, we want to educate society about contemporary democratic socialism, encourage critical thinking and show alternatives to capitalism. Rosa Luxemburg's thoughts are wonderfully suited to this because her political struggle is more topical than ever at a time when billionaires profit from the Corona pandemic, 80 million people are displaced, fascists are coming to power in so many countries across the world and climate change is rapidly advancing. I was wondering, do you know the office of the Rosa Luxemburg Foundation in Hanoi? They produced an animated film about Rosa Luxemburg's life called *The Eternal Rose* to mark the 150th anniversary of her birth. How do you like the film?

The famous Luxemburg researcher from the German Democratic Republic (GDR), Annelies Laschitza, once said to me: "Once you start researching Rosa Luxemburg, you can't stop." She was to be proved right. In 2014, I came across an exciting essay in literary studies by Prof. Helmut Peitsch. In it, he pointed out that Luxemburg had long since become a motif in literature. As a German studies student, I was so fascinated by this topic that I decided to deal with it in detail in a dissertation. After two years of initial research, my employers allowed me a sabbatical year. Thinking that I would be too distracted in the middle of the city, I looked for a quiet place in nature to carry out my research. At that time, a friend of mine ran the youth training centre of the IG-Metall trade union at Schliersee and he offered me a small room with a view of the lake and the mountains. Schliersee is located in the foothills of the Bavarian Alps and is described in travel guides as the most beautiful region in Bavaria. The lake in the town of the same name is surrounded by mountains and is

---

1 Brecht 2018: 532.

about an hour by train from Munich. From my window I had a direct view of the mountain where Rosa Luxemburg once stayed. In 1902, there was an SPD party congress in Munich, which Luxemburg attended. Afterwards, the comrades went on an excursion to mount Bodenschneid, where the following photo was taken:

For me, it was literally a great luxury to be able to spend a whole year exclusively with Rosa Luxemburg in the midst of a charming landscape. Rosa Luxemburg – who wrote herself into the canon of world literature with her poetic letters. On the one hand, her fascination and compassion for every creature on earth from ant, great tit, butterfly, bumblebee, robin, dung beetle to toad and caterpillar; on the other, her radical declaration of struggle against the class of oppressors, against capitalism, and her utopian belief in the imminent world revolution. These apparent contradictions prompted poets and thinkers, writers and playwrights like Heiner Müller, Alfred Döblin and Egon Erwin Kisch to include Luxemburg as a protagonist in their works. Among the abundance of poems, plays and novels, I concentrated in my dissertation on the image of Rosa Luxemburg in biographical and literary prose, analysing 14 biographies, eight literary works and two films. In each work, new facets of her personality were revealed: the revolutionary, the politician, the internationalist, the anti-militarist, the socialist, the communist, the democrat, the Marxist, the scientist, the economist, the teacher, the editor, the rhetorician, the lover of culture, the botanist, the universalist, the lover, the friend, the confidante, the comrade, the imprisoned, the dreamer, the writer, the fighter, the woman, the migrant, the lonely, the passionate, the undogmatic, the reflective, the murdered, the scorned, the misunderstood, the dangerous and the admired. The list could go on forever, but in the end it was the totality of these traits that made Rosa Luxemburg a human being. Her solidarity with mass suffering conditioned and finally justified her revolutionary struggle for the liberation of society from capitalism.

I would like to end my first letter to you with the words of Luxemburg, which should serve as a model for us leftists: "The most ruthless revolutionary energy and the most generous humanity, this alone is the true breath of socialism. A world must be overthrown, but every tear that has flowed, though it could be wiped away, is an indictment; and a man rushing to important action who tramples a worm out of raw carelessness commits a crime."[2]

With great anticipation I await your letter,
Your comrade Julia

2 See Luxemburg November 1918.

The Schliersee in Bavaria

April 20, 2021
Hanoi, Vietnam

Dear Julia,

I am very pleased to receive your letter although I know that on this occasion you are very busy. I am delighted that we have the opportunity to work together since first meeting at last year's Rosa Luxemburg conference in Berlin. As you said, we didn't have much time to talk together during the conference, so I hope that through this correspondence we can share more with each other, about our work, our socio-political views and the inspirations that Rosa Luxemburg brings to us.

First of all, thank you for your positive comments on my paper at the conference, which is now published in a two-volume book with the title *Rosa Luxemburg*, edited by Frank Jacob, Albert Scharenberg and Jörn Schütrumpf. It is one of the research results that I have after approximately four years of studying Luxemburg.

I would like to tell you a little about myself. I am 38 years old and a Master of Philosophy. Currently, I am a researcher at the Institute of Philosophy in the Vietnam Academy of Social Sciences (VASS). I have been working here for over 10 years now. Before that, I had different jobs: as an employee of a district party committee, and as a lecturer at a university where I taught about the principles of Marxism-Leninism (Philosophy, Political Economy, Scientific Socialism). It is my love for philosophy, my love for German thinkers (such as Hegel, Kant, Nietzsche, and of course Marx and Engels) that is the driving force that has helped me to choose my current research career (in fact I have a rather special love for Germany). Having become a researcher, I have more time and the right conditions to study many thinkers, and Rosa Luxemburg has fast become one of my favourites.

About your letter, thank you for sharing about your work and your life. It is interesting to know that you run the Rosa Luxemburg Foundation (RLS) in Bavaria. Like you, I am a member of a leftist party, the Communist Party of Vietnam. I also share the socio-political difficulties that you and the RLS-Bavaria are facing. I enjoy Oktoberfest even though I can't drink alcohol.

As I mentioned, I have been interested in Rosa Luxemburg since early 2017. One day, I had a conversation with one of my colleagues. We discussed the issues that I planned to study in the near future. She asked me if I knew anything about Rosa Luxemburg and suggested that I could focus on her as my main research assignment. At our Institute, for a topic to be accepted as the main research assignment, we have to present a research proposal for a period of 3-5 years, and it must be aligned with the general research interests of the institute. At that time, I knew very little about Luxemburg, although I had wanted to study her several times before. All I knew was that she was a Marxist and related to the women's liberation movement. I remembered that I had bought the Vietnamese translation of an old book about Rosa Luxemburg by Dominique Desanti, *L'oeuvre et la vie de Rosa Luxemburg*, but I hadn't actually read it. That was the only document about Rosa Luxemburg that I had and knew about at that time.

From then on, I spent most of my time and interest researching Rosa Luxemburg. It may surprise you, but in the beginning I faced many difficulties, even though Vietnam is a socialist country, a country following Marxism-Leninism. But the life and thought of Rosa Luxemburg has received little attention from Vietnamese researchers. It sounds a bit paradoxical, doesn't it? In my judgment, it could be for the following reasons:

First, the general situation: in the past, Vietnamese researchers when studying Marxism-Leninism often limited their research scope to the works of Marx, Engels and Lenin, with little regard for other Marxists. In recent years, however, the scope of possible research has finally been extended to other Marxists and Marxist schools, such as Western Marxism, the Frankfurt School and, fortunately, Rosa Luxemburg.

Second, historical factors: as you know, Rosa Luxemburg and V.I. Lenin had at times opposing views, and since the Communist Party of Vietnam always takes Marxism-Leninism as its ideological foundation, any views different from those of Marx and Lenin, even when coming from other Marxists, were/are not easily welcome. On the other hand, historically there were many articles in the newspapers of the Indochinese Communist Party (the old name for The Communist Party of Vietnam) praising Rosa Luxemburg's struggle and sacrifice for the world revolution and the liberation of the proletariat. She, along with Karl Liebknecht, was often put together with V.I. Lenin in writing. If we read Vietnamese documents about Luxemburg, we readily find Lenin's comments about her, both praise and criticism. However, analytical articles on her thought were/are almost non-existent. When assessing Luxemburg, she is placed somewhere between the two poles of Eduard Bernstein-Karl Kautsky and Karl Marx-V.I. Lenin, but closer to the Marx-Lenin pole.

Third, research conditions: there are no translations of Rosa Luxemburg's works into Vietnamese. If one wants to learn about Luxemburg, one must access documents in English or German. The few Vietnamese translations of Rosa Luxemburg's works that I know of so far only appear on the marxists.org site. But that's just a handful of essays.

So what I am trying to do to overcome these difficulties is to dedicate my time and love to Rosa Luxemburg. I am now in the "can't stop" state, to use Laschitza's words that you shared. My research and attitude towards Luxemburg's thought have also received much support from my colleagues, as I am opening up a new field of research. Having said that, for me, research on Rosa Luxemburg is more than just a profession. I have the feeling that when I introduce Luxemburg to others, publishing my research on her is like fighting for the values that she pursued: democracy, justice and equality. That is why Rosa Luxemburg herself became an impetus for my research work.

In your letter, you mentioned the animated film *The Eternal Rose* to mark Rosa's 150th birthday anniversary. Thanks for mentioning it, and I'm glad you know about it too. It is the video version of an art book of the same name that I had the good fortune to be part of as a member of the advisory board. With the support of the Rosa Luxemburg Foundation Hanoi office (RLS Hanoi), the book and video will help bring the image and life of Rosa Luxemburg closer to the people of Vietnam, especially young people. I am really happy that I was able to participate in a project that honours the life, thought and dedication of Rosa Luxemburg. The goals that she pursued, such as justice, democracy, human liberation and socialism, are the same values that the Communist Party of Vietnam and the Vietnamese people are pursuing. Therefore, I believe that the book will be easily accepted by young Vietnamese readers and that the image of Luxemburg fighting for socialism will spread in everyone's awareness. After reading this book, my friends expressed respect and admiration for Rosa Luxemburg – whom they knew almost nothing about before.

Currently, I am also trying to complete a draft of my book on the subject of Rosa Luxemburg's thought on democracy and revolution. I really hope it can still be published this year, in time to celebrate the 150th anniversary of her birth. In general, although my research experience of Rosa Luxemburg is not extensive, I realize that there are ideas and views of Rosa that can become lessons and suggestions for the road of building socialism in Vietnam.

For example, in my article "Rosa Luxemburg's Viewpoint on Democracy and Its Lessons for Practicing Grassroots Democracy in Vietnam Today" that you mention, I pointed out the similarity between Rosa Luxemburg's view on the necessary elements to ensure democracy and the basic grassroots democratic principles that are under construction in Vietnam. Luxemburg argued that democracy can only be achieved when the following conditions are present: people are aware of their political role in the development of society; mass participation in mass organizations and social movements; community supervision over the government apparatus. She wrote:

> This dictatorship [= socialist democracy] must be the work of the *class* and not of a little leading minority in the name of the class – that is, it must proceed step by step out of the active participation of the masses; it must be under their direct influence, subjected to the control of complete public activity; it must arise out of the growing political training of the mass of the people.[3]

> Public control is indispensably necessary. Otherwise, the exchange of experiences remains only with the closed circle of the officials of the new regime.[4]

These principles are similar to the main contents of grassroots democracy that we are implementing in Vietnam: *people know, people discuss, people do, people supervise*. Since the XIII Congress of the Communist Party of Vietnam (February 2021), we have added two more, namely: *people monitor* and *people benefit*.

In Vietnam, we are fortunate to have passed through the first phase of the social revolution: the political takeover. Vietnam is now led by a single party, the Communist Party of Vietnam, which is regulated by the Constitution of Vietnam. But besides that, there are still many more social goals that we need to achieve, including social justice: justice in the distribution and enjoyment of labour results, justice in opportunities and enjoyment of basic social services, such as education,

---

3 Luxemburg 2004: 308.
4 Ibid: 306.

health care, culture, living environment, etc. Disparities in opportunities and benefits appear between high and low-income people, between urban and rural residents, and between ethnic minorities and the Kinh people (the ethnic majority in Vietnam). Gender inequality, inequality in employment and income between men and women also still exist; consequently, women continue to be discriminated against when compared to men.

In your letter, you describe the life of the people in the state of Bavaria from a left-wing perspective. I was surprised by that information. It helped me see below the tip of the iceberg in terms of social life in Germany, a topic with which I haven't been familiar for some time. Perhaps the reason is that I have not had the opportunity to learn and interact with the workers you mentioned.

About income inequality, I think it is a worldwide problem and Vietnam is no exception. According to the GINI index, income inequality in Vietnam is at an acceptable level. In 2016, Vietnam's GINI coefficient was 43.1% and it will decrease to 37.3% in 2020. The GINI coefficient also varies from region to region due to differences in natural conditions, cultural level, educational level, comparative advantage, etc. But those numbers can hide the fact that the gap between the rich and the poor is widening. In fact, in 2016, the gap between the richest 20% of the population and the poorest 20% of the population was 9.8 times. This number increased to 10.2 times in 2019. But in 2020, under the impact of the Covid pandemic, the income of groups also changed. Because social security policies are more active in the low-income group, the gap has been reduced to 8 times.

In terms of occupations, employees who receive salaries from state agencies and companies have lower incomes than those in non-state companies or joint-stock companies. Most public employees have to work very hard to get a decent living in big cities. Their income seems to be just enough to cover rent and daily living expenses.

The Vietnamese government has also made and will make strategic adjustments to wages to improve income for people working in state agencies. However, the effect has been limited. From a gender perspective, female workers are paid lower wages than male workers. In 2016, male workers had a higher income than female workers by 11.9%. There are many reasons for this. First, the majority of low-paid jobs (sales, service, administrative assistants) are performed by women. Second, housework causes women to spend a lot of time with their families, which forces them to choose jobs with flexible hours (and often those with low income). Family responsibilities also cause women to share time between family and work, while men can comfortably spend more time at work. Long working hours also increase the income level of workers. Vietnamese women spend an average of more than 5 hours a day on household chores, while men spend 3 hours. Third, discrimination by gender and social norms. Women in families often suffer from gender stereotypes in the division of labour. Jobs such as cooking, washing, cleaning and even taking care of children are often thought of as women's work. Most of the work in the family is done by women. These are all unpaid jobs. This phenomenon reminds me of Rosa Luxemburg's 1912 analysis of unpaid work for women:

[The women of the proletariat] are productive for society like the men. By this I do not mean their bringing up children or their housework which helps men support their families on scanty wages. This kind of work is not productive in the sense of the present capitalist economy no matter how enormous an achievement the sacrifices and energy spent, the thousand little efforts add up to. This is but the private affair of the worker, his happiness and blessing, and for this reason nonexistent for our present society. As long as capitalism and the wage system rule, only that kind of work is considered productive which produces surplus value, which creates capitalist profit. From this point of view, the music-hall dancer whose legs sweep profit into her employer's pocket is a productive worker, whereas all the toil of the proletarian women and mothers in the four walls of their homes is considered unproductive. This sounds brutal and insane, but corresponds exactly to the brutality and insanity of our present capitalist economy. And seeing this brutal reality clearly and sharply is the proletarian woman's first task.[5]

Although Rosa Luxemburg was not one to write many articles or give many speeches about feminism and gender equality, I think she herself is nonetheless a symbol of feminism. She resisted gender stereotypes in Polish society by always pursuing her education, demonstrating to society the ability of women to excel at study through her academic and research achievements. When participating in the revolutionary movement, she worked tirelessly, and was in no way inferior to her male friends and comrades. At ideological forums, she was always ready to stand up for her views even though her opponents were influential theorists. This proves to society that, in political activities, women can do even better than men. On this point, I agree with the cultural historian Alhelí de María Alvarado-Díaz who wrote in her piece for *Rosa Remix*:

It may be unfair for us to impose our expectations and our contemporary definitions of feminism in judging Rosa Luxemburg's qualities as a feminist militant. The brand of Rosa's feminism was different and unique to her context and to the reality of her own trajectory as activist, as a minority and an autonomous thinker.[6]

And you, what do you think about Rosa Luxemburg and feminism? And what about you? Do you consider yourself a feminist?

In this first letter, I wanted to briefly introduce myself and tell you what I have learned during my research on Rosa Luxemburg. In addition, I wanted to share with you about the issue of income inequality in Vietnam today. I hope to be able to share more with you in my next letter. I am waiting for your letter.

---

5 Ibid: 241.
6 Alvarado-Díaz in Ehmsen & Scharenberg 2016.

Wish you all the best;

Hong Duc

PS: I want to send you the photo of the fence of RLS Hanoi, that I took one day at the end of 2020. The painting is so cool. I love it very much.

Chủ nghĩa Marx là một quan điểm cách mạng về thế giới, nó luôn nỗ lực không ngừng cho những khám phá mới, hoàn toàn coi thường sự cứng nhắc trong những luận đề đã từng hợp lý, và sức sống của nó được bảo đảm tốt nhất trong cuộc đụng độ trí tuệ của sự tự phê bình và sóng gió của lịch sử.[7]

---

7 "Marxism is a revolutionary world outlook which must always strive for new discoveries, which completely despises rigidity in once valid theses, and whose living force is best preserved in the intellectual clash of self-criticism and the rough and tumble of history." (Luxemburg 2015: 448-449)

May 14, Munich

Dear Hong Duc,

Thank you very much for your letter. Unfortunately, I am only now getting around to answering you. During the week, I run the business of the Rosa Luxemburg Foundation Bavaria. We are currently preparing a big congress against the International Motor Show (IAA), which will take place in Munich for the first time in September. Under the title "KonTra IAA - Congress for Transformative Mobility" we want to spend two days dealing with current transport policy, which we see as car-centric, climate-damaging and socially unjust. We demand that for a climate-just mobility turnaround, car traffic must be drastically reduced and public transport must be expanded quickly and consistently.

So I do my academic work, such as this letter, at the weekend. However, I had numerous political commitments over the last few weekends. On 1 May, I was at two demonstrations in Munich: the trade union demo with participants in the middle-to-upper age group and the revolutionary demo, which was organised by the left-wing autonomous scene and mainly attended by youth and young people. Sadly, there were clashes with the police and pepper spray was used. Then, the next day we had a party meeting for ten hours. Unfortunately, due to the pandemic, we could not see each other in person and had to hold the entire meeting digitally. There we elected the delegates for the upcoming party congresses. We have a lot to do this year because there are federal elections in September. Also 8 May – the day of liberation from National Socialism – fell on a Saturday this year so we also demonstrated in Munich for this important event.

Thank you very much for your letter. I am very pleased that you can give me an insight into research and politics in the Socialist Republic of Vietnam through our letters. This is really very exciting, and I would very much like to visit Vietnam one day. I would like to respond to your question and write something about me and Rosa Luxemburg as feminists. But first I would like to take up a topic that you also outline in your letter: Rosa Luxemburg's political stigmatisation after her death. I also dealt with this in my dissertation.

Already during the Weimar Republic, but especially during the Cold War, Rosa Luxemburg was instrumentalised for ideological and political purposes because of her political thinking and actions. Shortly after her assassination, social democrats and communists tried to appropriate Rosa Luxemburg for themselves. Among the communists, a new view of Rosa Luxemburg was established after her fragmentary writing on the Russian Revolution was published posthumously in 1922. In it, Luxemburg enthusiastically welcomed the revolution but criticised the lack of democratic structures. Lenin, who saw his revolution under attack, responded to this publication by Paul Levi with a sentence that was to shape Luxemburg's reception/historical fate within the communist movement:

We answer this with a few lines from an excellent Russian fable: "It is true that the flight of the eagle carried it lower than the flight of the hen, but the hen never flies to the height of the eagle. Rosa Luxemburg was wrong on the question of Polish independence; she was wrong in 1903 in her assessment of Menshevism; she was wrong on the theory of the accumulation of capital; she was wrong when in July 1914 ... she advocated the unification of the Bolsheviks with the Mensheviks; she was wrong in her prison writings of 1918 ... But despite all these mistakes of hers, she was and remains an eagle ..."[8]

Do you know the quote? After Lenin wrote it – but especially after his death – Rosa Luxemburg's political positions were devalued as erroneous by the leadership of the Comintern and the German KPD under the term "Luxemburgism". The accusation of "Luxemburgism" continued in the GDR, but was also prevalent in the Soviet Union and in West German K-groups.[9] This led to Luxemburg being stylised as a symbolic figure, as a martyr and co-founder of the KPD – but at the same time a theoretical examination of her political thought was prevented, thereby separating Luxemburg as a person from her work. Although her profile picture was emblazoned on flags, her writings receded more and more into the background. In my dissertation, I dealt with "Luxemburgism" in detail, and presented the different positions of Lenin and Luxemburg. However, it is important for me to emphasise that although Lenin and Luxemburg held different views on some points, they nevertheless appreciated and respected each other. I would like to see more of that in the Left parties and movements today.

In the FRG (Federal Republic of Germany, West Germany), the image of *blutige Rosa* (bloody Rosa) as the representative of communism, who wanted to bring Germany to ruin following the example of the Russian Revolution, was maintained. This image was shaped by the nationalist and bourgeois press from 1901 onwards, and from then on her opponents and enemies used it as Rosa Luxemburg's unofficial name. During the November Revolution, even the social democratic press railed against Luxemburg in this tenor. The extent to which this image of *bloody Rosa* shaped the political landscape of the FRG is illustrated by a dispute that flared up after Rosa Luxemburg was depicted on a postage stamp. The 40-Pfennig stamp appeared exactly on the day of Luxemburg's 55th death anniversary, 15 January 1974, in the stamp series "Important German Women" together with portraits of women's rights activists Luise Otto-Peters (1819-1895), Helene Lange (1848-1930) and Gertrud Bäumer (1873-1954). The first announcement in the daily newspapers was followed by a wave of public outrage: "Compared to this, [Red Army Faction member] Ulrike Meinhof is a downright harmless sheep [...]" wrote a reader in the *Rheinische Post*. Another reader found "the dedication of a special stamp to be the self-destructive glorification of a communist dictatorship." Institutions such as the Wiesbaden Chamber of Commerce and Industry refused to accept letters bearing the Luxemburg stamp. Even the German Bundestag debated the stamp. Federal Post Minister Horst Ehmke of the SPD (Social Democratic Party of Germany) government

---

8 Lenin 1977: 194-195.
9 The K-groups were active in West Germany from the late 1960s to the early 1980s. They were inspired by, among other things, the thinking of Mao Zedong as well as the early Soviet Union under Stalin, including the latter's critique of 'Luxemburgism.' See Kühn 2005: 13 ff.

defended the proposal of his department for postage stamps and received 200 protest letters in return, with Richard Stücklen of the conservative Christian Social Union (CSU) in Bavaria accusing Ehmke of "marching in the spirit of the SED."[10]

It was only towards the end of the 20th century that Rosa Luxemburg was freed from these political stigmatisations over time. The Cold War was over, and Rosa Luxemburg no longer had to serve the polarizations and demarcation of the two systems. When Luxemburg was included in the 20-part documentary series *The Germans* in 2010, there was no longer an outcry in society. However, she is still misunderstood in Germany today, which is particularly evident in the oft-cited quote, "Freedom is always the freedom of dissenters."[11] In a recent film documentary, historian Heinrich August Winkler interpreted the sentence as follows: "She was not thinking of freedom for the bourgeois democrats or the right-wing social democrats. It was a socialist pluralism that she envisioned. Freedom for the supporters of the revolution, but just more than freedom only for one party or its self-proclaimed vanguard." I would strongly disagree with Winkler. For her, freedom meant political freedom and the resulting social freedom in the revolution and the experience gained from it for one's own actions. For her, this freedom was the starting point for an emancipated society. She demanded that we engage with the positions of those who think differently, that we argue and fight for our own political demands and that we become better at this through constant education.

Anyway, perhaps these long-propagated negative views about Luxemburg also shaped the image of the Communist Party in Vietnam. Therefore, I am all the more pleased that you will be allowed to research Rosa Luxemburg for the coming years. This is really a great and very rewarding task because her thoughts are still highly topical. All over the world, her political thinking is seen as an untested socialist alternative.

But now to your question: Yes, I am a feminist. For me, socialism and feminism belong together and are interdependent. I was politicised by the sociology professor and Marxist feminist Frigga Haug. I don't know if you've heard of her. I admire this woman. For example, she developed the "Four-in-One Perspective."[12] It is about justice in the distribution of gainful employment, family work, community work and development opportunities. In your letter you point out that these four areas – in Vietnam too – are pursued separately. In the four-in-one perspective, these functions should be thought of and lived together. You quote a letter by Rosa Luxemburg on this very subject. The letter is from 1912. I find it appalling that 109 years later we still have to demand that housework be considered 'work' and be distributed fairly.

---

10 See German Bundestag 1974.
11 The quote is from Luxemburg's posthumously published manuscript *The Russian Revolution*, written in 1917 while in Breslau prison. The quotation is a marginal note. In full it reads: "Freedom only for the supporters of the government, only for the members of one party – however numerous they may be – is no freedom at all. Freedom is always and exclusively freedom for the one who thinks differently. Not because of any fanatical concept of 'justice' but because all that is instructive, wholesome and purifying in political freedom depends on this essential characteristic, and its effectiveness vanishes when 'freedom' becomes a special privilege." (Luxemburg 2004: 305).
12 See Haug 2009.

Fortunately, however, there is a new perspective today. Because alongside the international climate strike, the current feminist struggles form a considerable transnational movement: Whether in the Women's marches, women's strikes, #MeToo or *"Ni Una Menos"* – all over the world women are showing solidarity and struggling together for a just society. And it's not about who pays for meals, holds the door open or carries heavy things. Women finally want to have the same rights as men. We are fed up with being treated as second-class citizens, tired of being the servants of men. We are fed up that all the reproductive work, i.e. caring for children, the elderly, people with disabilities or nature, is left to us. We are tired of men deciding over our bodies and over our lives. We are fed up with being sexually harassed, earning less than men, being affected by poverty in old age, being dependent on men or excluded from certain professional positions. We are tired of being beaten, raped, sold, treated as war trophies, murdered and so on and so forth...

The Left international feminist movement – like Rosa Luxemburg – is resolutely opposed to capitalism, the system that stands for nationalism, wars, racism, oppression and exploitation. This welcome development is particularly well illustrated in the book *Feminism for the 99%: A Manifesto* by Cinzia Arruzza, Tithi Bhattacharya and Nancy Fraser, which I highly recommend if you haven't read it yet. The authors write that women are fighting for a just world where wealth and natural resources are shared by all and where equality and freedom are not the goal but the starting point. And this is where I come back to Luxemburg.

While researching the topic, I came across a very exciting text by Drucilla Cornell, "Rosa Luxemburg's Ethical Feminism." Cornell is a US professor of law, women's studies and political science in Cape Town. She calls Luxemburg an "ethical feminist" and after studying her text I would like to endorse this view. This feminism is not solely about the struggle for women's rights, but also about overcoming capitalism and nationalism. Cornell writes: "Their anti-elitism is integral to their argument that there are no first and second class people and that the same is true of the violent hierarchy between nations. [...] In Luxemburg's understanding, the transformation to a socialist society requires a radical transformation of every individual."[13] Rosa Luxemburg fought for a society in which all people should be equal. This of course includes women and men, rich and poor, etc. She also rejected the rule of a party elite as in Lenin's Soviet Russia (See: "The Russian Revolution"). Accordingly, you will find only a few texts in her work that deal specifically with the women's question. However, she had an intimate friendship with the well-known proletarian women's rights activist, internationalist and journal editor Clara Zetkin.

One of her most important texts on the women's question is entitled, "The Proletarian Woman." In it, Rosa Luxemburg points out, for example, the class differences between women and shows that the bourgeois woman benefits from capitalism as a consumer. As Cornell also argues, Rosa Luxemburg did not only focus on the situation of women in Germany – her view was international. Luxemburg writes:

---

13 Cornell 2018: 4f.

A world of female misery is waiting for relief. The wife of the peasant moans as she nearly collapses under life's burdens. In German Africa, in the Kalahari Desert, the bones of defenceless Herero women are bleaching in the sun, those who were hunted down by a band of German soldiers and subjected to a horrific death of hunger and thirst. On the other side of the ocean, in the high cliffs of Putumayo, the death cries of martyred Indian women, ignored by the world, fade away in the rubber plantations of the international capitalists. 18 Proletarian women, the poorest of the poor, the most disempowered of the disempowered, hurry to join the struggle for the emancipation of women and of humankind from the horrors of capitalist domination! Social Democracy has assigned to you a place of honour. Hurry to the front lines, into the trenches![14]

For me, it is always impressive how current Luxemburg's demands are. At the beginning, I told you about international feminism today. Because you wrote about the situation of women in Vietnam, I would like to briefly report on Germany. Even in times of a female Federal Chancellor, equality has still not arrived in our society. It is not only in politics that women experience gender discrimination. Whether at the local, state or federal level, the political field is dominated by men, especially in the top positions; the proportion of women in the German Bundestag is 30 per cent. Women in Germany work in occupations that are paid less than average. These include, for example, social professions. They also work part-time more often and are less likely to have a career. The majority of unpaid work – housework, childcare and nursing – is still done by women in Germany. As a result, women are often affected by poverty in old age because they earn less than men. The list could unfortunately be continued indefinitely. And I notice many similarities to the situation of women in Vietnam.

For me, feminism means emancipation, gender justice and the abolition of discrimination. It is a hard and long struggle. Even in the Left movement there are patriarchal structures and men (and unfortunately also women) who don't want to understand why the issue is so important. It gets on my nerves to always have to start from scratch; these endless discussions with people who think we live in an equal society. But for me, feminism is not only standing up for your own rights, but also for all those women who have no voice.

I would like to close with a quote from Rosa Luxemburg about the proletarian woman:

> As a modern female proletarian, the woman becomes a human being for the first time, since the [proletarian] struggle is the first to prepare human beings to make a contribution to culture, to the history of humanity. For the property-owning bourgeois woman, her house is the world. For the proletarian woman, the whole world is her house, the world with its sorrow and joy, with its cold cruelty and its raw size.[15]

---

14 Luxemburg 2004: 244-245.
15 Ibid: 243.

With great anticipation I await your letter,
Your comrade Julia

P.S. Thank you for the beautiful picture of the graffiti on the Rosa Luxemburg Foundation office in Hanoi. I saw a video of how the picture was taken at the birthday celebrations. I'm sending you a photo of the original stamps I wrote about above.[16]

16 Picture credits: Archiv der sozialen Demokratie – Friedrich-Ebert-Stiftung, 6/FOTA006448.

Eine Welt weiblichen Jammers wartet auf
Erlösung. Da stöhnt das Weib des
Keinbauerns, das unter der Last des
Lebens schier zusammenbricht.[17]

17 "A world of female misery is waiting for relief. The wife of the peasant moans as she nearly collapses under life's burdens." (Luxemburg 2004: 244)

Thank you for the story about the stamps.

This is quite an interesting coincidence. The image of the Rosa Luxemburg stamp that you shared is the image that was used by RLS-Hanoi as an illustration for the book *Eternal Rosa* that I mentioned in my previous letter.

And thank you for mentioning Frigga Haug. This is the first time I have heard of her. I will take the time to read her works (only the ones in English, of course) and I have already found some of her articles on the internet. Thanks also for recommending the book *Feminism for the 99%: A Manifesto*. I believe it will also be useful to me.

In response to one of your questions, as I said before, in general, Rosa Luxemburg's ideas have not been fully and objectively studied in Vietnam. Therefore, I am glad for the establishment of RLS-Hanoi and their/your efforts at reviving Luxemburg's works, writings and ideas, to give them their rightful place and value instead of looking at it one-sidedly for political purposes, as was done in the past. In fact, I want to share some good news with you about Rosa Luxemburg research in Vietnam. In October of this year, our Institute of Philosophy (VASS) and RLS Hanoi will organize a conference on the topic "Ho Chi Minh and Rosa Luxemburg's Thoughts on a fair Society." Ho Chi Minh, the leader of the Vietnamese revolution in the twentieth century, led Vietnam to independence and freedom in 1945. Currently, Ho Chi Minh's thought is a core foundation for all actions of the Communist Party of Vietnam. As you can imagine, I am very excited that we can explore the similarities in the thinking of Rosa Luxemburg and Ho Chi Minh on the socialist revolution and socialist society.

One of the points where I think Ho Chi Minh and Luxemburg meet was to affirm that the future of humankind will be socialism, and that the working class all over the world need to unite to successfully implement the social revolution and liberate working people. He wrote: "Because there is only one humanity, one socialism and one International for the entire working family and that International is born to destroy all capitalism, all imperialism no matter where it comes from or how it is. It is our duty as socialists to help each other in order to quickly win the revolution everywhere and finally liberate all the working classes."[18] I am curious, how familiar are you with the life and work of Ho Chi Minh? Who knows, you may even be able to present a paper for this conference, and hopefully, you can come to Vietnam to attend the conference.

But back to Rosa Luxemburg and feminism. Although perhaps Luxemburg did not spend much time writing in women's newspapers, this does not negate the fact that she was always conscious of the importance and hence supportive of the women's movement in general. By way of example, when the publication of *Die Rote Fahne*

---

18 Ho Chi Minh 2011a: 33.

began, Luxemburg asked Clara Zetkin to write a regular column about women's issues. Clearly, she saw the importance of having a voice for proletarian women in the official newspaper of a communist organization like the Spartacus League.

But unfortunately, not long after the newspaper came into being and the Communist Party of Germany (KPD) was founded, she and her comrade Karl Liebknecht were assassinated, and they were denied the chance to continue their revolutionary socio-political goals, among others:

- Abolition of all differences of rank, all orders and titles. Complete legal and social equality of the sexes.

- Radical social legislation. Shortening of the labour day to control unemployment and in consideration of the physical exhaustion of the working class by world war. Maximum working day of six hours.

- Immediate basic transformation of the food, housing, health and educational systems in the spirit and meaning of the proletarian revolution.[19]

This shows that Luxemburg and her comrades in the Spartacus League identified gender equality as one of the top tasks after the proletarian revolution took power. And although they themselves could not achieve this in their lifetime, the goals they set for "complete legal and social equality of the sexes" are increasingly being realized. Unlike in the time of Rosa Luxemburg, women today are clearly much more empowered and tend to participate more and more in the socio-political life of countries. At the very least, we can see how gender equality has been legislated in many countries, though I can only imagine how tired you and so many other women around the world must feel that patriarchy remains alive and kicking despite all the amazing efforts you mentioned.

In Vietnam, we consider two types of gender equality:

- Formal gender equality: This is equality on the basis of not discriminating gender differences between men and women, manifested in the application of laws, regulations and common standards for both men and women. For example, formally male and female students enjoy the same educational conditions and educational opportunities; men and women are equal in terms of career advancement opportunities, etc. Of course, a mere adherence to formal gender equality can lead in reality to substantive gender inequality in environments where gender factors significantly affect each person's work performance. For example, the birth and care of children can affect women's academic continuity, and thus they may lose their ability to compete fairly with men for work and promotion.

- Substantive gender equality: This is equality based on gender differences while considering possible causes leading to gender inequality so that

19 Luxemburg 2004: 355.

214

appropriate behavioral measures can be applied to achieve substantive gender equality. Given that men and women are different, if gender factors are not taken into account, women will be more disadvantaged than men, possibly resulting in a deepening of inequality. Therefore, certain discriminatory, affirmative-action type measures are needed to remedy the causes leading to such a situation.

The Communist Party of Vietnam and the Government of Vietnam believe that gender equality is one of the basic factors to improve the quality of life of each person, each family, and society as a whole. The principle of equality between men and women is institutionalized in the Constitution and most legal documents of the State of Vietnam. We already have a National Strategy on Gender Equality 2011-2020, and a National Strategy on Gender Equality 2021-2030. In addition, we also have the Law on Gender Equality (2006). These legalized contents show that Vietnam is trying to ensure gender equality in society in accordance with the spirit of numerous international conventions such as the Convention on the Elimination of All Forms of Discrimination Against Women (CEDAW) or the Beijing Declaration and Platform for Action (1995).

One of the results is that – similar to what you describe is happening in Germany – the participation rates of women in politics in Vietnam have increased. As you say, the proportion of women in the German *Bundestag* is 30%. In Vietnam, of the 499 members of the 15th National Assembly (2021-2026), 151 are female, accounting for almost exactly the same number, 30.26%, making it the highest rate we have had in the last 45 years. Meanwhile, in our current Communist Party Executive Committee only 9.5% are female. In other words, many of these policies and apparent developments only meet the formal gender equality issue mentioned above. They are, however, still gender neutral and do not take into account important gender differences. Consequently, ensuring gender equality in practice is still a distant goal to be achieved and it will not be easy.

As a matter of fact, gender equality relies not only on the will of the ruling party, the legislative apparatus, and the general population, but must also rely on social analysis and scientific research to be able to accurately calculate the factors that affect and impact gender equality. In addition to scientific bases, cognitive factors will also affect the implementation of substantive gender equality. What do I mean by this? The idea of gender prejudice is still quite common in our society, even among a large part of party cadres and civil servants. Also, the number of full-time staff working on gender equality is limited, in conjunction with limited gender knowledge and gender mainstreaming skills.

In Vietnamese society in particular, and from what I understand in East Asian countries in general, the issue of gender prejudice is associated with the idea of respecting men and despising women, as influenced by feudal and Confucian thought as their historical sources.In many families, especially in rural areas, women and girls are often more disadvantaged than men and boys. Girls often have to do more housework than their brothers. For families in economic difficulty, who do not have enough money for all children in the family to go to school, the first people forced to drop out of school will be girls. Instead of going to school, girls will have to work to earn money for their families. As for better-off families, boys will be more pampered, their individual needs more catered to.

In addition, there are still many people, many families, who value sons more than daughters. We even have an idiom that expresses this thought: "one boy means one, ten girls mean none." Consequently, instead of having only one or two children, they will try to have more children until they have a son. Others will use technical measures to be able to actively have a son at will. They can have an abortion if the baby in the womb is not a boy. This makes the birth rate in society unbalanced. Vietnam's The Single Resolution Board (SRB) in 2019 was 111.5 boys per 100 girls, a ratio similar to that in China. These are really alarming issues.

In other words, from early childhood on, women have been socialized to endure their situation and sacrifice themselves, if needed. As adults, many women accept giving up on their personal desires, on a better work environment and/or promotion opportunities, in order to spend more time with their family. Many young women, after graduating from university in the city, are expected to return to their hometown and get married, so they have to give up on their dreams and ambitions, and perhaps accept a breakup with the person they love, in order to get work and get married as arranged by their parents. Not only are there very few people who dare to oppose such a request, but many are also satisfied with that decision. Paradoxically, many women even consider this a form of happiness because they have pleased their parents. They are educated, know about gender equality and about freedom of choice, but once gender stereotypes have become an internalized custom and culture, it is so very difficult to change. For many Vietnamese women, the value of life is to make their loved ones happy, not to make themselves happy.

In recent years, activities and movements calling for gender equality, especially the elimination of gender stereotypes, have become more prevalent in Vietnam. The good news is that these events have received the attention and response of many young people; the elderly too have reduced gender stereotypes in some cases. It is clearly moving in a positive direction. In short, Luxemburg was right: "Those who do not move, do not notice their chains." So let me tell you about two (no, three) of the many Vietnamese women who did move, representing the struggle for liberation from oppression and exploitation.

Firstly, the Trung sisters, the first Vietnamese women to lead the people against the domination and assimilation of the Northern government (Han dynasty, China). In the 40s AD, the land north of present-day Vietnam was a part of the territory under the rule of the Han dynasty. In AD 40, Trung Trac's husband Thi Sach was killed by a ruler. Angered by this and suppression by the feudal government, Trung Trac and her younger sister, Trung Nhi, united the people to revolt against oppression. After their victory, they established a new state. Their reign lasted 3 years (AD 40-43), when the Han dynasty sent troops to attack. Not wanting to be captured by the enemy, Trung Trac and Trung Nhi jumped into the river to commit suicide. Trung Trac was the first woman to be a Vietnamese monarch.

The second female is a revolutionary activist from the early twentieth century. Her name is Nguyen Thi Minh Khai (1910-1941), and as a young woman she began to actively participate in the workers' movement. In 1930, when the Indochinese

Communist Party (now the Communist Party of Vietnam) was established, she joined the party. She worked in propaganda and the training of Party members. She was also a delegate to the VII Congress of the Communist International in Moscow in 1935, together with her husband Le Hong Phong (1902-1942), a famous Vietnamese revolutionary activist, who served as general secretary of the Indochinese Communist Party from 1935-1936. In her intervention at the Congress, Ngyuen Thi Minh Khai said the following on the important role of Indochinese and Vietnamese women in the revolutionary era:

> [...] Especially during the revolutionary climax in Indochina, women participated significantly in the revolutionary struggle movement. They participated in the protests and led some of them, spoke at rallies, many times women bravely took the lead in the protests and the soldiers had to retreat, had to agree.[20]

Over the years, due to her revolutionary activism, Nguyen Thi Minh Khai, like Rosa Luxemburg, was also arrested by the French colonial government many times. In 1940, after the failed Cochinchina uprising, she and many of her comrades were arrested once more and this time they were sentenced to death. Minh Khai was executed by firing squad on August 28, 1941.

When thinking of the two, I see Rosa's image in Minh Khai's life and vice versa, as the two of them had so many similar experiences. But perhaps Minh Khai was luckier than Rosa, as she always had her friends and comrades around her, and she didn't have to bother with political opponents such as Bernstein or Kautsky.

I would like to close my letter with a quote from Ho Chi Minh: "To mention women is to mention one half of society. If we don't liberate women, we won't liberate half of humanity. If we don't liberate women, we'll only build half of socialism."[21] Therefore, in Vietnam, the cause of women's liberation is not only the work of women but is associated with the cause of national liberation, class liberation and human liberation. I believe Rosa Luxemburg might have agreed with this.

It is summer now. And I wish you seasons in the sun.

Yours,

PS: I am planning to send you the book *Eternal Rosa* via post. Although you can't read Vietnamese, you can at least see the wonderful images drawn by the Duoc Moi group. I hope you like them.

---

20 Subboard of Party History Studies 1998: 85-86.
21 Ho Chi Minh 2011b: 300.

Bản chất của xã hội xã hội chủ nghĩa ở chỗ quần
chúng lao động vĩ đại không còn là một khối thống trị,
thay vào đó, biến toàn bộ đời sống chính trị và kinh
tế thành đời sống của chính họ và mang lại đời sống
đó một phương hướng có ý thức, tự do, và tự chủ. [22]

22 "The essence of socialist society consists in the fact that the great labouring mass ceases to be a dominated mass, but rather, makes the entire political and economic life its own life and gives that life a conscious, free, and autonomous direction." (Luxemburg 2004: 350)

Dear Hong Duc,

I was very happy to receive your letter. I was inspired by the examples of revolutionary and famous women in Vietnam. Thank you for your invitation to come to the conference. I would very much like to make the trip. However, I still have to learn a lot about Ho Chi Minh's biography. The first time I heard about him was when my mum told me about the student protests in 1968, where people were always shouting "Ho-Ho-Ho-Chi-Minh!" We even found a photo of the 68 student demonstrations. Rosa Luxemburg and Ho Chi Minh are both pictured.[23]

I have now begun to read the German-language biography: *Ho Chi Minh. The Mysterious Revolutionary* by Martin Großheim. It was published in 2011, so it's fairly recent. I'm already very excited about the book. As soon as I can think of a topic that I could deal with scientifically in relation to my Luxemburg research, I'll get back to you. Of course, I would also be particularly interested in the work of my colleagues at the Rosa Luxemburg Foundation in Hanoi, so I very much hope that this will work out.

I am also pleased that you are now engaging with Frigga Haug's Marxist feminism. Only now did I remember that she also spoke in English on Rosa Luxemburg's birthday on the topic of "The Enduring Question: Feminism and Rosa Luxemburg," which is exactly the topic of our letters.[24]

---

23 Picture credits: CC_Flickr_by_Haus_der_Geschichte_sa.
24 You can find the video on the Rosa Luxemburg Foundation's Youtube channel: https://www.youtube.com/watch?v=p5L-N0SCYP8&t=349s.

Finally, I have three comments on your thoughts and representations of feminism in Vietnam. Yes, it is true that women all over the world are fighting tirelessly for their rights, but in 2019, the Rosa Luxemburg Foundation organised an international feminist conference in Bochum. I was thrilled at how many (young) men were there, pursuing the goal of a gender-equal society.

My second comment refers to your description that women often have to interrupt their academic careers due to the birth of a child. And that is precisely the crux of the matter. Why can't men and women share the task of caring for children? Why is it not self-evident that both are 50 per cent responsible? I also think that the state should do more in this direction. For example, in the GDR there was all-day care for all children, which was free of charge. This allowed women and men to concentrate on their jobs. Politically, we should focus much more on creating a system that does not leave parents alone, but creates comprehensive and free childcare offers for education, leisure and culture. It cannot be that women decide against having children because they are afraid that they will no longer be able to pursue their work.

Third, on the subject of women in parliament, I regret to inform you that the proportion of women in Germany has unfortunately not increased but decreased. After the 2013 elections, there were still 36.5 per cent women in the German Bundestag; after the 2017 election, only 30 per cent. This has to do with the fact that we have had a new right-wing nationalist party in parliament for five years, the Alternative for Germany (AfD), which is represented in the Bundestag with a share of women of only 10 per cent.

I was particularly shaken by the fact that the Federal Constitutional Court rejected a complaint by a group of women for parity in the Bundestag – that is, equal numbers of women and men in the German parliament. The judges found that the claimants had not sufficiently justified why the legislature should ensure gender parity. After all, elected representatives are not only obliged to their constituency, a party or a population group, but to the whole people - and thus to women and men equally.

To conclude, much work to do, but in the spirit of Rosa, I am hopeful that we will get there eventually. I would be very happy if we could continue our exchange in person, and I certainly look forward to receiving the book *Eternal Rosa*. I thought the film produced for Rosa Luxemburg's birthday in Hanoi was great. I have watched it several times and I am sure the book will be great, too.

With warm regards from Munich,
Your comrade Julia

*Für die besitzende bürgerliche Frau
ist ihr Haus die Welt. Für die
Proletarierin ist die ganze Welt
ihr Haus, die Welt mit ihrem
Leid und ihrer Freude, mit
ihrer kalten Grausamkeit und
ihrer rauen Größe.*[25]

---

25 "For the property-owning bourgeois woman, her house is the world. For the proletarian woman, the whole world is her house, the world with its sorrow and joy, with its cold cruelty and its raw size." (Luxemburg 2004: 243)

Dear Julia,

Thank you for your letter, I'm glad to know that you're now studying Ho Chi Minh. I am sure you will like his ideas.

Regarding political parties in Germany, I am aware of the emergence of the AfD in the German *Bundestag* and their very rapid growth in recent years. I even occasionally follow the results of the polls for the upcoming *Bundestagswahl*, and of course I support the red color of your *Die Linke*. In fact, every time there is a *Landtagswahl* (State election) in the East German states, I try to update myself regularly, because I know those are the states where the possibility of the Left Party participating in government is highest.

I wonder if Rosa Luxemburg were alive today, what would her attitudes and views be toward political parties in Germany and especially the SPD and *Die Linke*?

Although, as we all know, in the twentieth century, there were periods where Rosa Luxemburg's thought was less studied both in the two Germanies and also here in Vietnam, the situation has changed and nowadays there is a great deal of new research and articles on Rosa Luxemburg, her thought and her legacy. They/ we are in the process of reviving Rosa Luxemburg in the twenty-first century, and dialectically we are ourselves revived by engaging with her.

To conclude, it may be that some of Luxemburg's views on the specific methods of struggle of the workers' movement and of the proletariat are no longer relevant today because the characteristics of world politics have changed, because the relationship between political parties is no longer one of absolute confrontation and because workers today are much less united than they used to be. Yet, in my opinion, the goals of a good society, a socialist society for all, free from any type of oppression, are still the goals that humanity is aiming for.

I am so glad that we had the opportunity to share our views on Rosa Luxemburg and one of the most pressing social issues that is happening around us – gender justice. As you say, fighting for feminism is not just women's work. Men should actively participate in this movement and in recent times I believe more and more men here in Vietnam are becoming conscious of this. So, what about the role of (male) researchers like me? It is very necessary to regularly study and approach new feminist and gender equality theories in the world. More importantly, we must not forget to listen to the voices and messages of the women in our lives, i.e. our grandmothers, mothers, wives, daughters, sisters, colleagues, friends, neighbors, etc. Each of them can show us a small but concrete picture of gender equality and its challenges in society. Based on this we can then write our articles and present our research in order to explain different aspects of patriarchy and the struggle for gender equality, so that other people can understand. In addition, through our research activities we can contribute policy advice to legislative bodies to adjust and promulgate legal documents and policies to promote gender equality in real life.

I learned a lot from the information you shared, and I believe more than ever that in many situations we can turn to Luxemburg's instructions and suggestions for the problems that we need to solve, whether personally or socially.

I hope we will remain in touch and can continue to share other matters of interest.

I would like to close my letter with a statement from Luxemburg about human beings and at the same time about her life:

> To be a human being means to joyfully toss your entire life 'on the giant scales of fate' if it must be so, and at the same time to rejoice in the brightness of every day and the beauty of every cloud.[26]

Your Comrade from Hanoi,

Hoàng Đức

---

26 Luxemburg 2013: 363.

References

Alvarado-Díaz, Alhelí de María (2016), "Heroine of the Revolution," in *Rosa Remix*. Eds. Stefanie Ehmsen and Albert Scharenberg. New York: Rosa Luxemburg Stiftung NYC, 43-49.

Brecht, Bertolt (2018), *The Collected Poems of Bertolt Brecht*. Eds. Tom Kuhn and David Constantine. Harrisonburg: LSC Communications.

Cornell, Drucilla (2018), "Rosa Luxemburg's Ethical Feminism." *Rosa Luxemburg Foundation NYC*. Accessed on 11.08.2021, at https://rosalux.nyc/rosa-luxemburgs-ethical-feminism/.

German Bundestag (1974), 80th session. Accessed on 29.06.2021, at: http://dip21.bundestag.de/dip21/btp/07/07080.pdf.

Haug, Frigga (2009), "The 'Four-in-One Perspective': A Manifesto for a More Just Life," *Socialism and Democracy*, 23:1, 119-123.

Ho Chi Minh (2011a), *Complete Works Vol. 1*. Hanoi: National Politics Publishing House.

Ho Chi Minh (2011b), *Complete Works Vol. 12*. Hanoi: National Politics Publishing House.

Kühn, Andreas (2005), *Stalins Enkel, Maos Söhne. Die Lebenswelt der K-Gruppen in der Bundesrepublik der 1970er Jahre*. Frankfurt a. M.: Campus.

Lenin, V.I. (1977), *Werke, Vol. 33*. Berlin: Dietz Verlag.

Luxemburg, Rosa (November 1918), "A Duty of Honour." *Marxist Internet Archive*. Accessed on 13.08.2021, at https://www.marxists.org/archive/luxemburg/1918/11/18c.htm.

Luxemburg, Rosa (2004), *The Rosa Luxemburg Reader*. Eds. Peter Hudis and Kevin B. Anderson. New York: Monthly Review Press.

Luxemburg, Rosa (2013), *The Letters of Rosa Luxemburg*. Eds. Georg Adler, Peter Hudis, and Annelies Laschitza. London and New York: Verso Books.

Luxemburg, Rosa (2015), *The Complete Works of Rosa Luxemburg, Vol. II: Economic Writings 2*. Ed. Peter Hudis and Paul Le Blanc. London and New York: Verso Books.

Subboard of Party History Studies (Nghe An Provincial Party Committee, 1998), *Nghe An: The Examples of Communists Vol. 1*. Vinh: Nghe An Publishing House.

Làm người có nghĩa là vui vẻ đặt toàn bộ cuộc đời mình lên 'những cái cân khổng lồ của số phận' nếu buộc phải như vậy, và đồng thời hoan hỷ trước sự tươi sáng của mỗi ngày và vẻ đẹp của mỗi đám mây.[27]

---

27 "To be a human being means to joyfully toss your entire life 'on the great scales of fate' if it must be so, and at the same time to rejoice in the lightness of every day and the beauty of every cloud." (Luxemburg 2013: 374)

Деятель германского, польского и международного
рабочего движения, один из основателей КП Германии
РОЗА ЛЮКСЕМБУРГ • 1871—1919

Пишите индекс предприятия связи места назначения

Куда _____

ПОЧТА СССР

8. Peter Hudis

Кому _____

&

Индекс предприятия связи   и адрес отправителя

Hjalmar Jorge Joffre-Eichhorn

Dear Kelvin,

It is often said the history of a book or work of art is the history of its interpretation. The same can be said for a life of a person. Rosa Luxemburg's life and works have been interpreted in a variety of ways over the decades. What explains these differing views? Surely, that each generation draws out dimensions of her work based on the problems of their own time. So, what problem faces our time that offers a vantage point for exploring her legacy anew? As I see it, two issues stand out: one is the utter failure of all 'socialist' and 'communist' regimes to lead to a transcendence of capitalism; the other is recognition of the thoroughly *racialized* nature of contemporary capitalism. These are the problems facing our era and we cannot expect Luxemburg to answer them, but we can ask what her work means in light of them.

There are many reasons to consider Rosa Luxemburg a pioneering figure in the battle against racial capitalism. She fervently opposed colonialism and imperialism throughout her life, beginning with her very first articles and essays for the socialist press in the 1890s. She carefully studied (and praised) the communal social formations of non-Western societies in a series of lectures, essays and manuscripts between 1907 and 1912, the foremost being her 300-page work, *Introduction to Political Economy*. In these and other writings, in which she meticulously absorbed the latest anthropological and ethnographic literature on what we now call the Global South, she argued that precapitalist social formations among Native Americans, Australian Aborigines, and indigenous peoples in South Africa, Algeria and northern India, provided important insights into how a future socialist society can be organized – this at a time when many Marxists dismissed such societies as 'backward' and 'uncivilized.' It is hard to name a single figure in the socialist movement of her time who more fervently opposed the oppression and genocide imposed by capitalism-imperialism on people of color.

Luxemburg did all of this *before* 1913, when she began writing what is widely considered her magnum opus – her 400-page book, *The Accumulation of Capital*. I begin here, because it is widely assumed by many recent commentators that Luxemburg's profound studies of the non-Western world were a product of her dispute with Marx's theory of expanded reproduction in *The Accumulation of Capital*. But this is not the case. She had already written hundreds of pages on the non-Western world *before* 1913, when the *The Accumulation of Capital* was first published. Nor did she express any disagreement with Marx's theory of the origin and development of capitalism up to that point. She was well aware that Marx tied the birth and expansion of capitalism to the trans-Atlantic slave trade and colonialism in such works as *The Poverty of Philosophy* (1847) and Volume One of *Capital* (1867), and she never uttered a word of criticism of either one of them. Nor did she accuse Marx of ignoring or downplaying the suffering imposed by capitalism on indigenous peoples in *The Accumulation of Capital*.

In fact, it was not her dispute with Marx which caused her to turn her attention to the non-Western world; on the contrary, it was her studies of the non-Western world that caused her to take issue (in 1913) with what she called a "technical" and "scientific" issue pertaining to Marx's mathematical formulas of expanded reproduction at the end of Volume Two of *Capital*. I cannot rehearse here the argument in *The Accumulation of Capital* or the criticisms that many (including myself) have leveled against it. But I wish to stress that Luxemburg was fully aware that Marx never claimed that expanded reproduction actually occurs irrespective of non-capitalist strata. Instead, she argued that his formulas on expanded reproduction at the end of Volume Two of *Capital* fail to provide an *adequate account* of exactly *how* this occurs, since it abstracts from foreign trade in treating capitalism as a single isolated nation. Marx did so *not* because he thought expanded reproduction can actually occur in a single isolated nation (that would be an absurd claim that contradicts the law of value); instead, he did so to highlight what *drives* capital accumulation – the domination of means of production over means of consumption, or the domination of dead labour (constant capital) over living labour (variable capital).

Marx held that this domination of dead over living labour represented a specific expression of class domination that pertains to capitalism and capitalism alone. Luxemburg disagreed, arguing that the domination of dead over living labour is a transhistorical reality that applies not only to capitalism but to the future socialist society as well. *This was the decisive issue in their dispute.* Luxemburg states it plainly in *The Accumulation of Capital*: "The growth in constant capital at the expense of variable capital is merely the capitalist expression of the general effects of the increasing productivity of labour. The formula c is greater than v ($c > v$), translated from capitalist language to that of the social[ist] labour process, means no more than this: the greater the productivity of human labour, the shorter the time needed to transform a given quantity of means of production into finished products."[1]

Luxemburg's *The Accumulation of Capital* dealt with a specific debate within *Marxist* economics at the time, and she cannot be blamed for how those who came after her (such as the followers of John Maynard Keynes) tried to use the book to argue that effective demand drives capital accumulation during their effort to save capitalism from collapse during the Great Depression. Nor could she have known that Stalin and his successors would argue that the domination of constant over variable capital is not specific to capitalism but characterizes 'socialism' as well. Luxemburg, of course, would have never considered the USSR 'socialist,' any more than she would support saving capitalism through a welfare state. Since she was a virulent opponent of both bourgeois economics and all forms of authoritarian socialism, I believe she would have revised her argument in *The Accumulation of Capital* had she lived to see Keynesianism and the horrors of Stalinism. That is of course mere speculation on my part. But what is not speculation is that we have experienced both, so we must be attentive to how the logic of her argument can be used to defend positions that are at odds with the liberatory ideals to which she was devoted.

What speaks much more to the present moment is the emphasis in her political writings that any transition to socialism is inconceivable without what she called "thoroughgoing democracy." This is one aspect of her legacy that the leading forces

1 Luxemburg 2015: 230.

of capitalist society fully understand, as seen in how hard it is working in many parts of the world to destroy even the vestiges of bourgeois democracy. Luxemburg did not oppose participating in bourgeois parliaments and repeatedly insisted that a *democratic republic* is the formation best suited for waging the class struggle to a successful conclusion. At the same time, she took issue with the presumption that the institutions of bourgeois society can be counted upon to forge the transition to socialism. What is *necessary* is not the same as what is *sufficient*, which is why she embraced the slogan "All Power to the Workers' and Soldiers' Councils" during the German Revolution of 1918-19.

Prior to 1917 Lenin had also argued that a democratic republic is the formation best suited for waging the class struggle to a successful conclusion. But he dropped that perspective after the October Revolution and proceeded to create the basis of a single party state that monopolized power in the hands of "the thin strata of Bolsheviks." And through such acts as the suppression of the revolt in Kronstadt of 1921 and numerous workers' strikes and peasant revolts that had broken out throughout Russia, he reduced the "dictatorship *of* the proletariat" to a dictatorship *over* the proletariat in which even internal party factions were banned.

Luxemburg saw this coming, as seen in her 1904 "Organizational Questions of Social Democracy," which opposed Lenin for imposing "the blind submission of all-party organizations and their activity, down to the smallest detail, to a central authority that alone thinks, acts, and decides for everyone,"[2] and her 1911 "Credo" which stated, "we felt obliged to stand up decisively against the organizational centralism of Lenin and his friends, because they wanted to secure a revolutionary direction for the proletarian movement by swaddling the party, in a purely mechanistic fashion, with an intellectual dictator from the central Party Executive,"[3] as well as her 1918 booklet *On the Russian Revolution*, which attacked Lenin and Trotsky for suppressing democracy, imposing a single-party state, and banning leftwing organizations. Her support of the Bolshevik seizure of power and opposition to efforts to overturn it did not lead her to mute her criticisms, even as they were in the midst of fighting a bloody civil war against imperialist forces, as seen in her brutally *realistic* assessment in the fall of 1918: "It is clear that, under such conditions, i.e., being caught in the pincers of the imperialist powers on all sides, neither socialism nor the dictatorship of the proletariat can become a reality [in Russia], but at the most a caricature of both."[4]

This is the Rosa that lives on and speaks to the thoroughly democratic and grassroots movements of our time – especially those that have arisen in the massive protests against racism over the last year. She did not view democracy as a mere tool to be used to obtain power, but as indispensable for fostering social consciousness and revolutionary initiative *both before and after the seizure of power*. For these reasons, Luxemburg is not in the same category as many of the other Marxists of the time, including Lenin, with whom she often collaborated. Their differences were not a matter of polite disagreements; they reflected radically different conceptions of what socialism is and what are the means to attain it. As I see it, one side – defined

2 Luxemburg 2004a: 252.
3 Luxemburg 2004b: 271.
4 Luxemburg 2011: 473.

by Lenin's post-1917 approach and those of his followers – has been left behind by history, whereas the other – expressed by Luxemburg's critique of Lenin and Trotsky – points to the path which history is calling on us to embark upon today.

There are many expressions of this, but I will conclude by mentioning just one, stated as she directly participated in the Russian Revolution of 1905-06:

> The freedom to speak and publish is one precondition to the attainment of consciousness by the proletariat; the second is that the proletariat not put any restrictions on itself, that it not say, "We can discuss this, but not that." Conscious workers the world over understand this, and they always try to give even the worst of their enemies the right to freely explain their views. They say, "Let even the enemies of the working people voice their own views, so that we may respond to them, and so the working masses can work out for themselves who is a friend and who a foe."[5]

If we can live up to Luxemburg's *humanism* – as seen in her unwavering opposition to all forms of oppression, as well as passionate support for all victims of imperialism and colonialism – we will have done much to make her legacy come alive for our time. For the rest, as has been said, let the dead bury their dead.

Best wish,

Peter Stein

---

5 Luxemburg 1906a: 2.

"Freedom is always and exclusively freedom for the one who thinks differently."[6]

---

6 "Freedom is always and exclusively freedom for the one who thinks differently." (Luxemburg 2004c: 305)

May 15-20, 2021
Wrocław, Poland

Dear Peter

Let the dead bury their dead… The final words of your letter have proven prophetic as Gaza is once again under attack and … … … Starting my letter to you has not been the smoothest of endeavors. In fact, just finding the serenity to sit down and begin writing has been very challenging for me in these tempestuous and deadly times across the world, including in my own private-political life. For quite a few years now I have found myself balancing on an increasingly thin tightrope between falling into the abyss of despair and hopelessness and continuing to partake and chip in to our gigantic, at times seemingly impossible (quixotic?) struggle(s) against barbarism and for some type of renewed socialist – and why not say it? – communist hypothesis-horizon-desire-necessity. And no doubt about it, Rosa Luxemburg has over time become one of my most trusted and cherished friends, companions and comrades in arms, with these 'arms' referring just as much to Rosa's work and struggle(s) as to the deep sense of caring embrace I have felt whenever engaging with her words, thoughts, affects and convictions-turned-actions over the course of her short but highly intense life.

And so yes, I totally agree with you that in relation to a person as diminutively gigantic in stature as Róża Luksenburg, each generation will necessarily draw out dimensions of her work, and I would add of her life and how she fused the two, based on the problems of their own time, or perhaps of their-our own time-space, the latter, I feel, being so important to our understanding of, dialoguing with and learning from our "yatichiri" (Bolivian Aymara for teacher) Rosa L. How does the importance of RL differ and change when viewed from once again military-ruled Burma, from Gaza under fire or from Colombia suffering ongoing state-sponsored terrorism? How does the use-value of reading and discussing Rosa vary and depend on whether we are overworked and underpaid health workers in Kenya, increasingly despondent peace activists in Eastern Ukraine or literally drowning climate justice warriors in the sinking Maldives?

Clearly, as I hear you suggest, it is our deep appreciation for "Luxemburg's humanism – […] her unwavering opposition to all forms of oppression, as well as [her] passionate support for all victims of imperialism and colonialism" that could serve as a possible red thread capable of weaving our hearts and minds together in struggle as we continue on the path(s) of liberation and emancipation so beautifully trodden by her and countless others over the past centuries. I am also with you when you highlight her strong commitment to "thoroughgoing democracy" as the "path which history is calling on us to embark upon today," though I have admittedly never been entirely comfortable with the Luxemburg-Lenin debate, because I do feel the fact that RL was never in a position to exercise or defend state power makes any affirmation that she would have kept her commitment even in the face of the most bloody and intransigent adversity a leap of faith that I have never felt the urge to make.

On the contrary, in the spirit of a critical, de-monumentalizing solidarity with Rosa Luxemburg, I have at times found myself slightly bewildered and concerned by what seems to me her occasional tendency – detectable especially in her letters – to patronize and know better than others, in line with a dialectic between the revolutionary vanguard and the so-called masses that has been plaguing us forever and which, despite all the powerful theory and rhetoric generated over the past century and a half, appears to be very difficult to sublate in practice. In this sense, who knows how much a Secretary General Rosa Luxemburg may have come to resemble *tovarish* Ilyich. Who knows how protective she may have become of a successful revolution (in the sense of winning state power) in which she herself participated.

In any case, perhaps due to the fact that my political socialization began just before and after the fall of the Berlin Wall, in a (West) Germany in which a triumphant, self-righteous spirit of "the end of history" was (and is) particularly virulent, I eventually came to the stubborn conviction that we must own the entire genealogy of attempts to overcome capitalism as the starting point for anything we do. That way our critique will always be an internal critique based on a critical solidarity with those who came before us, with those who tried and ultimately failed in what they set out to achieve. And fail they/we did. Quite miserably, if you ask me.

I suppose what I am trying to do here is to bring together Brecht's "To Those Born After," with its emphasis on thinking of those who came before us "with forbearance," and Beckett's "Try again, Fail again, Fail Better," i.e. engaging in a dialectics of victories & defeats, of fervent hopes & bitter disillusionments, of rousing revolutionaries & all too human fallen heroes and heroines. Yet we must keep trying. For me, the monumentalization is meaningful on the level of honoring those of us who tried to do the impossible, and who gave their lives to pursue this crazy dream of a world free of oppression. And crazy they were. Crazy we are. Beautifully crazy as the following song by Spanish duo Pedro Pastor and Suso Sudón describes:

> *Solo los locos colocan deliberadamente las piedras otra vez en el camino por el puro placer de tropezar de nuevo [...] Solo los locos vuelven a empezar con la pasión de los niños aquellas empresas que dejaron a medias.*[7]

In fact, maybe craziness is actually one of our starting points, together with indignation, rage, hope, tenderness, resolve, caring, passion, determination, courage, love, solidarity and so many other qualities that sometimes go astray or get the better of us, that sometimes end up turning us into the ugly opposite of what we set out to become. Little red Frankenstein's monsters.

The demonumentalization, on the other hand, appears to me to be needed not simply in a general humanization and de-idealization of our revolutionary ancestors but in the active seeking of connections with some of their greatest weaknesses, their most fatal flaws and/or those moments in their lives in which they least resemble the image that has been made of them and which at times may have even coincided with

---

7 "Only the crazy ones put the rock back onto the path for the pure pleasure of tripping again [...] Only the crazy ones start again with childish passion those tasks left unfinished" (Translation: mine). Listen at Pastor and Sudón 2014.

their very self-image. In the case of Lenin, I feel deep solidarity with the bedridden, frail, lonely and increasingly helpless man realizing that the Revolution was devouring its children and the quite visceral, willful desperation that exudes from his final writings. Concerning Red Rosa, the connection is similar. It is those periods during her numerous jailtimes in which her depression took over, she felt sad and alone, with suicide on her mind. Tired. Existentially exhausted, full of revolutionary anguish and despair.

"Despair fills the part of the soul that was [once] occupied by hope"[8] our comrade John Berger once wrote in one of his texts about the struggle of the Palestinian people. Elsewhere he writes, again in relation to Palestine: "Despair without fear, without resignation, without a sense of defeat, makes for a stance towards the world here, such as I have never seen before."[9] Berger – whose very own letter to Rosa Luxemburg is a work of art – calls this stance "undefeated despair." I would like to suggest that this describes not only the condition of the undeniably unvanquishable spirit of the Palestinian people – so admirably visible again today –, but it appears to me that "undefeated despair" may in fact be one of the constituent, inescapable, individual and collective affects in any prolonged, against-all-odds struggle for liberation. Or rather, given the generally very unfavorable conditions in which we wage our dreams, despair must surely be expected to invade and inhabit us at one point or another. The question then is how to make this despair productive as opposed to dragging us down into the depths of resignation and ultimate defeat. How to make our despair and therefore ourselves undefeatable? Wouldn't you agree that the Rosa Luxemburg of the "Prison Letters" (but not only) incarnates powerfully this spirit of "undefeated despair"? How did she manage to keep fighting the good fight despite all the setbacks she experienced, despite all the verbal aggressions and physical violence inflicted upon her by false friends and real foes alike? It surely could not only have been her steadfast faith in historical materialism, as some would have it?

Interestingly, the Spanish word for despair is *"desesperación"* and someone who is desperate is *"desesperado/a/e"*. It has to do with no longer being able to wait for something to happen (*"esperar"* means both to hope/expect as well as to wait). The German word, on the other hand, is *"Verzweiflung"* and could be translated as "being negatively impacted by doubts (*Zweifel*)." So if we add to the original decrease or lack of hope (from the French *"desespoir"*), a growing weariness to wait and an equally intensifying tendency to be overwhelmed by doubts, I propose that one possible response to our condition of despair must be a systematic politics of comradely encouragement. Encouragement in the sense of giving each other courage to engage with and eventually – temporarily? – overcome our doubts, but also in the sense of cheering each other up when the going has gotten too tough to bear. Finally, encouragement in the sense of the Spanish *"ánimo"* and *"aliento"*, which refer to "inspiriting" and "giving breath" to others in order to stop waiting and start again on the path towards the communist horizon.

---

8 See Berger 2008.
9 See Berger 2006.

Believe me, Peter, when I tell you that over the past few years the time-space(s) I have inhabited, and vice versa, were often beset by a seemingly unstoppable growth of individual and collective despair and a big question mark as to what a politics of solidarity and encouragement could look like in practice, in particular in Afghanistan, my political home of 13 years. Over the past few months the security situation throughout the country has gone from very bad to beyond nightmarish and a whole range of absurdly ingenious targeted attacks against individual human rights activists, journalists, civil society organizations as well as the civilian population in general, and especially against members of the minority Hazara ethnic group, have become so commonplace that people are beginning to consider digging their own graves and writing their own obituaries in an attempt to have at least some type of micro-control over what appears to be their unavoidable destiny: premature, violent death. But really, Peter, "for how many more years can we ask the people of Afghanistan, day after day, to rise from the ashes of the corpses of their own mutilated dreams? How many more times can the Phoenix resurrect before it finally dies of exhaustion and despair?", as one of my friend-comrades recently asked (again) after yet another vicious attack against an educational center, with 70+ deaths, mostly young schoolgirls, in the capital Kabul.

How not to be murdered by exhaustion and despair? How to rise from the ashes of our mutilated dreams? How to go on? – "in spite of everything," an expression our *yatichiri* Rosa so often used to encourage, in the various possible meanings of the word mentioned above, her despairing and wavering friends and comrades, and, I suspect, herself as well. In spite of everything. *Trotz alledem*. What is perhaps lost in the English translation from the German is its history pre- and post-Rosa Luxemburg. In a few words, from what we know, "Trotz alledem" was the name of a song written by German poet Ferdinand Freiligrath (1810-1876) after the failed revolution of 1848 and inspired by Robert Burns' (1759-97) famous egalitarian call "A Man's a Man for A'That/Is There For Honest Poverty." The lyrics were later published by Karl Marx in his *Neue Rheinische Zeitung*, and the song and lyrics have since played a prominent role in the German workers' movement, thanks in large part to Luxemburg's and Karl Liebknecht's own frequent use of the expression, and further popularized post-Rosa & Karl through the interpretations of Communist singer and actor Ernst Busch (1900-1980) and, my personal favorite, the following version by recently retired *Liedermacher* Hannes Wader: https://www.youtube.com/ watch?v=AUUfuW-Pr3M.

Returning to Rosa, the Encourager, of course we know from her letters to erstwhile friends such as Mathilde Wurm that she could also be quite punishing with people she perceived as overly whining and contaminated by bourgeois self-pity.[10] Then again, so many of her letters are indeed full of not only "ruthless revolutionary energy" but also the "tender humanity" she affirmed to be the "true essence of socialism." For me, this "tender humanity" – the need of which was a few decades later reinforced by Che Guevara's unforgettable *"hay que endurecerse, pero sin perder la ternura jamás!"* ("One has to grow hard but without ever losing tenderness!") – is perhaps most powerfully expressed by Rosa

---

10 See Luxemburg 2013: 362-364.

Luxemburg's tireless efforts to encourage others to "be cheerful and serene," "to be but brave," "to be calm and happy all the same," to realize that "this too will pass," "to keep cheerful whatever happens," and therefore "to take [life] as it is, valiantly, heads erect, smiling ever – *trotz alledem*." Bless you, Rosa. You don't know how happy it makes me that after all your efforts to persevere, and support others to do the same, you got to be part of and experience, together with millions of workers and soldiers, the *Novemberrevolution* of 1918/19. It may have been short-lived and ultimately deadly, but the Phoenix rose valiantly once more, and so it shall again, in spite of everything.

In my next letter to you, Peter, I hope to expand a little more on Rosa's politics of encouragement and undefeated despair. In the meantime, I am very much looking forward to hearing your thoughts on this, perhaps aided by examples from your own life, if you feel like it. For now, I shall close with two gifts from Afghanistan, both of which I trust our friend Rosa Luxemburg might have appreciated – a photo of an indomitable plant known as *bot-e khar*, plant with thorns[11]

Bot-e Khar

and an Afghan proverb, a *Zarbul Masal*:

"Dawn will follow even the darkest of nights."

With that in mind, *la lucha continúa*!

In Solidarity,

Hjalmar

---

11 *Tashakor* to the photographer, my "brother" Saleem Rajabi in Afghanistan, currently battling to stay alive and sane with his family of 5 all the while continuing the struggle for justice and peace – despite all.

HÄNSCHEN, SEIEN SIE DOCH
FRÖHLICH, DAS LEBEN IST
SO SCHÖN. DIE WESPE HAT
ES WIEDER GESAGT, UND
DIE WEIß BESCHEID.[12]

---

12 "Hänschen, be cheerful and happy, after all life is so beautiful! The wasp has said so again, and it knows what it's talking about." (Luxemburg 2013: 389)

May 30, Chicago

Dear Ajohra,

Israel's war against Gaza, the West Bank, and the Palestinians within Israel has also weighed heavily on my mind over the past weeks, and your comments raise an array of questions about how Luxemburg's life and work speaks to such calamities. The events provide plenty of reason for despair and hopelessness – Netanyahu's regime has murdered hundreds of Palestinians (including dozens of children) with its attack on Gaza, while neofascist Jewish mobs (many but not exclusively from illegal settlements in the West Bank) have launched outright pogroms against Palestinians in parts of Israel (such as Lod) that had long been defined by Jewish-Arab cohabitation. The one image that sticks in my mind is Netanyahu supporters verbally assaulting an Israeli Jew and his wife from southern Sudan by shouting, "You n…..s have no right to be here, get out of this country!" How, I asked myself, could we have reached the point wherein a significant number of Jews, part of the most discriminated and oppressed group in European history, have sunk so low as to employ the exact words and practices once used in anti-Semitic pogroms against their forebearers? If this is not a descent into barbarism, what is?

With this in mind, I turned again to Luxemburg, and came upon an article in *Vorwärts* of November 3, 1905 (recently published in Volume III of *The Complete Works of Rosa Luxemburg*), which discusses the outbreak of anti-Jewish pogroms. She writes, "The Jews were blamed for behaving in an antipatriotic manner, for causing disturbances of the peace by political agitation, and for instigating and leading the revolutionary movement."[13] The upsurge of anti-Semitism during the 1905 Russian Revolution was a direct response to Jewish political militancy. Likewise, Israel's murderous assaults against Palestinians today is a direct response to its failure to eviscerate Palestinian political militancy. What does this tell us? That we should not be consumed by despair over the many setbacks faced by the Palestinian movement over the past decades, since it is Israel's failure to silence this movement that explains the intensity of its attacks upon it.

The human spirit of resistance is at issue, and the point is never to lose sight of the fact that it cannot be completely expunged by even the most horrific repression. Yes, capitalism compels human relations to take on the *form* of relations between things – but it is incapable of making us *into* things, since without *living* labour there is no source of the value that sustains it. *Things* cannot resist; *people* can. Herein resides our hope for the present – and the future.

But we have still not answered the question posed at the end of my opening paragraph. For some, the answer is simple: this is what you expect in colonial settler states. But does this really suffice? Israel was clearly founded by forcibly displacing the Palestinians; yet there are different kinds of settler states, and many Jews came to what is now Israel for reasons that were not reducible to the machinations of the

---

13 Luxemburg 2019: 267.

Western powers or the Soviet Union (let's not forget that the latter cast the deciding vote at the UN that created Israel). Obviously, explicating that history is not possible here. But if there is a straight, uninterrupted line between any and all calls for Jewish self-determination and what Netanyahu is doing today, it follows that there is absolutely nothing to learn from the tragedy that is Israel, because it means there is no tragedy. Predictable straight lines teach us nothing. But there is a terrible tragedy we *must* learn from: how can those who suffered such repression use that as an excuse to turn around and impose vicious repression on others? If it can happen to a section of the Jewish people, can it not happen to anyone?

If there is something to despair about today, it is that this question not only remains unanswered, but that it is too rarely asked. This is especially troubling in light of the unfinished, failed, and aborted revolutions of the last 100 years, in which members of downtrodden classes and groups again and again became the new oppressors. Immanuel Levinas once stated, "The circumstances of Marxism's having turned into Stalinism is the greatest offence to the cause of the human, because Marxism bore the hopes of humanity: it may be one of the greatest psychological shocks for the twentieth-century European."[14] It remains a great offence and shock today, because Stalinism arose from *within* the revolutionary movement—and on more than one occasion.

This frames my entry into the central issue posed in your letter: "We must own the entire genealogy of attempts to overcome capitalism as the starting point for anything we do." I agree, though perhaps in a different way from what you intend. Yes, we must own up to the fact that history shows that fighting against the status quo does not necessarily point the way to a new society; if undertaken from an erroneous standpoint or perspective, it can just as readily lead to a new kind of tyranny. But we must not "own" the wrong turns and failures that led to our present predicament – except as signposts for what must be avoided. Otherwise, all we have to offer at the end of the day is despair and hopelessness in the face of defeat. And no one needs us for that.

Instead, let us "tarry with the negative" (as Hegel put it) by asking which paths potentially lead to the overcoming of human self-estrangement and which do not – regardless of how committed we may be to a particular political cause or theoretical perspective. Hegel declared, "But the life of the spirit is not a life that shuns death and bewares destruction, keeping clean of it: it is a life that bears death and maintains itself in it. Spirit gains its truth only through finding itself within absolute rupture."[15]

What goes by the name of 'Marxism' today is defined by an "absolute rupture," and we must own up to *this* as we try to move forward. Paul Mason captured this in a recent essay on the Marxist-Humanist philosopher Raya Dunayevskaya (who happens to be my mentor): "Since the rediscovery of the 1844 Manuscripts the dilemma for Marxism has been clear: either it is a theory of the liberation of individual human beings or it is a theory of impersonal forces and structures, which can be studied but very rarely escaped."[16] Luxemburg clearly understood Marxism

14 Levinas 1999: 107.
15 For a version of this quote, see Hegel 2018: 20.
16 Mason 2021: 204.

as the liberation of the individual; this is especially clear from reading her political works alongside her letters. In contrast, those who tried to read her out of Marxism – Stalin, Mao, as well as figures like Althusser – did not understand Marxism as a theory of the liberation of the individual. We know the consequences, and there is no point following the approach of those who continue to treat Marxism as a theory of impersonal forces and structures – whether they are opposed to Stalinism or not.

This is not to suggest that those associated with what Ernst Bloch called "the warm current" of Marxism did not have limitations and contradictions of their own (as suggested in my first letter, I find Luxemburg's economic theory and *a priori* rejection of the emancipatory potential of national liberation movements to be at odds with her overarching humanism); nor does it suggest there is any assurance that those associated with such "warm currents" today will point us in the right direction. The dialectical principle of *transformation into opposite* (which Lenin directly drew from his reading of Hegel's *Science of Logic* in 1914 in response to the offence and shock of the Second International's capitulation to imperialism) can apply to any individual, situation, or movement.

I recall many years ago a young activist who attended a talk by Dunayevskaya on the Russian Revolution and the rise of Stalinism asking during the discussion, "What guarantee do we have that a revolution in the future will not end up leading to some totalitarian regime?" When Dunayevskaya answered, "There's isn't any guarantee," she burst into tears. But was another answer really plausible? But that hardly means we have to reinvent the wheel: we have a clear idea today of what is the road that is best *not* taken, so we start from there.

No work by Luxemburg more powerfully addresses this than the critique of Kautsky, Lenin, and Trotsky in her 1918 work, *On the Russian Revolution* (it is often forgotten that it was just as critical of Kautsky as the Bolsheviks). It argues that shutting down freedom of speech, press and assembly and turning the "dictatorship *of* the proletariat" into the rule of a single party *over* the proletariat through "revolutionary" terror undermines the possibility of a transition to socialism. You say you are not comfortable with this since she was never in the position to manage a seizure of power of her own. But let's keep three things in mind: 1) Luxemburg was no shrinking violet when it came to employing violence against the ruling class: she knew as well as anyone that even the most peaceful seizure of power would be met to by a violent counter-revolution by the old order. At issue was how to combat it without turning a necessity into a virtue. 2) What most worried her was that the Bolsheviks turned the apparatus of repression *against other leftists*; she surely knew that one of the first acts of the Cheka (headed by her former close colleague and supporter Feliks Dzerzhinsky) was to go after the anarchists. 3) In contrast to the standpoint of Kautsky and others, hers was an *imminent critique* of the Bolsheviks – and not solely because she supported their seizure of power in October 1917. Her insistence in *On the Russian Revolution* that the *Marxist* concept of "the *revolutionary* dictatorship *of* the proletariat" involves "unrestricted democracy" threw back at Lenin the very words inscribed in his party's program since 1903, which read: "The Russian Social Democratic Labor Party therefore sets as its immediate political task the overthrow of the tsarist autocracy and its replacement by a democratic republic whose constitution would guarantee…unrestricted freedom of conscience, speech, press and assembly." Yes, such a democratic republic is what Marx and Engels – as well as Lenin prior to 1917 – meant by "the revolutionary dictatorship of the proletariat."

Hence, I'd like to turn your point on its head, by saying it is rather easy to proclaim the need for "unrestricted democracy" before the revolution, when one is part of a besieged minority, but quite another after the seizure of power, when one is in a position of authority. And yet it is affirming and implementing democracy *after* the revolution that is the measure of whether one is seriously committed to democracy in the first place. Lenin and Trotsky failed that test, which was bad enough; but even worse, it became the template for revolution after revolution that followed. And as Luxemburg feared, not a single one of them produced a transition to socialism; what resulted instead was a new form of capitalism, *state-capitalism*. So perhaps it was Luxemburg who was the greater realist.

But am I guilty of issuing such criticisms with the privilege of hindsight? There's much truth to this: no one, including Luxemburg, anticipated that something as egregious as Stalinism would emerge from *within* the revolution. But that's still not a reason to reject the criticism, first, because what is the point of being a historical materialist if one does not learn from history, and second, a decade *before* the 1917 Revolution she offered an alternative to the path later taken by Lenin. It is found in an essay (of 1908) entitled "Lessons from the Three Dumas." It tackles what would face a revolutionary regime that came to power in Russia without accompanying proletarian revolutions elsewhere. She wrote,

> The working class cannot delude itself that, having overthrown absolutism and attained a dictatorship for a certain period, it will establish a socialist system. The socialist revolution can be only a result of international revolution, and the results that the proletariat in Russia will be able to achieve in the current revolution will depend, to say nothing of the level of social development in Russia, on the level and form of development that class relations and proletarian operations in other capitalist countries will have achieved by that time.[17]

That a revolution in a single country, even one as big as Russia, cannot by itself produce a transition to socialism does not, however, negate its importance, since the creation of a *truly* democratic republic, "however temporarily, would provide enormous encouragement to the international class struggle. That is why the working class in Poland and in Russia can and must strive to seize power with full consciousness." She is fully aware that in lieu of an international revolution the dictatorship of the proletariat cannot survive for long; she cites the "inevitable removal of the proletariat from power by a counterrevolutionary operation of the bourgeoisie, the rural landowners, the petty-bourgeoisie, and the greater part of the peasantry." Hence, "Revolution in this conception would bring the proletariat losses as well as victories. Yet by no other road can the entire international proletariat march to its final victory. We must propose the socialist revolution not as a sudden leap, finished in twenty-four hours, but as a historical period, perhaps long, of turbulent class struggle, with breaks both brief and extended."

---

17 To be published in *The Complete Works of Rosa Luxemburg. Volume IV* (forthcoming).

Luxemburg was essentially saying that the defeat of a revolution in a single country is not the worst outcome – so long as its promotion of proletarian self-emancipation through "unrestricted democracy" inspires workers elsewhere to take up the fight. This is in marked contrast to Lenin's approach after 1917, which sacrificed democracy for the sake of staying in power. It *seemed* to offer a successful model to many in the following decades. But it no longer does today, and for good reason – instead of promoting socialism, it ended up discrediting it.

You raise a good question – who knows whether Luxemburg might have taken a path similar to Lenin had her party come to power in Germany or Poland. Under the pressure of events, would she have abandoned her perspective of 1908 and 1918? There's no way to know. But *if* she had done so, it would do nothing to undermine the validity of the principles projected in those writings. She would instead come to us as a *tragic* figure – not in the way we understand that today, as a dedicated Marxist murdered by the counterrevolution, but as someone who failed to live up to her own liberatory principles. And that would be a far greater tragedy.

For this reason, I am not sure that "undefeated despair" is the existential standpoint that is most appropriate for our time. There are two types of despair when it comes to political commitment: one is despair when you put up the best of fights but still lose to forces stronger than yourself; the other is despair at self-inflicted losses. The latter is always more painful, since the defeat cannot be blamed on anyone else.

Of course, these two senses of despair are not always neatly distinguishable. One moment of my political personal life may speak to this. Although I am now a professor of philosophy, that has been my vocation for only one-fifth of my adult life: prior to earning a Ph.D or even imagining having a position in academia, I spent two decades as a full-time organizer for News and Letters Committees, the Marxist-Humanist organization founded by Dunayesvskaya; I served as her secretary from 1986 to 1987 and following her death in 1987 became national co-organizer (in 1988) of the group. Though it was not easy living a hand-to-mouth existence for 20 years on a below-poverty stipend with no health benefits, I treasure the years I spent working to advance the ideas I had come to cherish. But by 2008 it became clear that the organization was no longer viable in its existing form, and it was time to leave it behind. As the group began to fall apart, I had no idea how to support myself, nor was it clear whether an effort to form a new Marxist-Humanist organization would prove successful. It was the closest I had come to being immersed in personal and political despair in my entire life. Fortunately, thanks to the work of a number of close comrades, I was able to get back on my feet, obtain a Ph.D in philosophy and a job at a local community college, and assist in forming a new group, the International Marxist-Humanist Organization, in which I remain active to this day. It is painful to experience the demise of an organization one is deeply devoted to, but parties and groupings are ephemeral – they inevitably go under when they have outlived their usefulness. But if the ideas you are committed to stand the test of time, it becomes easier to surmount the despair one feels when their particular embodiments prove inadequate.

To return to Luxemburg, she surely suffered serious setbacks – especially the Great Betrayal of 1914, which was a far greater defeat than anyone of my generation experienced. But I do not think the despair she felt in the face of her closest colleagues supporting an imperialist war was self-inflicted. She was able to carry on even after Great Betrayal, and even after the defeat of the Spartakusbund Uprising of January 1919, because she stayed true to herself "in spite of everything." The tides of history were too strong to realize her principles, but staying true to them is what enabled her to end her last piece ("Order Reigns in Berlin") with the words, "I was, I am, I shall be." That is how not to be murdered by exhaustion and despair.

As for Lenin, I too feel for the bedridden and increasingly helpless man in his last days realizing that the revolution was taking a course contrary to what was expected. Was that an expression of *defeated* or *undefeated* despair? It's hard to tell. But I would say this much: even putting aside Luxemburg's 1918 criticisms of his policies, Lenin could have changed course after the Kronstadt Revolt, which signaled that his party was losing connection with the working class. But instead of loosening centralized control, allowing greater workers' input, and including other Left tendencies in the government, he went in the opposite direction by banning party factions and imposing greater repression on other Leftwing forces. Did he realize by 1923 that this was a wrong turn? If so, he may have experienced a very different kind of despair than Luxemburg.

Of course, we have to manage the despair we so often feel at the state of the world – especially since committing to the cause of the disenfranchised and powerless means putting yourself in a position in which you are more likely to lose than win. But new passions and new forces constantly arise, which call upon revolutionaries to provide them with theoretical direction, and no amount of defeats frees us of that endless responsibility.

Best wishe,

"Being human means joyfully throwing your whole life 'on the scales of destiny', when need be, but all the while rejoicing in every sunny day and every beautiful cloud."[18]

18 "To be a human being means to joyfully toss your entire life 'on the great scales of fate' if it must be so, and at the same time to rejoice in the lightness of every day and the beauty of every cloud." (Luxemburg 2013: 363)

Dear Peter

How are you? I cannot believe it took me such a long time to respond to your very engaging letter. This is totally ridiculous and I apologize profusely for making you wait so long. The truth is that, apart from working on this very book and the enjoyable but time-intensive labour it takes to coordinate and support 20+ author-comrades in their writing endeavours, the past few weeks have been psycho-somatically very challenging and oftentimes quite immobilizing. In fact, I increasingly feel that I must begin to face the scary possibility that my own, long-term battle with despair I alluded to before is moving ever closer to becoming the precise opposite of the (undefeated) despair that Rosa Luxemburg may or may not have experienced – and (eventually) made productive – at various moments during her life-long struggle for a socialist world, free(ish) of oppression.

I find it very interesting that you use the more-than-proverbial "getting back on one's feet" to describe how you "surmounted" your own period of despair thanks to the support of close comrades and a commitment to a set of ideas and convictions (?) that have stood the test of time. I say interesting because the German word for defeat – or shall we say de-feet, as in swept off one's feet – is *Niederlage*, which literally means to "put/lie down something," supposedly one's weapons after military loss, but which can also be the implosive lying down of exhausted and politically wounded bodies. Thus, in order to overcome the (repeated and seemingly predictable) experience of *Niederlage* in our ongoing struggles – as Luxemburg said: "the whole road of socialism is paved with nothing but thunderous defeats"[19] – our individual and collective bodies must perform, and likely more than once, the strenuous task of hapless angels[20] getting back up from underneath the rotten mount of shattered illusions, mutilated hopes and yes, those vanquished bodies of friends and comrades no longer able to rise up together with us. No hyperbole here. Defeat is real and fucking hurts, getting back up on one's feet is darn hard and premature death for those comrades who suffer it is likely just that, death, even though we may later imbue it with mythical-poetic content and despite the fact that for some of us death may simply be the worst option except for all the others, a necro-staying true and committed to our "I/We shall be" principles and ideas, which those of us who remain shakily on our feet must acknowledge and value.

In keeping with the theme of death, apart from the ongoing slaughter of the Afghan civilian population and the increasingly Zombie-like existence of many a close friend in Kabul going mentally berserk over the prospect of the Taliban returning to power soon – shame on you, Uncle Sam – the recent suicide of Queer Communist Sarah Hegazi is one of those moments that have kept me firmly nailed to the ground. Living in exile in Canada after being subjected to constant harassment and threats

---

19 See Luxemburg 1919.
20 See Heiner Müller's interpretation of Walter Benjamin's reflection on the Angelus Novus (See, e.g., Rizzo 2020: 73-76).

in her native Egypt in the aftermath of the 2011 uprising, Sarah took her life in 2018, leaving the following note:

> To my siblings – I tried to find redemption and failed, forgive me. To my friends – the experience [journey] was harsh and I am too weak to resist it, forgive me. To the world – you were cruel to a great extent, but I forgive.[21]

Rest in Power, Sarah. *A luta continua.*

I should say that I did not know Sarah or anyone close to her personally and hence by no means do I intend to instrumentalize her death for the sake of my own, possibly naval-gazing argument. It's just that her words so deeply resonated and shook me – in particular, the self-blame and subsequent asking for forgiveness – and because in light of recent "journeys" of my own, unfortunately far removed from the "Acid Communism" our comrade Mark Fisher started to dream up before he took his life in 2017,[22] I believe they make reference to a series of predicaments too many of us on the political Left often refuse to deal with on a personal, visceral level as opposed to our willingness for engaging with it as a mere set of de-personalized abstractions. Speaking with Frantz Fanon, who I know you greatly appreciate, I am talking about the "lived experience" in political struggle of moments-cum-sustained periods of a sense of individual failure, weakness, powerlessness, guilt, loneliness, amputation of one's enthusiasm (Fanon again[23]) and indeed hopelessness and defeat – partially due to the (in)actions of our very own comrades and our quite well-developed capacity for Left cruelty and Self-Lefteousness – which, if not taken seriously and unaided, may culminate in that ultimate anathema of Left (macho) ethics, that ultimate act of uncomradely self-indiscipline, that is, at long last giving up and in to the harshness of the struggle and the unacceptability of the world, succumbing to Left Depression, Left Self-Harm and/or – "anticipating the butcher"[24] – Left Suicide.[25] "Serve them right, those lunatics!"[26]

Of course, Rosa Luxemburg herself was no stranger to depressive episodes and suicidal thoughts, including at least three direct references to feeling suicidal in her correspondence, for instance in the following passage from a letter to Clara Zetkin written on June 4, 1907, after returning from the Fifth Congress of the Russian Social Democratic Labour Party:

> I just got back from London, dog-tired and down with a cold […] I did some real brawling and made myself a mass of new enemies […] By the end I was so tired, and had such a hangover mood of depression, that thoughts of suicide came to me. – You know that state of mind from your own experience.[27]

---

21 See Unknown author 2020.
22 See Fisher 2018.
23 See Fanon 1967.
24 After the 1940 suicide of Walter Benjamin, Bertolt Brecht wrote: "I am told that you raised your hand against yourself. Anticipating the butcher. After eight years of exile, observing the rise of the enemy. Then at last, brought up against an impassable frontier, you passed, they say, a passable one […]" (See Unknown author 2015)
25 For a recent engagement with personal-political suicides in the former USSR, see Fitzpatrick's 2011 insightful review of Kenneth Pinnow's *Lost to the Collective: Suicide and the Promise of Soviet Socialism*, 1921-29.
26 Lenin 1973: 205.
27 Luxemburg 2013: 243-244.

Then, on October 17, 1914, a few months after the "great betrayal" as you call it, Luxemburg writes to Paul Levy:

> Yesterday I had another of those "pleasant" [party] meetings. I finally went to bed at 1am with suicide on my mind.[28]

At the risk of misinterpreting your words, this last quote dialogues almost literally with your "[o]therwise, all we have to offer at the end of the day is despair and hopelessness in the face of defeat. And no one needs us for that." Here I find myself quite fundamentally disagreeing with you and probably Luxemburg herself – her rather harsh letter to Mathilde Wurm comes to mind once more – because at the end of the day I consider despair and hopelessness to be forms of (self-)estrangement born in and out of struggle, which we must also learn how to "tarry with" if we indeed believe that the socialist revolution is not a "sudden leap [but] a historical period, perhaps long [...]" Hence, if we dream of ensuring that next time round – preferably starting later today – a veritable, decolonized and depatriarchalized dictatorship *of* the proletariat will materialize and do better than the (self-proclaimed?) ones before, well then I strongly feel we must develop asap a series of affective-epistemic-political responses and spaces where we can individually and collectively face *all* our multiple, possibly intersecting estrangements – no matter how long it takes – and thereby begin to organize both our actually existing pessimism as well as the consequences of our repeated defeats,[29] with the aim of continuing to limp along "on the Golgotha-path [...to] the victory of the great million-strong masses of the socialist proletariat."[30]

In short, I don't think we have a chance of winning unless we treat the experience of individual and collective political defeats and their difficult consequences for our psycho-somatic health as something that should become one of our de-pathologized default elements when assessing political struggles past, present and future. What's more, given the double nature of Left despair – vis-à-vis the world we live in as well as in relation to our own shortcomings and fuck ups in the struggle for revolution – we are urgently invited to create a type of collective organization based on a phenomenology of spirit, an ode to our powers, that understands, values and encourages that every individual will be politically present and active in accordance with their current state of body and mind and their subsequent possibilities for action: From each according to their ability, to each according to their needs,[31] creating one day of struggle at a time, *together*.

Returning briefly to Hegazi and Luxemburg, what haunts and enrages me in their combined confessions of weakness, exhaustion and depression – thank you for your honesty – is the former's repeated asking for forgiveness and the latter's reference to party in-fighting as the main cause of her suicidal thoughts. Why am I so angry? Because the bad old Show Trial logic is still with us, Left-wing policing and propagating of guilt are real[32] and there are way too many so-called comrades "capable of saying smart things, but idiots on a human level, ruthless and damaged,

---

28 Luxemburg 1987: 458 (Translation mine).
29 See Hamza & Tupinambá 2016.
30 Luxemburg 2004: 357.
31 See Marx 1875.
32 See Fisher 2013.

who don't know anything about cultivating friendships or how to party, and who are way too puritan in everything they do."[33] Amen! We are, of course, talking about our inner red Torquemada here: We spot mistakes, we call out, we judge, we condemn, we know better, we banish etc. etc. In sum, we wag our finger until the whole hand straightens, extending the right arm from the neck into the air and we say ... *Himmelkreuzhageldonnerwetter!*[34] No wonder Rosa sometimes longed to live among animals. Our frequent lack of social-affective competence is literally mind-blowing. So, can we please get a grip on ourselves? And yes, in case you were wondering, I am absolutely guilty of some of the above. If there is one thing I can't stand, it's self-lefteousness.

To conclude, I totally agree with you that "new passions and new forces [will] constantly arise," I just wonder what that actually means to many of us in the period before and after the "constantly," in those "breaks both brief and extended," Luxemburg warned us of. May these perhaps be the "times of monsters" our friend Gramsci was talking about? Is this the time where we are most at risk of drowning in the tides of history? And if yes, how to dig ourselves out from underneath the sand the current order is trying to suffocate us with? How to continue wagering on the possibility of a successful revolution fomenting a process of constant self-liberation when clearly the odds are so overwhelmingly stacked against us? How to stay politically, mentally and physically alive and sane in a context marked by "so many occasions for giving up! So many temptations to bow one's head and submit to expediency!"[35] How to truly embrace the *trotz alledem* when it is the source of so much pain? What *is* to be done?

Call me a romantic or even a utopian – both words that, I propose, should be among the most cherished rank and file expressions in our liberation vocabulary – but in the spirit of your critique of "predictable straight lines" and regurgitating once more Fred Jameson's by now slightly tedious but nonetheless still accurate "it's easier to imagine the end of the world than the end of capitalism," can we not spend a little more time harnessing our individual and collective capacities to dream? Can we not work on pushing the currently very limited boundaries of our *Möglichkeitssinn*, i.e. the sense of the possible, as Austrian novelist Robert Musil called it? Whatever happened to Che Guevara's *Seamos realistas y hagamos lo imposible*? (Let's be realists and do the impossible)? I don't know about you, but I keep meeting way too many self-infatuated realists, including among Leftists, and I am really tired of their professional eye-rolling. Isn't realism in times of barbarism a type of (self-)thingification or at least false consciousness? Let's bring in Jameson's buddy Žižek: "It starts with: dreams are for those, who cannot endure, who are not strong enough for reality; it ends with: reality is for those, who are not strong enough to endure, to confront their dreams."[36] Isn't that It, Peter? Isn't that one of the urgent tasks we have today that may help us get back up on our feet and win against the multiple barbarisms and their barbarian goons out there, a new politics of dreaming and desire?

---

33 Malzahn 2015: 171.
34 Luxemburg 1987: 69.
35 See Bensaïd 2001.
36 See Slavoj Žižek's film *The Pervert's Guide to Cinema*.

In fact, isn't this where the two tragic figures of Luxemburg and Lenin can be(come) comrades again? They both endured reality and died confronting their dreams, and neither of them gave up on their desire, *trotz alledem*. I mean, we keep bashing Lenin for all his (apparently) predictable authoritarianism, but did his 1902 *What is to be done?* not also contain a wonderful passage about the importance of dreaming in a revolutionary movement?[37] Is it not curious that his very last signed article, "Better fewer, but better," in spite of its rather realist title, ends with "[t]hese are the lofty tasks that I dream of for our Workers' and Peasants' Inspection."?[38] Lofty Lenin, Lofty Luxemburg. I say the struggle for socialism is also a struggle for liberating our Enlightenment-repressed loftiness.

So let's finish with Rosa. German Queer Communist Bini Adamczak recently re-discovered a 1951 book by Georg Glaser, *Secret and Violence*, in which Glaser relates a meeting between Rosa Luxemburg and Margaret, as told by the latter:

> "When I saw her [Luxemburg] for the first time," she mused before us,[39] while we scrutinized her face, looking for a special glimmer left behind by the meeting with the great deceased. "[...] I said to myself, such a little woman, how can she do what she does with the market square all packed with people." She interrupted herself proudly: "Well, when you heard that Rosa was giving a speech, no worker stayed at home. And when she started talking – then I got it, it hit me straight in the heart."[40]

Adamczak writes: "[...] how easily we hear *mused to herself*. But she said *mused before us*. Musing before. The dream is not some privatized beyond, an ineffable experience of the 'dreamer' turned in on herself with vacant eyes, fleeing into a magic world she alone has access to, no, it is a shared, collective activity. Common invocation of the absent, which is a projection in a twofold sense: imagined and presented – that is, demonstrated. The demonstration of a dream."

I like that. A lot. Why not spend more time dreaming and musing together collectively – with as many people as possible, again and again – in the spirit of Rosa L. and Margaret, invoking the (still) absent, demonstrating it and, PLEASE, fucking making it a lived reality LEFT NOW. We deserve as much. Time to get going.

In Solidarity,

Hjalmar

---

37 See Lenin 1977: 509-510.
38 See Lih 2010.
39 Editor's note: The German original says 'vorträumen,' which is not an official word in the German language and literally translates both as 'to pre-dream,' which could be figuratively interpreted as to viscerally inhabit a particular dream, and 'to dream in front of someone.'
40 See Adamczak 2021.

References

Adamczak, Bini (2021), *Yesterday's Tomorrow: On the Loneliness of Communist Specters and the Reconstruction of the Future*. Cambridge: MIT Press.

Bensaïd, Daniel (2001), *Résistances. Essai de taupologie générale*. Paris: Fayard.

Berger, John (2006), "Undefeated despair." *openDemocracy*. Accessed on 13.08.2021, at https://www.opendemocracy.net/en/palestine_3176jsp/.

Berger, John (2008), *Hold Everything Dear: Dispatches on Survival and Resistance*. New York: Vintage.

Fanon, Frantz (1967), *Black Skin. White Masks*. New York: Grove Press.

Fisher, Mark (2013), "Exiting the Vampire Castle," *openDemocracy*. Accessed on 10.08.2021, at https://www.opendemocracy.net/en/opendemocracyuk/exiting-vampire-castle/.

Fisher, Mark (2018), *K-Punk: The Collected and Unpublished Writings of Mark Fisher*. London: Repeater.

Fitzpatrick, Sheila (2011), "Deaths at Two O'Clock," *London Review of Books*. Accessed on 10.08.2021, at https://lrb.co.uk/site/the-paper/v33/n04/sheila-fitzpatrick/deaths-at-two-o-clock.

Hamza, Agon and Gabriel Tupinambá (2016), "On the Organisation of Defeats," *Crisis and Critique*, 3:1, 427-441.

Hegel, Georg F. W. (2018), *The Phenomenology of Spirit*. Cambridge: Cambridge University Press.

Lenin, V.I. (1973), *Collected Works Vol. 33*. Moscow: Progress Publishers.

Lenin, V.I. (1977), *Collected Works Vol. 5*. Moscow: Progress Publishers.

Levinas, Emmanuel (1999), *Alterity and Transcendence*. London: The Athlone Press.

Lih, Lars T. (2010), "'We must dream!' Echoes of 'What Is to Be Done?' in Lenin's later career," *Links International Journal of Socialist Renewal*. Accessed on 10.08.2021 at http://links.org.au/node/1980.

Luxemburg, Rosa (1906), "Krytyka w ruchu robotniczym." *Czerwony Sztandar*, No. 39, January 9, pp. 1-2.

Luxemburg, Rosa (1919), "Order Prevails in Berlin." *Marxist Internet Archive*. Accessed on 13.08.2021, at https://www.marxists.org/archive/luxemburg/1919/01/14.htm.

Luxemburg, Rosa (1987), *Gesammelte Briefe. Band 5*. Institut für Marxismus-Leninismus beim ZK der SED. Berlin: Dietz Verlag.

Luxemburg, Rosa (2004a) [orig. 1904], "Organizational Questions of Russian Social Democracy," in *The Rosa Luxemburg Reader*. Eds. Peter Hudis and Kevin B. Anderson. New York: Monthly Review Books.

Luxemburg, Rosa (2004b) [orig. 1918], "Credo," in *The Rosa Luxemburg Reader*. Eds. Peter Hudis and Kevin B. Anderson. New York: Monthly Review Books.

Luxemburg, Rosa (2004c), *The Rosa Luxemburg Reader*. Eds. Peter Hudis and Kevin B. Anderson. New York: Monthly Review Press.

Luxemburg, Rosa (2011) [orig. September 30, 1918], "Letter to Julian Marchlewskli," in *The Letters of Rosa Luxemburg*. Eds. Georg Adler, Peter Hudis, and Annelies Laschitza. London and New York: Verso Books, pp. 473-6.

Luxemburg, Rosa (2013), *The Letters of Rosa Luxemburg*. Eds. Georg Adler, Peter Hudis, and Annelies Laschitza. London and New York: Verso Books.

Luxemburg, Rosa (2015a) [orig. 1915], "The Accumulation of Capital, Or, What the Epigones Have Made of Marx's Theory – An Anti-Critique," in *The Complete Works of Rosa Luxemburg, Vol. II: Economic Writings 2*. Eds. Peter Hudis and Paul Le Blanc. London and New York: Verso Books, pp. 345-450.

Luxemburg, Rosa (2019), *The Complete Works of Rosa Luxemburg Vol. III, Political Writings 1: On Revolution – 1897-1905*. Eds. Peter Hudis, Axel Fair-Schulz, and William A. Pelz. London and New York: Verso.

Malzahn, Rehzi (2015), *dabei geblieben: Aktivist*innen erzählen vom Älterwerden und Weiterkämpfen*. Münster: UNRAST.

Marx, Karl (1875), Critique of the Gotha Programme. *Marxist Internet Archive*. Accessed on 13.08.2021, at https://www.marxists.org/archive/marx/works/1875/gotha/.

Mason, Paul (2021), "Why Twenty-First Century Marxism Has to Be Humanist," in *Raya Dunayevskaya's Intersectional Marxism*. Eds. Kevin B. Anderson, Kieran Durkin and Heather A. Brown. Cham: Palgrave Macmillan, 185-208.

Pastor, Pedro and Suso Sudón (2014), "Solo los locos/Viva la Libertad." *YouTube*. Accessed on 13.08.2021, at https://www.youtube.com/watch?v=Aa394I6bq78.

Rizzo, Jessica (2020), *Waste. Capitalism and the Dissolution of the Human in Twentieth-Century Theater*. Santa Barbara: punctum books.

Unknown author (2020), "Egyptian LGBTQI+Activist Sara Hegazy Dies Age 30 in Canada." *Egyptian Streets*. Accessed on 13.08.2021, at https://egyptianstreets.com/2020/06/14/egyptian-lgbtqi-activist-sara-hegazy-dies-aged-30-in-canada/.

Unknown author (2015), "On the Suicide of the Refugee W.B." *Red Wedge*. Accessed on 13.08.2021, at https://www.redwedgemagazine.com/online-issue/suicide-wb.

Wader, Hannes (2014), "Trotz Alledem." *YouTube*. Accessed on 13.08.2021, at https://www.youtube.com/watch?v=AUUfuW-Pr3M.

DER GANZE WEG DES SOZIALISMUS IST
– SOWEIT REVOLUTIONÄRE KÄMPFE
IN BETRACHT KOMMEN – MIT LAUTER
NIEDERLAGEN BESÄT. UND DOCH FÜHRT
DIESE SELBE GESCHICHTE SCHRITT UM
SCHRITT UNAUFHALTSAM ZUM ENDGÜLTIGEN
SIEGE ! [41]

---

41 "The whole path of socialism, as far as revolutionary struggles are concerned, is paved with sheer defeats. And yet, this same history leads step by step, irresistibly, to the ultimate victory!" (Luxemburg 2004c: 377)

9. Asma Abbas
&
Jigisha Bhattacharya

Letter 1: Bats, Words, Birds, Flight

Dear Jigisha,

I apologise profusely for the delay in sending this letter. Addressing oneself, let alone another, requires a presence that reliably looks back at you with some kindness, a luxury I just haven't had in a while. Even automatic writing requires a stillness in time and place, lost to me since I feel both locked in and in constant motion. On a lucky day, it is only my mind that I cannot still, looking to park it anywhere I run into sleep; on other days, I feel I am carrying my whole body in a bag and can't find a place to keep it, and moving gives the illusion of deferring gravity.

I wonder a lot what that stillness is that anticipates the motion of language, and if it's meant for all of us. I recall Vilfedo Pareto comparing Marx's words to bats, "One can see in them both birds and mice."[1] While Pareto sees it as a problem, I don't. It shouldn't come as a revelation that he's not a big deal in my world, as the purveyor of the kinds of social science that I find deeply reactionary to the possibility of a world suggested by those bats. What I see in the likeness is an invitation to a reader to give an account of an entire world in her practice of reading, and hence inaugurate what it means to read politically (which, to me, is different from tactfully or strategically in the normal logistical sense of the word politics). That normal logistical sense is not present in the Marx I read, but was always there for my father (though it still looked so different from all that these leftist upstart party political experts in the US tell us). The idea is not that meaning has to be administered, but that it has to be taken responsibility for – such a fundamental difference in orientation and provenance. I trust that you know that Rosa herself often spoke about birds, especially in her captivity, in a way that of course, as the convention goes, might have equated birds with freedom. But that wasn't all. They also allowed her to imagine and visualise the forms of relationality that engender formations and flights that were crucial, sadly lost today on so many of our friends and comrades, some of whom we truly trust and who don't want to complicate things, and those who presume to speak for us because our common enemies find us on the same side.

Freedom and flight, though joined in the birds that Rosa learns so much about and of which she writes to her friends in letters (like birds themselves), are conditions with such different kinesis and potentia. A form of motion that may involve fleeing from something, yes, but also flight toward. Again bringing origin and directionality to the fore, this recalls Isaiah Berlin's freedom from and freedom to, as well as the fugitivity that suffuses Sheldon Wolin's fugitive democracy and Fred Moten's discussion of fugitive blackness and planning. Then there's my own attachment to

---

1 Ollman 1976: 332.

the 'fugue state' that, by connecting the refugee to the exile to the slave to the native by shunning the nation-state (which I find to be settler-colonial in all its forms), signals the possibilities of a politics that defies the deathful congelation in the idea of the nation-state as the locus of existence, desire, or politics. (I have been studying the fugue with a senior colleague in Music here, but am at a loss as to how to connect it to a form in the classical music of the South Asian subcontinent...so if you have ideas, please do share.) I won't pursue this digression, since there are many more to come, but all this to say that between Marx's bats and Rosa's birds, I find possibilities of language, reading, and writing that far surpass the normalisations and administrations that shape our performances in the academy, pervade the fetish relations to thinkers that I was completely unaware of until I came to this country, and which constantly feel antagonistic to the enamouredness our world actually deserves and needs.

I am sorry to begin writing a letter by speaking about reading but it seems important given how much of our lives are spent arriving at how to live with and read dead thinkers, what they owe us, and what we owe them. (I guess, I should add, if we are lucky enough not to have been decided for.) By beginning with Marx, I don't mean to indulge in questions of legitimacy, or over-determine our relation to Rosa, or turn to her *in his name*. Nonetheless, the lineages are important if they were important to the Rosa that we read today, as ways in and out and about, not as justifications of inheritances or accumulations. There is a way in which the whole industry of "what is living and what is dead in ____" lives by sparing no one... Recall the *Jacobin* (eyeroll) article this spring that tried to instruct us, this time, in the right way to read Rosa.[2] The writer Daniel Finn admonishes us that turning to the "personal" hurts Luxemburg's politics. Notwithstanding the condescending gall of this man conducting a rescue operation (to protect and to serve, yessir!) that no one asked for, it is just a replay of the boring presumptuous messes that happen when we all take ourselves so seriously, just a breath away from that secular 'will-to-administer' gaze ever ready to discipline and get us on the right path. If we indeed even fear that her person compromises her message, how ridiculous and insulting is that! Who are we trusting to draw the line between the personal and the political, the partition between concern and rigour – a gratuitous rigor mortis that sets in time and again when Marx's many boys endeavour to set us straight and direct the right kind of joy and cheer around the imminent liberation of all and the end of this world?! More on the perils of happy communists later – trust me there are many! Most days, I feel everyone hates birds and is willing to turn into the mice of meaning at the drop of a hat – whether chasing the *one* correct way of reading, or inheriting the prophecy of what Marx wanted to be done. Wasn't he much more interesting than that?

The entire slew of false equations between privatising, domesticating, and reducing Rosa's personality and politics to each other, seems so awfully sophomoric, and says a lot more about the writer than the reader. Why is such writing completely devoid of whom it is addressing, unlike a letter? Or is it just that it feels righteous leaving the reader completely unimagined and unnamed, but the writer cannot actually accomplish that? Obviously, the epistolary mode of address makes all sorts of assumptions, just as I am making about you, an act that perhaps enframes you

2 See Finn 2021.

without your consent... But, perhaps, the saving grace is the honesty that owns and names those imaginations in the vulnerability of such address itself. No wonder that the journalist – that 'universal' writer qua purveyor of meaning if there was ever any, right next to the lawyer – was seen by Weber as part of the professionalisation of politics that goes hand in hand with the expropriation of power and bureaucracy's separation of the means of production from the producers (in this case of political power). While such a bureaucratic relation to political knowledge can seem very philanthropic and altruistic, I know that Rosa had a special nose for this impulse and hated it, as do I. Who gets to create the order in which spontaneity is anathema, and where crisis is not centrally defined without democratic agonism? Who gets to sanction and vindicate the violence done in the name of political discipline if we aren't seen as co-constituting meaning? Who, in the end, gets to write something to 'rescue' Rosa? What kinds of words are these, and to whom are they addressed? Why can't we write more letters, and let others in on our relations, beyond the depersonalisations, arbitrary secularisations and partitions that actually underwrite violent intimacies, invasions, appropriations, and disciplinings?

What could be more ironic than these definitive accounts invested in neutralising or killing the living labours of those whom they seek to follow! For years, no wonder, I have harboured a desire to write a polemic responding to all the 'corrective' orthotic readers of Marx – all his boys who lunge forward without the grace of the sufferer on the path of History, but seek to show us how to move – and call it *Of Marx and Men* (you'd recall the Steinbeck here, I hope...). So, perhaps the choice between birds and mice is not mere superstition (or it is a good, useful one), and actually suggests a choice between entire ways of reading and being. That the bat shares the night with the owl, its natural enemy and undetected predator, suggests a relation between Minerva's owl (that takes flight at dusk and times philosophy after the event) and the batlike quality of words. Do you also see how this might resonate with the difference suggested in Marx's famous thesis eleven on Feuerbach about philosophers interpreting the world and the need to change it...? That the alternative to the philosopher's words is not the opposite of philosophy or words, but the ability of the words to morph and manifest, be differently sentient, nocturnal, and discover the world in practice that is not merely the kind of production and labour of the 'useful' work day? I feel many of us dwell in this strange interstitial place where the binaries and dualities that are proposed just don't make any sense. Where philosophy is not opposed by practice, or day by night, or utility by loss. Where theory does not look always the same or need to be in a conflictual relation to action. Where fetishists of theory are as off-putting as fetishists of action. Where study and political knowledge resist codified expert wisdom, whether it comes from the activist, or the academic, or the technocrat. Many of us are trying to escape all these enclosures. I bet the bats and the birds that are continuous between Marx and Rosa know something about these impositions.

This also brings us 'home' in a way, Jigisha, to ask why those of us who are policed in the 'west' for our relation to these thinkers have had to constantly work through so much crap. We must first generously address all that is important to those who call the shots here – make sure they are okay, even if some concerns are completely not ours – before we can get on with our own business. Who holds the power to determine the kinds of thresholds, the permissions, the barriers to entry that are erected and maintained here? Is this a matter of place or milieu? What do you feel? How have you come to these thinkers, and to Luxemburg herself? Who and why are we answerable to the academic or to any other canonising fetishist? Are our claims irrelevant if they do not seek to affiliate in proprietary ways, in order to produce certain kinds of capital and celebrity, certain kinds of bodies to eat off? (I often think about what bodies get produced when women thinkers are canonised, and the permission to violate and abuse that accompanies that corpus/corpse. My mind races to Hannah Arendt and how the right-Arendtians continue to violate her and capitalise on her.) What happened to those of us who have had to live under the dead bodies of thinkers and leaders past? Wouldn't we rather be haunted by their freely roaming spirits? Wouldn't that have let ours soar in turn – something not altogether unknown to us, given our abundances of history – with some kind of poetry, some kind of lightness? Do you feel free of all this waste because you are at least *home*?

Even in my own Shia communist non-nuclear household, where oddly I knew and felt a lot more about Spartacus than about the Spartacists – maybe because all of the big questions had been figured out and channelled into some kind of habit – there was no need for a kind of fetish or romance or table-talk on Marx because there was another embodied history that had gotten past the theory-practice hatred or rending that I discovered only once I came to study in the US. When I look back, it seems to me that most US academics – and not just the 'men' among them – were like those who filled the rooms into which Rosa walked. Meetings of professional associations, which play a big role in turning a collective into a gatekeeping bureaucracy where we are all clients or consumers and not co-producers, demarcating who inhabits the inside and outside of various professions and the academy. Recall the opening scenes of Ralph Ellison's *The Invisible Man* where the narrator performs in a big hall, entering a room full of future traitors, of class enemies pretending to be friends and comrades. It makes me think of how long it takes us to realise that, or if we can ever identify a future traitor, or a crash of hope. For people like Rosa, and also my father, a few decades apart from each other, the love of the people gathered in those large halls held sway over all the muck brewing. Did they not know, or were they ignoring it? It made it easier for me to visualise Ellison because I had a feel for the pride and dignity that walked into those rooms with Rosa and my father. How were they able to pull off being outsiders, but never guests in the workshops of new worlds, something that seems so impossible nowadays? That permutation was key to their life – being the outsiders, but still our hosts in worlds to come, needing no permission and having no complaint. I struggle to remember if I ever saw my father wracked by a crisis mentality – whereas I spend my time pushing back against everyone's attachment to crisis, and the status quo ploy crisis is, feeling erased and distorted and betrayed. What Rosa and Abbu had, in the face of great erasure, distortion, betrayal, was the confidence that the world they were fighting for was theirs as much or more than those who sat across from them or who continued to see themselves as the owners of the world and of life. What they had was the dignified assertion that the institutions these people owned or ran wouldn't be a thing without them. Can you imagine contemporary neoliberal University allowing us anything like that confidence? In what ways has it, instead, not sought to destroy it? If I have anything like a love of the world, and a claim on that, even if unrequited, it is because of what I saw and learnt as a child, not needing the legitimacies to which we are now beholden, fraying at our edges because of the misrecognitions and exploitations that fuel these factories and plantations of knowledge production.

Even today, when my faith falters, in myself and/or the institutions within which I labour for a new world, awaiting the next betrayal, never too sure what form it will take, I go weak in the knees and turn back to some kind of weird fabulated capital of sentiment, history, or form. On certain days it's just a defiant claim to culture, or history, or a kind of music, or a particular way of thinking about words, or a relation or love (and all of them together). But I wonder, increasingly nowadays, what Rosa fell back upon, because she was constantly spurned for *not* choosing to fall back on what others thought was appropriate to own, rest, claim, proclaim, and count on. Perhaps she paid heavily for still trusting against trust, for counting on her own sense of the capacities of others, like we do every day, stubborn against those who foreclose possibility and rule over big and small wastelands of so many spurned desires. It isn't accidental that we turn to people like her and Walter Benjamin, for a relief from the calculus of realpolitik (even, and more troublingly, the pathologising gaze of our friends on the "Left") that gives us no place to put down heavy bagfuls of our bodies if we pursue forms of belonging that are anti-nationalist, anti-Zionist, anti-imperialist, and internationalist.

I do realise that different enactments of this relation to the 'history' of communism and its key figures have much to do with training in the imperial university and working in the bourgeois academy. In other words, there is something to be said for what I saw in my home: the freedom from constant masquerade and re-enactment, the freedom from that history as "taste" (to recall Simon Gikandi), where I was surrounded by those who had already metabolised a lot, and whose lack of patience with the flexing of bourgeois performance searching for redemption amid thinkers or certain kinds of academic validations never amounted, as it often does today, to a lack of patience with theory, or with the abstract, or with words. Maybe that is where I learnt to just think of theory as language, as a *way*, and not as a profession or a medium. Reacting to the overly managed relation to theory driven by Western social science that makes its way into our universities in the Global South, I feel I have moved on from saying that "these thinkers don't need us (to get them right) but it is we who need them," to saying that "we don't need them if they look like this in the hands of these establishment experts, mediators, and translators." The response to rampant anti-intellectualism cannot, sadly, be an instrumentalist relation to theory and to study. I just want to be allowed the people I care about and still share with others in quiet tones without borrowing phrases or thesis sentences, a prescribed way to love them and be close to them, a way to let their words be bats and birds. Besides, I feel completely uninspired to 'lead' anyone to their salvation in thinkers, or to establish a new museum of dead objects. If we find them and in turn are found by them, I want the benefit of silence and notetaking.

I feel this so strongly, thinking about how Rosa's language of the birds sought the same kind of flight, the same kind of yet-undetermined possibility, a disciplined anti-disciplinarity that is a slap in the face of all those who have reduced politics, and knowledge of it, to a commodity or to a set of logistical operations. This is happening everywhere – even in the alleged revivalism on the Left, which comes with a developmentalist discourse of sorts, which adjudicates the right consciousness, calibrates who is at which stage of democratic or communist denouement and what is the correct stage-appropriate expectation to be had, shortlists our preferred guides, cedes the question of freedom to the right-wing, stays opportunistically silent and uncritical of the nation-state form and mistrusts citizens' own views for not being fully aware and needing another round of some gospel. I feel the creep into the Left of the Global South – in countries like Pakistan, perhaps even India, I think, but you tell me – of a jargonic attachment to certain homogenising ideas of what it means to act politically, to have political knowledge, and to perform a politics, that seems reminiscent of the turn away from the party to NGOs at crucial moments in history – for my father, Leftists who saved themselves by creating NGOs destroyed the communist movement. Certain ideas of political modernity, throwbacks to a century ago, find interesting allies in conversations about a misled demos, rather than making institutions learn to hear better or destroying them! The acceptance of working 'inside' the institution as the only way forward is phenomenally greater than it's ever been – I recently came across an article about an artist trying to correct the misperception of the Middle Eastern woman away from being either "radical" or a "victim," to highlight all those doing the good work that is keeping things afloat! Why have we normalised this? I strongly believe that Left bourgeois academics and liberal reformist cultural experts have a big role in sustaining and guarding the institutions that assure them a position in the regime of value and inheritance. The next problem, their fresh neoliberal technocratic analysis of the contemporary political moment says, needs just the expert they have in mind!

Now, it needs to be said that neither Rosa nor I romanticise the birds in a boringly symbolic way – flying free, unattached, and so on. She was moved by how they move in formation, and what relationalities they can teach us. After all, they do break their flight, reset their anchors, teach each other what they know, including the courage to bear that there is no simple return to where we begin. We have a robin's nest on our porch. We have been a stopover for three or more years now. Steve and I remain extremely superstitious about animals. Too many stories to narrate, but since we are speaking about birds... The week in April that my mother had her (first) stroke, the first nest came crashing down (unable to stabilise itself on a little makeshift shelf Steve had made for them to give them more room above the light fixture where they usually build). One egg cracked. Robin blue egg. Robin 'neel' egg. (Did you have Robin Neel powder in Calcutta, to soak white school uniforms in?) Five and a half weeks later, Steve improved on our offering, and the robins returned. We named them Rubina and Mint, and our cat Tipu stands guard from across a screen. Rubina laid four eggs, and they hatched today. My mother hasn't had that linear of a recovery or outcome — preserving life has meant something very different inside the home as compared to just outside the door. But it feels as if we weren't abandoned altogether. All this to say, I am no one to project our own bird issues on to Rosa, but my version of Donna Blue Lachman's *The Language of Birds: Rosa & Me* would certainly look very different from the 1993 play by the performance artist. Based on Luxemburg's prison letters, the play performs the service of returning Rosa to our memories when she is all but erased or seen as a foil in the history of communist struggle. You can find it here,[3] and here's the poster I made for its online screening on Rosa's birthday this year:

---

3 Watch it at https://mediaburn.org/video/the-language-of-birds-rosa-luxemburg-me/.

ROSA is 150

The Language of Birds: Rosa Luxemburg & Me

written and performed by
Donna Blue Lachman

COME WATCH WITH HIC ROSA
on Sunday, 7 March 2021
https://w2g.tv/tmf5bnk6l6u7eu4hru

HAPPY INTERNATIONAL WOMEN'S DAY

It's 1993 Chicago after all, and I cannot help but think of how perfectly it captures the zeitgeist of (neo-)liberalism, even in those who resist, and anticipates the domestications that plague our ideas of theory, practice, politics, art in this country (and is fast pervading the country I left behind). It's a very American thing, to basically convert the question of nature, of the transcendent, to one that is entirely internalised, squarely lodged inside the body. The recording of the play that I saw was filmed from behind a pillar, in a theatre that was very small and enclosed, with a stage overbuilt to look like an underbuilt, plain apartment. Our actor – a struggling artist who is working on a one-woman play about Rosa in this one-woman play about Rosa – embodies and disembodies Rosa in front of us. Rosa's letters are our birds in and out of the character's enclosed apartment, reminiscent of the prison. If I am to compare different representations of Rosa in a fixed space without exit, theatre seems woefully inadequate (precisely because of its literal resemblance to the prison) at capturing Rosa's relation to the space of her imprisonment, and her motion within and beyond it. This speaks to my own issues more than Lachman's or Luxemburg's, but this framed stillness feels like a conventional 'close reading,' a rigorous excavation or representation that misses the chance to create an actual moment of redemption. In contrast, Margarethe Von Trotta's film has room for more breathing, because it allows those suffocations to yield to a timescape – where space, in this case visual space, is produced through time and motion – rather than to a spacetime, where time is subsumed into space. I understand why Tracy Strong speaks about theatre as a kind of an anti-political space that insists on the stillness of characterisation (what political theorists would hold akin to a perfectionism) that I just cannot afford to pin on Luxemburg, for anyone's sake right now. Years of being occupied with colonial optics and the positive dialectic of recognition (embedded in the way we think about characters and what to do with the time of their suffering short of turning it into productive identities), leaves me with a feeling that a counter to both is possible only in film and music, not in theatre.

I am thinking about how this domestication and the anti-politics of theatre – even in the way the interiority of Rosa's prison and being is presented – symbolise the liberal deceptions or delusions about secularism that Marx was so keen to point out any chance he got. Secularism as the supposed independence of different spheres of life from each other which becomes pathologically mechanistic and dissociative, an imposition or privilege depending on who you speak to and on what day. Not unlike the lockdowns of the past year and a half. How lucky one must be to not feel abandoned by god during the pandemic! An already failing society got a chance to justify its shrinking constellations of care, as its cartographies of emotion and intimacies became ever more subsumed by state-centred geopolitical ones. My mother even got a vaccine – oh that grand gesture of hospitality, the first really, that this country extended to her, a kind of pandemic refugee in her immigrant daughter's house. We saved her from the virus but welcomed these strokes so far away from home, so now we cannot predict or choose the day we get to move toward health or just away from mortality. I wonder what has happened to me as a political being that placing us all inside has felt as a kind of 'protection.' Wherefrom emerged the 'desire' that these lockdowns have fulfilled, to not populate the world I so love, to not expose ourselves anymore, to not feel humiliated? Now, withholding one's gaze or turning it away is not even an ocular act; it just requires pressing a button to mute or to turn off a camera. For those of us constantly trying to disappear, but

263

also constantly witnessing our own disappearance, it is interesting to no longer have the choice. There is no record of either being disappeared or watching it happen... we can just mute and yell, or reach for some orange oil and smell it, or have the twentieth cardamom from the jar to the left of the screen.

Okay, perhaps the dominant, in my view flawed, visualisations of Rosa's various spatial and bodily interiorities have to do with her leg and her limp. There is something about her motion that bothers people, the inability to place her, her resistance to take those roots they want her to cling to as lifelines, to blame her for her own isolation and abandonment. If placing her on the stage in theatre can be extended to other ways of placing her in history, we as the audience claim the power to keep time, rather than allowing her to keep time for us. If sensuousness, as Marx says, is embodied time, and we know how our bodies came about, by way of their disposability and pulverisability, to serve as means of production, I take extremely seriously the indirect and direct time-keepings that range from the policing and normalising of individual bodies all the way to Hegelian narratives of history. So much of our lives are led holding ourselves and others hostage to this idea of time, that other subjectivities – other configurations of time, that is — are pathologised and are seen as needful of our orthotic intervention or guidance. So many on the Left have accepted this mode, flustered by all the calls to crisis and order, mindlessly performing the efficient orderings of dead bodies, dead women, dead women thinkers, thereby suffocating their living meaning. As materialists, weren't we supposed to resist the scaffolding away of time and motion, to defy the reduction and domestication of our bodies and thoughts? I want to defer to the way Rosa embodies time, in her movement through the world, as a signal to new relations to time, embodiment, and being. I am confronting the big question of who is keeping time just as we are hurriedly asked to move out of the time of quarantine into the quarantine of time in this delusional victory in the war against the virus – Benjamin's empty, homogeneous time, inhering its own sensuousness and comportment through the world, understood anew as that of grief, of shrinking emotional geographies, and of the evacuation of political possibility signalled in the joint fascist and liberal hatred of the political, adopted with relish by Leftists who think it's their chance to be policemen and bosses.

Not sure what more to say for now... this is one of those moments where the desire to constantly engage with these thinkers feels exhausting and draining, precisely because of the fear of what else it will have us confront in others. What will we do if our go-to philosophy of relation continues to be completely upended by the sneaking suspicion that there isn't a relation worth having, and that we have been barking up the wrong tree, worrying about the wrong things, and putting our bodies and trust in the wrong place?

When sleep finally finds me, I might have a chance to wake up to find myself alive in the world I make and love even if it evades me when I am trying to fall asleep. Perhaps I am particularly raw right now. There is this scene in the movie *Haider* where a little kid rises up from a mound of the dead and runs out of a truck and exclaims he is not dead. We have to constantly remind ourselves nowadays, in an extended unfolding of pandemic fascism, that we aren't dead and the convenience that our dying will create for others should not be facilitated. No matter what time our bodies keep, and in which parts of the world simultaneously. So we rise up, to counter the discordant liveliness, the allergy-inducing vitality of the world of "the Left" as we know it today, and to counter the murderous stupor of the fascists. Rosa did the same. She began again, constantly.

To close, I think of a photo I saw this morning of a student activist in India – let's call her N – dressed in a light orange kurta, returning to jail at the end of her three-week parole at the passing of her father. She brings a bag with her. Rosa's prison cell is presented in many visualisations like a place where one could continue to befriend life. I don't know if and how N gets to keep time in defiance of the timekeepers. And the young academics in prison or those extrajudicially executed for the blasphemy law in Pakistan.

And Obaida,[4] who hated prison but learnt to cook there. And was then killed by the Israelis.

With love, and thanks in advance for your patience

Asma

PS: One of the things I sneaked into the ICU ward my mother was in two days after her stroke were readings in English, Urdu, and Arabic, just to make sure she could read. For the sake of the bats and the birds that might yet show us all a way out (and a world we want to return to).

---

4 See Abunimah 2021.

And now they have all turned to Martinique, all one
heart and one mind again; they help, rescue, dry
the tears and curse the havoc-wreaking volcano.
Mt. Pelee, great-hearted giant, you can laugh; you can
look down in loathing at these benevolent murderers, at
these weeping carnivores, at these beasts in Samaritan's
clothing. But a day will come when another volcano
lifts its voice of thunder: a volcano that is seething
and boiling, whether you need it or not, and will
sweep the whole sanctimonious, blood-splattered
culture from the face of this earth. And only on its
ruins will the nations come together in true humanity,
which will know but one deadly foe — blind, dead
nature. [5]

5 "And now they have all turned to Martinique, all one heart and one mind again; they help, rescue, dry the tears and curse the havoc-wreaking volcano. Mt. Pelee, great-hearted giant, you can laugh; you can look down in loathing at these benevolent murderers, at these weeping carnivores, at these beasts in Samaritan's clothing. But a day will come when another volcano lifts its voice of thunder: a volcano that is seething and boiling, whether you need it or not, and will sweep the whole sanctimonious, blood-splattered culture from the face of the earth. And only on its ruins will the nations come together in true humanity, which will know but one deadly foe – blind, dead nature." (See Luxemburg 1902)

Letter 2 | Flowers, Borders, Poetry

Dear Asma ,

Firstly, let me take this moment to apologise to you for the delay in responding. It's funny how we both start our letters apologising to each other for delayed responses. It seems the times are such that certain luxuries, as you've mentioned, have been denied to us. I am so sorry for the difficult times you have been going through, as we say amongst friends, 'Hugs.' For me too, to imagine a fond presence to address and respond to, seemed like an almost forgotten exercise. Partially because of the pandemic-induced habits (or lack thereof), partially because of our own individual situations, perhaps. But I must say this, it was not only a logistical problem, but a problem of ideation and imagination. I should have also taken a lesson from politics, that collaborative works are way more difficult than individual ones; and way more rewarding.

Letter writing truly seems like an art form – to not respond instantly to individual messages, and to see, understand and respond to someone's thoughts on a much more expansive canvas. No wonder so many took to the epistolary form as their genre of writing. I remember, when I was young, I used to have a 'Dear Diary' exercise myself, even before reading Anne Frank's. Interestingly, what you say about language resonates with me so vividly – the difficulty of it, the difference in speech and writing. The way placement and choices of words work. Sure, there have been structural studies of linguistics, and post-colonial deconstructions of it. And yet, so often language evades us – there are widely different responses to language it seems. In a crisis, one either lets go of it, or vehemently takes to it – what shapes such responses? Why do I keep saying, 'you said in your last letter' – when in actuality you wrote it, and I read? Is this verbal quality intrinsic to the letter, or is it something through which we find ourselves in closer proximity to each other? How did people feel proximity when the only means of communication was through the written word, stamped and posted? How do we access it now, when the epistolary form, in its traditional sense, has become more and more obsolete? I particularly remember Eliot Katz's letter[6] to Luxemburg where he pulls in Adrienne Rich and Rosa in an intimate tangent of a conversation to think through the present realities of socialism, democracy and politics.

You have asked why can't we write more letters? Sometimes I associate the violent (and often nasty) factionalisms which we have within the Left (and here I am using 'Left' in its broadest possible sense that we politically aspire towards), globally and in India, as a contributing factor to that. Surely, political questions need political debates and resolutions. Surely, political strategies and goals are also determined through the political manifestos of parties and organisations. Surely, the vitriolic attacks and counterattacks often stem from disillusionments with others' politics. And yet, it seems like there is such a lack of communicating to the other, of knowing

---

6 See Katz 2012.

and responding to the audience one assumes to debate. One almost gets the sense that a wider people, who do not necessarily share the same dreams of emancipation, has been assumed as the audience of one's position papers or debate answers. It hardly ever tries to strike a conversation with the one (not necessarily individual) it attempts to critique. It hardly embodies the care and empathy that the letter often demonstrates. There is a certain assumption in the letter of knowing the addressee, of trying to create a space where the interlocutors care about the other's opinions and contexts. Perhaps, that is what has made the letter-form more susceptible to life-writing than political-writing historically? Now, this is not to endorse the 'woke' Left that we see today, who believe only debates and discussions can solve all issues – because there would be some issues, some political angles, some orientations which can historically not be resolved, and for good reasons too. But this 'de-personalisation' you talk about, seems to be costing the Left heavily – and yet, there is hardly any attention to it – all the more when we need it in our neoliberal regimes, with a de-personalised individualisation of everything. The lines between internal and external critiques seem increasingly blurry, and the light at the end of the tunnel increasingly faded.

On the other hand, the 'letter' form has been a part of so many stories of resistance, of movements. Whether publicly addressed, whether personally addressed and then made public – the letter form has a certain intimacy that is undeniable. The letters from prisons, the letters from one comrade to another, the letters across borders – have had this somewhat visceral quality to them. So many stories of the refugees made by Partition who kept writing letters to the remnants of their families and friends in the other nation. You talk about your father, and the logical sense he found in Marx; – my father too read Marx in that sense. It might seem too abrupt a decision to spend such a long time discussing the word, the letter and Marx. Incidentally, through my father, I can connect all three. I lived away for a couple of years from my father, and I used to write him letters – using the phonetic Bengali script (my mother tongue), not adequately knowing the standard spellings. And he responded to them with equally detailed descriptions of squirrels or flowers or birds. It was through these letters that we formed our mutual space for conversing about anything and everything under the sky and beyond. Later when I was growing up, he would explain how 'time' was quantified through 'human bodies' as per Marx. I could never think of my hand in the same way again, as the image of a hand moving wheels in a factory, being forced to become measures of a clock, became deeply ingrained in my head (it's interesting how in contemporary theoretical paradigms so much has been spoken about *bodypolitic*, but the labouring body itself has hardly been a part of that discussion). Only later, I learnt during an ongoing strike in a Maruti automobile factory that a Maruti branded car takes 45 seconds to be produced. My father is an old-school leftist activist, who perhaps liked the clear resolution which Marx's writings proposed to the misery of the world. A misery he long dreamt of resolving. The first de-personal letter that I ever saw, too, was from one of his diary notes, a poem of Nazim Hikmet, translated. I call it de-personal, as it was addressed as a love letter to his wife but was imagined as if it was an announcement to the world, and was in fact later made public. He mentions Dachau concentration camp in that poem, and I remember the first time I stepped on the Dachau grounds, the image of Hikmet anticipating Dachau from a jail cell was the first to come to my mind, standing under the cherry blossoms. I picked some blossoms from the ground and kept them hidden in the journal I was carrying, thinking, merely sixty years ago, this tree was perhaps there, witnessing one of the supreme horrors of humanity.

Photograph of Red Bougainvillea at JNU campus, New Delhi

Sezgin Boynik, while discussing Lenin's language, calls it a "coiled verbal spring."[7] This has always struck me, how languages refer to images – literal and metaphorical. It is not a spring in its exuberance, but it is a coiled one; one that has been deliberately folded to fit its mould. Yet it is a spring nonetheless; yet the coil expresses that it indeed contains the spring. The verbal spring is everything that the spring is supposed to offer, but it also is intentional, and measured, and roped in from slippages. When we come to Rosa, however, it seems the spring is not constrained – it is set free in her. I am not saying that Rosa was impulsive, of course, as we both know her position against impulsive actions, but I am pointing to the wider intimacy that we may find in her words – speeches and writings. She *knows of no formula to write us for being human* she wrote to Mathilde Wurm. It is this brilliant excess that captures for me Rosa's language, that is not afraid to be intimate, close, affectionate and passionate. I do not intend to say Lenin was less passionate, or that there is only *one* way to read Lenin or Rosa – unlike the fellow men that you mention, and the men who have held sermons on ways of reading

---

7 See Boynik 2018.

historically. I mean to say, perhaps this quality of language – which has now been termed *domestic*, and by extension her politics too has been perceived as such (I fully agree with your frustration there) – sets her free from the coil of political writing.

Rich once wrote of Rosa that her words seem powerfully akin to the experience of writing poetry.[8] Of course, it is not the provenance of a poetic language per se that she is speaking about, but the intimacy a reader feels when reading Rosa, and to imagine Rosa through her writing. Rosa's language was spring in its fullest, spring as it should be. It is deeply frustrating, and even sad, that the men on the Left, through their prescribed readings of Marx, Engels and Lenin, never learnt to truly examine their assumptions and decisions regarding what Left leadership ought to look like. This is reflected in their gendered understandings too and continues to form similar reiterations from other interlocutors. I truly believe the three had much more to offer, beyond such 'correctional' readings – and thankfully, many women political writers have pointed that out as well. They have rather read Rosa's writings through her life, and not the other way around. As the genres differed, Rosa did change her ways of language, and yet, that intimacy of addressing the partially real, partially imagined reader never left her completely. Those who try to limit Rosa within the ambit of domestication, altruism, and emotionality, perhaps fail to understand that it is also a democratisation of political language that she attempts (and possibly performs). It is a question of appealing intimately to the audience, to the addressee, "to the masses," to see them not solely in terms of utile bodies, but as fully human, to make connection from human to human. It might seem like I'm trying to preach some form of Enlightenment Humanism here, but it really is beyond that. It is a question of assuming political position, as much to oneself as to others. It is a question of challenging, and transforming the political language, which is not devoid of the 'personal.' For the personal indeed is manifested heavily within the political conditions one finds oneself in. Even though the earlier instance is from one of her letters from prison, we find similarly poignant prose in her 'political' writings as well. The way she appeals to the question of imperialism and colonialism – the primary entry-point is not through the historicity of it, but through the plight of the colonised people (thinking particularly of "The Proletarian Woman"). In Kalahari, in Putumayo, Rosa looks out for the "human cost," to quote Scott and Le Blanc,[9] above others. It is a visceral compassion she extends to proletarian women across the world, invoking them and their plight intimately, and yet never losing her voice. Now, it has been widely assumed by commentators that she owes such an early understanding of colonialism to her Polish lineage, yet the question also becomes about how she channelises her own *personal* point of departure with those of the many from Africa and Asia whom she has never seen; how she appeals to them, addresses them. It does not deter her political charge one bit, and yet it makes possible the imagination of an intimate bond that is beyond polemics. It was never personal in the sense of her individual identity, but it was personal as *human* is. *Nothing human was alien to her.*[10]

---

8 "I could feel around me – in the city, in the country at large – the 'spontaneity of the masses' (later I would find the words in Rosa Luxemburg), and this was powerfully akin to the experience of writing poetry." (Rich 1993: 25)
9 See Scott and Le Blanc 2010.
10 Inspired from a line from the play *The Self-Tormentor*, which was written in 165 B.C by Roman playwright Terence (Publius Terentius Afer).

Photograph of poster from JNU campus walls, New Delhi

You talk about the need to place the lineages in relation to Rosa, while not taking the route to Rosa as necessarily overdetermined by them. And for me, strangely enough, it has been through Lenin. Within the political spaces I found myself in, the debates around party-structures and organisational-structures between Bernstein and Rosa, and the debates around *mode of production* in relation to Lenin, were a staple. For an erstwhile colonised nation, *The Accumulation of Capital*'s critique of the empire somehow was far too seldom discussed (I have things to say about the place of women thinkers and women activists in relation to this, but more on that later so that I can process my rant more cohesively!). This is also one of the reasons I believe Leftist critiques of the British Empire did not gain enough traction in India, for it was only through the post-colonial school that the thoughts were popularised. Like many others on the socialist spectrum, Rosa too was either clumped to the 'Women's Question,' or not widely prescribed to be read and discussed. It was only the male-thinkers of the Marxist tradition who were read widely on matters of class, state and polity, while the women thinkers were traditionally denigrated to the question of gender. I say denigrated because the gender question was not seen alongside the questions of class or state, but rather was seen as a mechanical subset of the class question. It was almost as if the category of women was always to come after the other pressing political matters determined by the male-bastion, no matter the contexts. On the other hand, despite the lack of popular circulation of Rosa's writings within the male-dominated political realm, Rosa remained in people's minds in less orthodox spaces like my university. I remember on my campus, one of the popular slogans in student protests was the two sentences – 'Marx, Lenin, Bhagat Singh – We shall Fight! We shall Win! / Rosa, Clara Zetkin – We shall Fight! We shall Win!' There were many others it recalled from India and around the world, a wonderful way to pay homage to the political lineages that shape our politics today. It was a juxtaposition of multiple departure points of one's political imagination, but that imagination embodied a sense of people's liberation, of emancipation and freedom as we want it. *For freedom is always and exclusively freedom for the one who thinks differently.*[11]

You speak of N, and N happens to be a dear friend and comrade – one of the reasons why I took time to respond to the letter. The passing away of N's father, and the expressions on N's face – it was too much to bear. It was a question of the punitive state, but it was also a question of political parentage; a parent, let alone a father, sharing the imagination of a free world alongside the daughter, daring to *think differently*. And what human cost such thoughts incurred. The order prevailed in Berlin, after Rosa was murdered and washed away in Landwehr. The order still prevails as many political prisoners are battling for their basic rights under a raging pandemic in India, where hundreds of thousands died just for the lack of basic healthcare. The order still prevails here after comrade M, N's father, succumbed to an ill-managed raging pandemic. But this order cannot thwart freedom forever. We must remind ourselves of Rosa's last words, "Your order is built on sand. Tomorrow the revolution will rise up again, clashing its weapons, and to your horror it will proclaim with trumpets blazing: I was, I am, I shall be!"[12]

What words to have, as last words, Asma? You have asked whether I feel free of the waste of impositions because I am, at least, home. You may have understood, by now, that the Leftist traditions in India have been no different. It is eerie, reassuring, saddening – and all such emotions together – that we have similar inheritances when it comes to the 'history' of communism in India. So many men, so many dead bodies, so many dead thoughts being nailed to gold frames. How does one even try to fathom it, and scrape away the interpretations of interpretations of thinkers? As one reads Marx and Lenin, one finds there's so much more to the carefully selected portions and carefully curated understandings. I am not trying to completely erase the history of communist thought traditions here, and I am willing to acknowledge the limitations of space, and time too. But it does seem like Benjamin's *Angelus Novus*, if you look at the current situation of political resistance to a Hindu-Right nationalist regime: one is propelled backwards with the weight of this history. So, no, I do not feel at-home, at home. The difficult terrains of communist thought and activism in India – I draw inspiration from them, but also find myself in what you call an 'interstitial' space in relation to the political formations. Increasingly, as I venture as a young researcher into the world of academia, I encounter new ways of manipulation, new ways of making sellable heroes, new ways of *mainstreaming* resistances.

To begin with, I never had high hopes of bourgeois academia, given how the university space itself has been a site of exclusion; yet, as a part of student protests and resistances, and difficult thoughts that the university-space made possible, even if in a limited capacity, it indeed is a complex relationship. After all, our inheritance from the university is also Mai '68, Baader-Meinhof, Rhodes Must Fall, and Fees Must Fall. The JNU campus that I experienced – which is no longer there under the state onslaught, but was the closest to what I could call home – was a bubble, far from a perfect one, but a bubble that upheld difficult dreams. We could take

---

11 See Luxemburg 2002: 305.
12 Ibid: 378.

long walks freely late at night – can you imagine, Asma, what that meant in my early twenties, in our realities in India or Pakistan? And strangely enough, I too owe my faith in activism or imagination towards people's emancipation at large, not to academic knowledge production but to everything I have done outside of its ambit: the political induction I had in my childhood, the activisms I've experienced, or the thinkers and poets and artists I've been introduced to, largely outside academic classrooms: Adrienne Rich, or Nazim Hikmet and Faiz Ahmad Faiz, or Marx, Althusser, Gramsci and Ranciere; or Anuradha Ghandy. In the deeply competitive, heartless and shrewd space that academia is, under its garb of free-thought and free-associations, I completely echo your sentiments about the lack of collaborations, the lack of collective work, of collective thinking. I see similar things happening within political circles as well – albeit without the cultural and economic capital that academic works garner.

And yet, there are so many people I've seen who have tried, or have been trying. I have seen my father never abandon the hope of a changing, transforming world throbbing with life, even as movements after movements fizzled out, and the stories of activism became increasingly marred by manipulations driven by self-interest. I have seen women fight tooth and nail within and beyond the party to uphold their autonomy, and their dreams of an emancipated world (and I always imagine Rosa in this difficult space too, trying to battle her way – in her thought, vision and activism – through the controlling faces of her time and organisation). And here, perhaps, we are indebted to Rosa most crucially – for teaching us through her life to keep dreaming "despite all." Her struggles are echoed in the many people around the world who have kept fighting the bigger and smaller battles within political organisations and beyond, just to keep dreaming for that free world.

I remember being asked in Berlin, "How do you know about Rosa Luxemburg?" And it was a perfectly well-intentioned question. How do I explain the complex calibrations of our political lineages which owe as much to our imperial past, as to that of the anti-colonial resistance, as to that of revolutionary thoughts? How do I explain to a binary understanding of Rosa, that Rosa came to me as a child, through translated Soviet Books and the reading practices they inspired, which made my childhood a better place? As I was speaking amongst so many comrades about Rosa's ideas, it seemed we – the Global South – had all been drawing inspiration from Rosa to battle our neoliberal realities, which were deeply marred by our colonial histories, and yet, that part of Rosa's influences and contributions hardly finds a space in her normative, Eurocentric readings. I'm glad I found comrades in Brazil, in Argentina who – even without discussing – had very similar inheritances from Rosa. And it is this, the difficult political solidarities, friendships and camaraderies, that I feel at-home with.

Photograph of poster from JNU campus walls, New Delhi

Incidentally, as I am taking a much-needed break from academic works – by teaching in a university, ironically – I teach a particular text by Meenakshi Chhabra on the histories of the British India Partition,[13] and how education was communalised institutionally. It is meant to act as a text that helps students see 'history' itself as a contested space, beyond what is taught in the school-education systems. And so often, I do see the same binaries that Chhabra warns us about in this essay – how India-Pakistan fast turns into Hindu-Muslim – so often I see my students, growing up in a Hindu-Right India, taking to these same binaries, involuntarily. And perhaps the involuntary, subconscious aspect of it is what scares me the most – how have we become these forces that we call the Left, which only now answers to the demands set by the Right? How has our activism turned into issue-based, momentary, reactive movements solely? In the past several years, as I am in the middle of this political situation in India, I have felt that the terms of the debate are no longer even fathomed by us – let alone set by us; that we are merely trying to barely keep our relevance as the 'Left' in the popular domain through our reactive measures. We have not dealt with the trauma of Partition; have not dealt with the increasing communalisation of society; have not dealt with how the family-space becomes the microcosm of the bourgeois state's mechanisms, have not dealt with

---

13 See Chhabra 2015.

how capital, state, academia, family – and all other institutional set-ups – actually contributed to such a reality, and now when we find ourselves in this spot, we are unable to shape our political approaches.

I remember watching Abbas Kiarostami's *Shirin*, where the entire film only looks at the faces of female spectators as they watch a staging of the Persian myth of Khosrow and Shirin. We do not have an appearance on the stage, we are just spectators, trying to emote ourselves as the drama unfolds – on the stage and our faces. Why can't we imagine our 'history' as a 'history' against this sense of an ending? Perhaps similar to Carl Einstein as he stood beside Landwehr that January, forcing himself to address the crowd after Rosa's death? In one of the imaginative constructions of his speech[14] that was never found – beyond its precise mention in all narrations of Rosa's murder – Derek Horton makes an anagram out of Rosa – *Soar*. If only we could imagine endings not as final limits, but as something that births countless possibilities too. If only we could imagine Rosa – not in her tragic death, but as someone who registered her protest through the inevitability of her death – 'soaring' to liberate us from our contracted political presents.

Sometimes I understand why Rosa would make herbaria while tending to plants. It's powerful, how 'womanly' 'domestic' 'private' chores can give one a sense of solace, of freedom too. This brings to mind Sabeen Mahmud, who said her revolutionary aspirations were stoked by her mother Mahenaz,[15] and died voicing the disappearances of activists around Pakistan, who dared to think differently. When will we talk about women's spaces and domesticity, of this 'private' world they have been relegated to, and the revolutionary thoughts and acts it has inspired in a complete subversion of what that 'assigned space' was supposed to be – beyond the boundaries of market-driven romanticisation of 'choice' and liberal academic theorisations of 'agency'? In the lockdown, as I understand the domestic space perhaps more crudely than ever before, I have turned to another kind of life. Holding petals and leaves gently so that they don't crease, looking for hidden bursts of protest in the most uncommon of places, to have slumber with the full possibility of waking up to life. I see them grow, I try to understand why their leaves are yellowing, why their branches are drooping, and try to tend to them. Against the advice of fellow plant-lovers, I never trim them regularly, and let them grow at their own pace – and see how they bloom when in full life. As I stood on Lichtenstein Bridge at Tiergarten in Berlin, I put down a couple of randomly collected flowers I had in my journal.

Here, take some petals of bougainvillea – when they bloom to the fullest, during the hot months of summer, I always feel it to be the onset of a crimson dawn they are announcing.

---

14 See Holmes and Kivland 2019.
15 See Answer 2019.

Photograph of fallen petals from my Bougainvillea plant

Warmly,
Tigisha.

" Only the revolution of the world proletariat can bring order into this chaos, can bring work and bread for all, can end the reciprocal slaughter of the peoples, can restore peace, freedom, true culture to this martyred humanity. " [16]

---

16 "Only the revolution of the world proletariat can bring order into this chaos, can bring work and bread for all, can end the reciprocal slaughter of the peoples, can restore peace, freedom, true culture to this martyred humanity." (Luxemburg 2004: 349)

Letter 3 | Place, Politics, Scatter, Boats

Dear Jiglsha,

Thank you for the gift of the bougainvillea photos, such a red that I don't often associate with the bougainvillea. Seeing them makes me reinvent the original on which my memory riffs! It's otherwise always been either a deep magenta or an almost-red, and then it dissolves into something close to the oh-too-abbreviated flesh of the *falsa*, a swatch right out of my mother's fascination. My khala, responsible for a lot of beauty in my life, used to make the same clothes for her two daughters and me – which often required buying a lot of the same cloth and having it dyed different colours. That was my first time with a colour my ammi called *falsai*. In memory of that moment, I got myself another *chikankari* kurta shalwar a few years ago, which still runs colour even after fifty washes.

It felt so good to read your letter. I learnt so much from it, savouring your scholastic and activist entanglements with Luxemburg and her place in the world of our many men, and reverberating with the familiarities that must remain uncatalogued until we meet in person. I hope that my mention of N didn't feel intrusive or offhand – our cartographies of care are both simple and not straightforward, so sometimes our solidarities accrue greater familiarities than we have often earned, but I assure you they are in earnest. I am relieved that she is back and hope that you will be able to spend time with her. "Hugs," as you said, aplenty.

As you pulled together a vivid, achy, vital, sketch of the moment and your location in it, I remain struck by how completely different the idiom or systematicity of Left activism is in India as compared to Pakistan, especially inside bourgeois academic institutions. Perhaps it has to do *literally* with the *angrezi* and the citationality, even in the posters you show, and the conversations you relay, that I don't think have been the dominant modalities or poetics of student politics in Pakistan. Perhaps it has had a lot to do with the public manifestations of politics in an actual democracy, the literalities (and, as Jacques Ranciere would have it, *literarities*) allowed or even necessitated in the spaces that have not been populated in Pakistan because of a host of other impossibilities. I don't say this to make a crude developmentalist judgment about political modernity comparing the two countries, but to register how qualitatively divergent the political cultural denouements are within that which was, not very long ago, undivided (which itself only raises questions about the nature of political space beyond geopolitics). I am intrigued by what certain absences enable *and* what certain presences disable in different institutional spaces across polities, and how traditions develop in order to arbitrate where and when political agonisms are fought out, which partition of the sensible needs to be negotiated when, where, and by whom. Spaces get carved out with their own resident poetics of politics which we have no choice but to proliferate, in the face of what seems to be an overwhelmingly bothersome uniformity of idiom across incommensurate spaces and institutionalities. The variations in politics and its poetics that we find along different trajectories of the state, despite being cut from the same cloth, must at least allow us to dismantle any assumptions about the undulating flat spatialities of politics, which are sadly also at work in an increasingly theatrical and secularised Laclauian space of political (over)articulation that is so pervasive in some modes of professional political organising.

When you speak of the trauma of partition – even further unaddressed for Pakistanis thanks to the obscurantist narrative of independence – it is not hard to see how discrepant temporalities and institutionalities of the political are attached to that, as cause, as symptom, or as aftermath. Things in India have been completely different from the formations and forms they have taken in Pakistan. Today, when I see a kind of bourgeois nostalgia around the Left emerging in Pakistan, it feels like I am experiencing the bends under the sea… Maybe it's just a question of who gets to write a history of the present and of spaces where these things are being worked out, what pasts can be erased, and which can be capitalised on in the moment. I refuse to see it as progress, even if it feels like something's being recovered in the context of lost possibilities in Pakistan. Such a gross over-articulation of the political, no dearth of those who begrudge the philosophical and at the same time constantly see themselves as translators in the guise of political educators. Internationalism in the hands of these self-loving political actors looks like an economy of citation qua inheritance and lineage, even on the Left. But where is the method, the kind of pluralistic and abundant space that might provide some relief by jettisoning canonisation as the dominant modality of politics, even in bringing down the saints? There are times I feel desperate for something that doesn't walk in with a claim to inheritance or tradition, doesn't have to build itself on a monument to the past (or to the known future!), because of the violence it does to those it is bound to bulldoze in order to produce the edifice of the present, and the present as edifice.

As it is, I have been feeling very strange about the vanguardism of institutions and the assumptions we are allowed to make about who we are encountering, why we are increasingly able to handle only one set of political questions and orientations at a time, and why we accrue certain authorities to ourselves or cede them, fixated on the state as the key interlocutor that affirms and disaffirms, recognises and misrecognises. Why do I always fantasise about a conversation or negotiation among us that ends up never happening, since we are constantly standing in some court awaiting both surveillance and legitimacy? Why aren't all our embodied relations to the same histories sufficient to produce a new world? Have we left no secret languages, no desire to speak to each other without the mediation by the Leviathan? Perhaps I could never get this right and have become allergic to authorisations – and translations – if they aren't actually held in common across from the grand and transparent public sphere. Where do the questions go – of freedom, trust in each other, and love for the world – when people are tangled up with the state or other state-like institutions to which they must first answer, ready to betray friends at the drop of a hat when that happens?

So many political conversations feel like discussions about tools, and the university itself becomes a kind of idealised institution in a way it has never before been in Pakistan. There is something about the overwrought institutionalities experienced as spaces where certain recognitions and affirmations are made possible, and in this way the question of class seems so very crucial. What exactly do these interesting fascinations, these self-orientalisms, mean when we only ever seek to build that which will recognise us as we are now. What kind of self-undermining politics is that in the guise of self-affirmation? How has the Left been affirming this relation to the state, and state-like institutions, in an extended play of the creepy 'I will change you with my love' kind of desire? I was just speaking about this earlier today with a student, about how the regime of value and instrumentality of politics remains unquestioned the more the sense of crisis heightens, when we know so well, in our bones, how crisis is always used to return us to order. Perhaps my traumatising lack of reliance on institutions and what comes off as a weird disdain for US-style pragmatism comes from not having a history of institutions being there for us, to respond to us let alone do anything for us. I keep wondering if there were times more subtle, more poetic, yet more effective, with spaces and trust in agonism and battle, when one kind of presence, publicity, exposure, visibility, and publicness was not dictated to us. How can we empower organised intellectual spaces within which political work has happened, and continues to, that are not administered by the university, and which do not take political education to be, erroneously, an education in politics — as a paltry set of instructions rather than a set of intuitions and sensibilities? But maybe this is my own nostalgia, delusion, and fantasy crafted to give me permission for my politics.

What exactly was Rosa's relation to time and place? What did it take for her to claim her work *as* politics, and who was adjudicating it then? From the powdered wigs of German Social Democracy to Lenin on the national project, the judges were many, as there are now, constantly instructing us in instrumentalist and utile politics, devoid of any distinction between waste and loss when it comes to such things as time, worldmaking desire, and political struggle. Nevertheless, she didn't waver. Hers was an avid and unequivocal resistance to the national project – to its temporalities, and not only to its reference to space and identity – and that is something really important to me. I see myself in that, and at the same time, can't for the life of me understand why most people aren't able to give Rosa's understanding of the colony due credit, by actually understanding that all states are settler-colonial in one way or the other, and that anchoring our desire in the state, or in the world understood as a grand state, or in institutions mimicking the state as the uber-institutionality, is only to give in to the inevitability of colonisation, and to accrue to oneself the privilege of deciding the temporality of different disposabilities. Don't you think it is just a matter of time until the next betrayal comes, when we are told not only that our lack of nationalism is a problem, but that our lack of behaving properly as a global citizen or good internationalist is a problem too? What gets the Left as upset with the impolitic as the liberals and the right wing get? The pandemic has left me more world-weary than before, as I await the demand to give up on yet another claim that I never made. It's as if the demand for evacuation comes first for those who are seen as homeless to begin with – a strange message that comes to us by way of how Zionists understand Rosa's lack of Jewish identification and finds it punishable, or her fate somewhat deserved, because she didn't find refuge in the right identities, regardless of all the ablism, misogyny, xenophobia, and antisemitism she dealt with all her life. There is much written on Rosa's 'rootlessness,' her lack of claim on her heritage, her 'unaddressed scar,' her betrayal of her history. One day soon

I am sure that we will see the move from Rosa's flawed and false consciousness to some kind of quasi-eugenicist interpretation of the same, linking it to her physical disability. Why was Rosa, why are we, not allowed to live in a world where we are not constantly protecting a deep scar?

This brings up something so important about my relation to Luxemburg and her insistence on the international and the anti-national. At some point, I believe, as is happening today, the seriousness of one's political contributions depends on whose dominant ideas of the political one reaffirms. The state has inevitably been the dominant locus, for understandable reasons. But what did *we* do by surrendering our imagination to it in a way that allows other forms of the political to feel like a distraction, or secondary to the question of state power? Perhaps this is my completely unhinged attachment to a history of defeat as essential to the experience of politicisation, strangely common between my life in Pakistan and the US, where the public spaces of politics remain brutally separated by a thick glass wall from where the rest of life and politics happen. When I attended my first conference ever, on the occasion of the 150th anniversary of the publication of Marx's *Eighteenth Brumaire* – held in New Orleans, where I also discovered, to my sheer joy, balconies and bougainvillea to match anything I grew up with — it became clear to me how European and English Marxists were doing very different things with Marx. Seemingly, I had fallen into the 'trap' of the wholesomely political – philosophical, existential, humanistic, visceral, poetic – Marx. I felt so outside of the strategy and programmatisation, lacking in the confidence that comes from seeing ideas manifested in certain lived realities not enclosed within your will or intellect. While the Europeans had other evidence, all I knew was fidelity understood as either the power of stubborn insistence on the validity of ideas and dreams, or the subjunctive act of reading when it becomes a prayer and appeal in the kind of non-secular way that doesn't quite match what the functional politicians and preferred political actors of the world do with the same words. This realisation allowed me to understand better why my father and uncle worried that my going to the US had 'confused' me and might potentially render me not useful to the masses. I was simply too indulgent of the entrails of meaning-making and being human that felt like a digression from pressing questions of socialist strategy. I guess I haven't learnt much, except that I feel that my pathological recalcitrance towards instrumentalism and opportunism, and my disdain for functionalisms and positivisms as paltry ways of knowing and being sciences, have always been in the service of effecting different spaces by embracing discrepant and impolitic temporalities. This is something I believe we learn from Rosa, not because she did the same thing, but because her relation to space was not indentured to the question of state, nation, and other grand institutions that *keep time for us*. The fact that she remains confusing and dispensable to the Left, as well as maligned by the Zionist Right, is because she didn't stick to a space that was marked for her, she wasn't imprisoned by the imagination of the state, didn't claim the territory she was granted, and refused to abide by the prescribed forms of identifications and performances – as woman or as Jew – that might have had the some people trying to claim her and save her life *as if* she were one of their own. We know, instead, what she got, and that her community abandoned her for not claiming her Jewishness in the right way, and so on.

So, there's her internationalism, the nature of which has to be investigated further, given what your letter has made me think of: the limitations of an expansionist or uniform idea of the international. A universalism that does not heed histories of politics and lifeworlds themselves, that ends up impelling a meeting in a homogenized present that prescribes the spatiality and the institutionalities meant to organise our labour, together with the understandings predestined for us. This is a real question to struggle with, but it's hard to articulate it to those who are ready to just take advantage of it, since the only way they can see it is from the administrative lens of conflicting priorities and assigning resources to them. What role have those of us inside institutions played in normalising a particular kind of infrastructural positivism – afflicting academically-inclined activists as much as activistically-inclined academics – that oversees the segregation of space and time in thinking about politics, spaces, and people in both, and that has figured out the world and just needs to 'make it happen'? Maybe our concepts are so rotten at the core, that our politics has become relegated to reproducing what little it is we do understand; we cling to it as if our life depends on it. The art of connecting various times and spaces to each other must be more of an act of making constellations between endemic knowledges and experiences rather than an expansionism that assumes that capital and colony produce and colonise spaces and lifeworlds similarly everywhere. What exactly are we struggling with theorising here? That different planes and temporalities of existence co-exist? That they cannot be simply overwritten by the dominant temporality of the state, and that they must not be allowed to be? Is this my privilege speaking? Is my discomfort with a prescriptive, public, and performative Left politics something I can get over, that comes in the way of me actually working with others in the mediatised, 'transparent' public sphere?

Rosa kept going somehow. And I feel reassured by the fact that betrayals energised her. Up to a point. Because they do the same to me. I can't even get to enemies ever because I am constantly thinking about what supposed friends and comrades are up to. Is that a blessing, or a curse? She isn't some rationalist denying her own suffering; she sees it as tangled up with the sentimental world writ large rather than a dualism of pain and pleasure, suffering and joy, and so on. What is the visceral materialism here that evades the grasp of the vanguards of the grand march? I am certainly with you on the issue of a certain kind of responsibility and accountability, and Lenin looms large for me too. I am actually never even able to see the two as violently dualistically as they are often read. When I read Edmund Wilson describe Lenin on his journey back to Russia, there is such familiar pathos, a kind of relation to the suffering of others that was also not merely seen as the stuff of pathology and abject victimhood. In that sense, the historical materialisms of Luxemburg and Lenin – which I cannot help but understand as containing the history of materiality, *in addition to* the materiality of history – together make for a mode of study, relation, and practice that neither could on their own. Neither of them files away the visceral or fetishises the concrete. Neither reduces history to the monologue of personal lived experience or agentic manifestation. I really love how you speak about Lenin's language, Jigisha, something I rarely ever encounter. One realises how each of their poetics and aesthetics always feel like they have been squared away, or put away on an unreachable shelf. In his case more like an Apollonian statue, in her case an unkempt Dionysian melody, maybe a fugue, or maybe atonal. An embalmed body, or one eaten by fish in a river.

I wonder, though, had Luxemburg lived longer, confronted with the question of home and to what and whom she belongs, what would she have answered 'to the revolution'? At what point do these questions arise in the life of an activist? In my darker moments, I often think of Tom Paine when I think of Luxemburg – that perhaps in her early death she was spared the fate that befalls those of us who belong everywhere and nowhere, and hence are easily abandonable and disposable when revolution (and other wishful homes) cease/s to be a 'place' for the very people who build it (like Paine). It reminds me also of Hannah Arendt writing about Stefan Zweig in "We Refugees," leaving us with the heavy question of the delusions that allow us to live but which end up being lies that never save us. Zweig's and other refugees' memory of Vienna, of a Europe that was a kind of unproblematic home in the past, certainly had a fallacious quality, leading to many of them taking their lives once they were deprived of what they at least thought was theirs. There, too, as with Rosa, one might imagine there is this insistence on a filiality, that was not to be requited. Once the social disintegrates, life also departs. And if the social has always been full of betrayals, not quite there as we imagined it – as we are also seeing the pandemic expose – then the task of returning to something will augur another kind of finitude. I can't say what Luxemburg's fate would have been had she lived to see WWII. But if she did, what might circumstances have impelled her to avow and bind her flesh to?

I wonder even more what would have happened if the truly internationalist, anticolonialist and abolitionist beginnings that were born of the rejection of empire would have put up a resistance to the form of the settler-colonial nation-state. Those of us not sold to the sovereign nation-state as panacea must constantly work ourselves out of the sinking spiral of the same and the notions of 'human' it underwrote, and never quite reach a self-fashioning of an international and anti-national demos that we dream of. I wonder how this failure of ours is qualitatively different from those who began without these boundaries in their struggles but had to eventually buckle in the face of insistent demands to territorialise, domesticate, and contain, themselves. How are both these imaginations and their limits different? Why was Luxemburg so much more prescient when thinking about the fate of colonised people and her mistrust of the way in which leaders tended to cast their desires? That absolutely must have something to do with what she was able to see in her own relation to state, to place, and to world. Might she, like Rousseau's foreigner as legislator, be the one most able to not only see but also feel? I ask this because of how I feel unsustainable as a political actor, looking back at so much labour, inherited, genealogical and my own, that just *does not accumulate*, or manifest itself outside of a blur of a photo of perpetual motion, or a scatter of stars when I feel a bit better – each in good aesthetic and poetic taste, for sure, but so beside the point of 'History.' Is this inability to accumulate, make matter, translate – trauma, abundance, labour, home, being-in-the-world – a particular kind of disorder of the *misplaced* rather than the displaced? An affliction of the historical materialist. It can't end well, can it now!?

In this set of very well-to-do impasses, I must admit that I find Rosa's relation to happiness and internal bliss — in her letters especially to Sophie Liebknecht who is often distraught – sort of intolerable at this point in my life and our history. (Really, what would she think of positive psychology and the neoliberal discourse on individual resilience and self-care within contemporary movements?) I have spent a lot of time trying to speak about hope as a kind of dead love, so I know that Rosa's relation to revolution and its joy is not simply a kind of "cruel optimism," to recall the late Lauren Berlant whom we just lost this week. Yet Rosa's sentimentality cannot just be set aside and must be reckoned with precisely because misunderstanding it has consequences. So often, especially within Left and progressive circles, conversations just end, and the spaces get closed for those who don't perform these joys and happinesses. I have also been with Marxist boys/Marx's boys who walk the earth lunging ever forward, the opposite of the angel of history. I don't know what to do with this. I remain deeply suspicious of happy communists. If I don't tell myself, as Steve reminds me, that Rosa's sense of bliss might have something to do with being in prison and that the expansiveness that she can muster has to do with what she has no choice but to counter, I would be so put off by the cloyingly positive psychology type stuff in her letters.

I don't know how to deal with this particular way of transcendentalising the personal, and hence the political, taking it out of the realm of a relation to others. But maybe we do that when, as I gestured above, the social that we have imagined gives way under our feet. My distrust of happy communists is ever greater today, as I remain suspicious of a kind of heraldry of the future that comes with those who instruct and direct the course of history, who narrate themselves as its agents. I just don't understand if I am so completely broken as to no longer be able to rejoin that river flowing ever forward. When I am feeling fairer to Rosa on this matter of happiness, I understand her joy as something different, as an assertion of a spirit, a love for the world, that isn't *merely* matter – which, when in Benjamin can lead to losing one's life to a world unrequited, and when in Arendt, can lead to an embrace of miracle and natality. Rosa's ability to endure and continue faced with what she is, is key. But what do we make of those who don't endure the way she does? What is their sense of glee and purpose and forward march countering? Where do they get their faith, and what is that faith trying to counter? I am so curious. I feel that the happy communists are afraid of suffering, of allowing suffering to be present, to matter, unless it's converted into something else, something useful, harnessed in some way. And I feel, deeply with Rosa, that this is connected to the manner in which the question of accumulation has to be understood philosophically, socially, psychically, existentially, and hence politically. The university is a pretty sordid place for an actual honest reckoning of this, it seems – and from what you say, *wherever* it may be.

I keep reminding myself of how much I felt that my father was never quite happy about me trying to make my own life here, where I wasn't able to articulate a wellness for myself because I wasn't sure if it would be seen as betrayal of those I love and had left behind. Much of the time, especially later in his life, he couldn't even fully understand what I might feel good about – maybe I stopped translating, maybe there was nothing beyond the reassurance of voice that we could give ourselves at the growing distances that I always felt were populated by more imagination and thought than was possible in proximity. It was a slow reduction of syllables over time. Once I was back with him for the last year of his life, those syllables almost disappeared because we could see each other. There was so much to say but too late for it. When we did, earlier, speak and listen to each other, over my many years here, I continually tried to tell him I had no comrades to come back to in Pakistan like he had when he was young, and that he couldn't even imagine how that would feel. The truth is, I don't even have those comrades in this place and time, but yes numerous 'open boat' relationalities one nurtures and steps out of, one foot serving as the oar. Academia as a space to remake the world was and is a ruse, an occupation and not the collective project that tempted me because it reminded me of what I did at home, and which I left too early to have friends as a grownup. Perhaps there could have been a weird kind of displaced community, all of these named rooms that people have entered. I was not taught to pick a room (or a cage). But I also chose, and continue to choose, not to pick one.

The emotional and geographic cartographies of our lives far exceed the constant labour of subsisting that fills the day materially, especially in the isolations and heartbreak of the pandemic, already lost, already a non-memory to those who refuse to grieve anything, and hence will never allow another, better, world to come to pass. What we have are the effortless meridians of lives past and present, here and there, beautifully nourished and nourishing. Your bougainvillea have found a spot. I only worry that when I hit a wall or disappear into one, no one will know its coordinates.

Standing Here Wondering Which Way to Go (Zineb Sedira, 2019)

Blessings and beauty, always, Jigisha.

Warmly,
Umar

As regards the question of being an expatriate,
I would not swop with the public prosecutor on any
account. I have a dearer, greater home than any
prosecutor... What other fatherland is there
than the great mass of working men and women?
What other fatherland is there than the improvement
of life, the improvement of morality, the improvement
of the intellectual strength of the great masses
which constitute a people? [17]

---

17 "As regards the question of being an expatriate, I would not swop with the public prosecutor on any account. I
have a dearer, greater home than any prosecutor. What other fatherland is there than the great mass of working
men and women? What other fatherland is there than the improvement of life, the improvement of morality, the
improvement of the intellectual strength of the great masses which constitute a people?" (See Nettl 2019)

Letter 4 I **Home, Death, Care**

Dear Asma ,

It was so lovely to read your last letter. The moment I read *falsa*, I was excited, as it reminded me of a falsa-tree (are we talking about the same berries?) I had at home, growing up. I know exactly the colour you are talking about, and your associations bring up so many different memories for me as well. That house with the falsa-tree was one my paternal grandfather had built in the 1940s with his own hands – literally, making bricks out of a kiln, and building that house brick by brick. They left behind everything when they left their homes during Partition, and wanted a life out of the refugee colonies. Not many had that option; they could still make do, amidst extreme poverty. Whenever I think of that house now (we don't live in it anymore), I am reminded of so many things from my childhood, and one of them is my mother stitching. She was learning to sew and stitch, and made a red and black shalwar-kameez for me. I hated it, because in the 1990s I was just getting introduced to the new-found fascination for readymade clothes enabled by the onset of the neoliberal market.

This, in a very organic way perhaps, brings me to the question of our shared stories, shared histories of women's labour. Growing up in a progressive household where the women's question was viewed as an excess to class, and therefore secondary. Funnily enough, in a strange way this allowed me different ways of freedom which were not offered to other girls my age. I was told from the very beginning – you don't have to think of yourself as any less. Now, that's a luxury most of the people in South Asia don't get, and I am thankful for that. What I am trying to say here is that this progress, this freedom happened (like within much of the Communist/Leftist movements/spaces in India) at a cost. The cost of non-recognition of my girlhood, non-recognition of the divide between the public and the domestic, and a botched understanding of the women's question so to speak, that was propagated in much of the male-led interpretations and organisations of the time. This is how labour was read. This is how labour was taught to be read. And it was convenient.

The massive weight of Uncle's wedding band
Sits heavily upon Aunt Jennifer's hand.

As I grew up, the gendered understanding of labour was a tough realisation to arrive at. Gender was important as long as it was related to the working class. It was merely something the rulers used to divide the working class. It was something that was absent from within the family – definitely the families of the Leftists, but from the family-structure as well. People were happy reading and discussing only state and private property without ever bringing the family into it. It was only a 'family' as long as it was of a worker they visited as a part of their organisational work. No family existed beyond that. That too, the women workers would be the responsibility of the women's wings or women members of the organisations – not because women experientially were able to form solidarities, but because this work itself was seen as a subset of the central problem (and women were seen as lesser organisers), the central problem of class that was arrived at leaving the family out of the question. What do we do with women who stitch for their children? What do we do with women who are allowed to learn only those skills which are womanly in a household? I remember that the moment I saw somewhere that most of the professional chefs in the industry were male, I was shocked (I was very young, in my defence). The way tailors are male, cooks and chefs are male – the way the entire gamut of the public labour force has been male. And yet, the family has to be left out of it in the cultural elitism that vanguard Leftist spaces have kept spewing.

When Aunt is dead, her terrified hands will lie
Still ringed with ordeals she was mastered by.

I'm not denying that the Leftist organisations have been at the forefront of leading struggles for the women's cause, neither am I denying that many women did try to fight it wonderfully on their own accord even within such male spaces of the organisations. After all, we draw our daily inspirations from them as we find ourselves within this strange rift between our ideological beliefs and political practicalities. Women like us – where do we belong? This brings me to the question of Rosa and her home that you wonderfully raise. Within Indian political spaces (not academic ones, which derived insights from her economic works, even if late), Rosa was just a woman leader, a woman ideologue. As you know, the 'just' here is necessary again. Growing up knowing her, and yet not quite knowing her, when I actually started to read her work I was surprised that she actually did not limit herself to the women's question – not in the traditional understanding of it. When one reads her, there is such a keen empathy and clarity which characterises almost all her writings (as we were discussing earlier – those ones which have been read as her feminine trait). Yet, she was seen as just a heroic female face from the West within these milieus, lesser still, as a woman ideologue. And that stemmed from the mechanical understanding of labour, of contradictions, of unity that she so sternly refuted all her life: "Comrades! Do not let yourselves be taken in by the old catch-phrase that in unity there is strength. Now even Scheidemann and Ebert of the Party Executive are trying to peddle that one. Yes indeed there is strength in unity, but in a unity of firm, inner conviction, not of an external, mechanistic coupling of elements which are inwardly gravitating away from each other. Strength lies not in numbers, but in the spirit, in the clarity, in the energy that inspires us."[18]

This spirit, this clarity, this energy that she speaks about – can it be achieved, or even attempted, without this "inner conviction"? This conviction that is so utterly different from the discomfort with a certain kind of programmatisation of Leftist writings that you speak about. I don't know as closely about the European Left (I must note that once at a conference I heard someone look at Rosa's writings through the municipal policies of a German city and lost it), but this seems to have been the case in this part of the world too – perhaps with less of a claim on her lineage. Perhaps that's why I can relate to the frustration, the hopelessness and the political opposition to such institutions, authorities and their impositions that continue to

---

18 See Luxemburg 1916.

dominate our political imaginations. You write that if Rosa were to answer this question, her home perhaps would be the revolution itself. And yet, when one sees the 'revolutionary' tools which are there in front of us, how can one feel at home? We see the programmes being mechanically transacted, with the 'convictions' and ideologies continually settling to the demands of capital, with the revolutionary project being compromised – justified by selective readings of political conditions, by people and parties as it suits their agenda. The entire gamut of political analysis, of emancipation of people, of freedom and equality – all seem to be nicely fit into neoliberal transitions, or market-driven 'strategical' programmes for the socialist outfits. And those who still aspire to imagine beyond the claws of the state-capital nexus, are termed 'fringes' of the emancipatory project, or 'reactionaries' with no grounding in realpolitik. How do we even talk about freedom, of belonging? And then I think, perhaps in this unease, in this recognition of the situation as is, there is a certain sense of difficult solidarities that we are able to share. Perhaps, in finding ourselves in this space which is ours and not ours (popular academicians call this liminality these days), and still trying to seek clarity, there lies hope?

I have been fortunate to have been part of such difficult solidarities, I think. It is so troubling to learn from you that the situation on the other side of the border – has not quite been the same. With all its drawbacks, I took such a kind of a university-space as given. Especially as I would always be looking up to the limited news that we are able to get from the student-youth spaces there. I particularly remember a demonstration at the Faiz Aman Mela festival in Lahore sometime back, where very spirited young protestors were sloganeering to the tunes of Bismil's *Sarfaroshi Ki Tamanna Ab Humare Dil me Hain*.[19] I also remember the beautiful and exciting song from the Women's Democratic Front there, *Hum Inquilab Hain* – it has been my favourite ever since. In contrast, I always used to regret that the situation in India has been so neoliberalised that we do not have the capacity to produce cultural interventions beyond remixes. It is too disheartening to learn that this might be a part of the uniformity of idiom that you speak about, across polities, across state-formations and across public spheres. Increasingly, I feel the same about the homogenisation of our political articulation – the purity espoused by philosophers all around, and the dogged opposition to it – none of which is rooted in material conditions, or in a conviction for freedom, as Rosa keeps reminding us. The revolutionary framework seems to be caught up between an overly deterministic plateau of all resistant articulations and imaginations, and a compromised yet loud opposition to all existing frameworks, where the questions of by whom, towards what end – none of these have any clarity. The attack against dominant history that such spaces claim to lodge, ends up becoming a further justification and legitimisation of the status-quo – what you call 'preservationist.' There is a carnivalesque expression of political actions, which, with each passing day, and each passing 'event,' gets increasingly closer to Debord than to Bakhtin.

Every time I am stuck in such spaces, I have to remind myself of Gramsci's "optimism of the will." I'm glad you brought up N again, she has been enjoying her occasional lockdown rides around Delhi, and has been trying to recover to the fullest. The trial, however, has not started yet, and she has to appear in front of

---

19 This revolutionary poem written at the wake of the anti-British, anti-imperialist freedom struggle in India, can be loosely translated as, "now we have the desire to lose ourselves (towards the goal of freedom)."

the great Indian judiciary six times a month. Their bail judgement was challenged in the Supreme Court, and they have suggested that this particular ruling cannot become a precedent – it is singular, only applicable to their 'unique' case, and can never be cited in cases of other political prisoners. As I am writing this to you, Stan Swamy – another of the numerous political prisoners rotting in Indian prisons – has died. The punitive state did not allow him a sipper bottle that he needed. He was 73, worked all his life as a Jesuit in the remotest parts of Indian tribal belts, and had Parkinson's. Reading his last pieces of writing, I am baffled by the amount of conviction, faith he had in us, in humans at large. From the Taloja prison, where he was convicted alongside numerous other activists, he wrote, "Despite all odds, humanity is bubbling in Taloja prison." He wrote that he could see God in the faces of the ordinary prisoners there. Sometimes I wonder how this amount of conviction is possible. And then I am reminded of Rosa's letters from prison to Sophie Liebknecht. While attempting to imagine a trip to Corsica from behind the bars, she writes, "Every time I was so profoundly stirred that involuntarily I wanted to kneel, which is always my inclination when I see anything perfectly beautiful. There the Bible is still a living reality, and so is the classical world."

Yet we both know how different this utterance is from the prayers of the functional politicians that you talk about. There is a non-programmatic here that is not entirely made up of privileged dreams and aspirations to luxury. There is a conviction in the idea itself – of freedom, of devotion (even though it has such Christian connotations, it is difficult to use in a secular sense), of poetics, of care and empathy. The empathy which makes it possible to rekindle the belief in the revolution again? Or the peace-utopias that she situates so boldly. How is it that from within clamour, one is able to think of such utopias – neither as unattainable designs, nor as programmatic causation, but as something rooted within the idea of freedom itself? Perhaps there lies the secret to our homes, our communities, our belongings? Maybe that is where our realisations would attain expressions? It's truly insightful the way you talk about the correlation between Lenin and Rosa – their historical materiality, and their material history. So much charge had been put on both of their performative actions (albeit, very differently analysed), it seems that we have made products out of them, neatly divided on to shelves – one for polemic, one for perlocution, one for ephemera. I'm reminded of Danish Siddiqui here – a phenomenal and brave photojournalist who was reportedly killed in an open fire between the Taliban and the Afghan military this week. Danish, being a Muslim photojournalist in today's India, captured the most visceral, atrocious, horrific of events. One of his 'iconic' photographs was of a Muslim man during a pogrom in Delhi, who is trying desperately to save himself from the communal Hindu mob. Zubair, the subject, after recovery, said he could not look at the photograph. Danish made note of it, visited him regularly at his relatives', and captured many more photographs of Zubair, just to cure him of the visceral trauma of the earlier one. He used to state that he refused to see the people he photographed as mere subjects, products. I wonder where we can situate these lost, marginal narratives of care.

The care that you find intolerable now, Asma, and rightly so within the neoliberal regimes of self-care (I cringe every time someone mentions soul-cleansing and good vibes). Yet, when I see Rosa and Sophie's communications, for me it becomes an instance of these difficult solidarities – not the liberal bourgeois sisterhood, but truly political forms of solidarity. Where something is at stake, and that cost is acknowledged and reciprocated (hopefully). These, perhaps, are Rosa's real remains.

The tigers in the panel that she made
Will go on prancing, proud and unafraid.[20]

Would the free world we seek, too, be born from our labour?

Love,

Tigisha.

---

20 See "Aunt Jennifer's Tigers" in Rich 2016.

References

Abunimah, Ali (2021), "Israel kills boy featured in film about imprisoned kids." *The Electronic Intifada*. Accesed on 27.08.21, at https://electronicintifada.net/blogs/ali-abunimah/israel-kills-boy-featured-film-about-imprisoned-kids?fbclid=IwAR3vpBLGrFfEUmAOvLSKa8qHXVpJ2xH5iHs8Frzc1WJo-atw6V06lUcgq7Y.

Anwer, Zosya (2019), "After Sabeen is a story about two women who lifted each other up." *Dawn*. Accessed on 27.08.21, at https://images.dawn.com/news/1183755.

Boynik, Sezgyn (2018), *Coiled Verbal Spring*: *Devices of Lenin's Language*. Helsinki: Rabrab Press.

Chhabra, Meenakshi (2015), "Memory Practices in History Education about the 1947 British India Partition," *Journal of Educational Media, Memory and Society*, Vol. 7(2), 10-28.

Finn, Daniel (2021), "We Need to Rescue Rosa Luxemburg From the Soap Opera Treatment." *Jacobin*. Accessed on 08.08.21, at https://www.jacobinmag.com/2021/03/rosa-luxemburg-socialism-history.

Holes, Dale and Sharon Kivland (Eds.) (2019), *The Graveside Orations of Carl Einstein*. London: MA BIBLIOTHÈQUE.

Katz, Eliot (2012), "Reaching out to Adrienne Rich: An Activist Poet's Tribute." *Logos*. Accessed on 25.08.21, at http://logosjournal.com/2012/spring-summer_katz/#:~:text=Dear%20Rosa%20Luxemburg%2C,for%20freedom%20and%20egalitarian%20democracy.

Luxemburg, Rosa (1916), "Either/Or." *Marxist Internet Archive*. Accessed on 26.08.21, at https://www.marxists.org/archive/luxemburg/1916/04/eitheror.htm.

Luxemburg, Rosa (1902), "Martinique." *Marxist Internet Archive*. Accessed on 29.08.21, at https://www.marxists.org/archive/luxemburg/1902/05/15.htm.

Luxemburg, Rosa (2004), *The Rosa Luxemburg Reader*. Eds. Peter Hudis and Kevin B. Anderson. New York: Monthly Review Press.

Nettl, J.P. (2019), *Rosa Luxemburg – The Biography*. London and New York: Verso.

Ollman, Bertell (1976), *Alienation: Marx's Conception of Man in Capitalist Society*. UK: Cambridge University Press.

Rich, Adrienne (1993), *What is found there. Notebooks on Poetry and Politics*. New York: W.W. Norton & Company.

Rich, Adrienne (2016), *A Change of World*. New York: W.W. Norton & Company.

Scott, Helen C. and Paul Le Blanc (Eds.) (2010), *Socialism or Barbarism: Selected Writings of Rosa Luxemburg*. London: Pluto Press.

"Order prevails in Berlin!" "You foolish lackeys! Your "order"
is built on sand. Tomorrow the revolution will "rise up again,
clashing its weapons," and to your horror it will proclaim
with trumpets blazing: I was, I am, I shall be !" [21]

21 "'Order reigns in Berlin!' You stupid lackeys! Your 'order' is built on sand. The revolution will 'raise itself up again clashing,' and to your horror it will proclaim to the sound of trumpets: I was, I am, I shall be." (Luxemburg 2004: 378)

Novemberrevolution in Deutschland
Gründung der KPD
70.JAHRESTAG

PHILATELISTISCHER
JUGENDWETTBEWERB
1987/88

Annex: Letters from
Rosa Rosa Gomes

Dear g.[1]

Thanks for your mail. You've brought a lot of topics to be discussed already, but let me first briefly present myself.

My name is Rosa, I was born in São Paulo, the biggest city of Brazil, in the Southeast near the coast. But I grew up in a countryside city, Cuiabá, located almost in the middle of the South American sub-continent. I came back to São Paulo to go to college, and I've stayed here until today. I am a Historian, graduated from the University of São Paulo, where I also got my master's degree in Economic History. I first got interested in Rosa Luxemburg through Margarethe von Trotta's film and then started studying her book *The Accumulation of Capital* when I was an undergraduate student. Afterwards, for my master's degree I kept studying Rosa Luxemburg's accumulation theory. One of the things that left a deep impression on me was that she was the only woman at the time who developed an economic theory, debating with all the men around her. Today I work in heritage centers as conservator of paper and photography, and I teach classes about Rosa Luxemburg and economic history.

Because I grew up in a city far from the economic center of Brazil, São Paulo city and state, I used to think I was different from my *paulistano* friends, but that is not actually true, as the milieu in which I grew up was composed mostly of people from São Paulo or some other part of southern Brazil. This happened because of the migration movements in the 1960s in which the foundation of today's capital Brasilia played a major role. From that time on west-central Brazil started to be invaded by farmers whose aim was to expand the agricultural frontier in a natural environment called *Cerrado*.

In the beginning they raised cattle, nowadays the region is also one of the largest areas of soy production in the world. This type of expansion, which still happens in today's Brazil – for example in the Amazonia region – always looked to me like the process described by Luxemburg in *The Accumulation of Capital*:

> In other words, while this noncapitalist milieu is indispensable for capitalist accumulation, providing its fertile soil, accumulation in fact proceeds at the expense of this milieu, and is constantly devouring it.[2]

In other words, Capital advances through land-grabbing and dispossessing the inhabitants of those lands. In the process mentioned in the 1960s and 1970s, many indigenous peoples that lived in those places were killed and their territories broken up. Of course, these were different times for capitalism, different from the ones lived

---

1 Editor's note: For a variety of reasons, both private and professional, Rosa Rosa Gomes' partner was unable to finalise his contribution. As a result, only Rosa's correspondence is published here, with a number of footnotes to add contextual clarity.
2 Luxemburg 2015: 302.

in by Luxemburg and from the ones we live in today. Yet, I always ask myself how much the times have *really* changed for those of us living in the peripheral countries, at the frontiers of capital advancement, having to deal daily with the destruction and be in a permanent state of resistance. It is very tiring and difficult to sustain resistance in the long run since people must deal with their everyday survival – food, housing, and so on. So, most people tend to mobilize themselves for campaigns, that can last months, and then go back home in order to survive until the next campaign.

You talked about the changes in the 1970s and mentioned industrial production expanding in, or moving to, the "Global South." In Brazil, this process brought some industries to the country, but they were all products of the Second Industrial Revolution. Central countries got rid of their polluting industries by sending them to the peripheral ones at the cost of big loans, of course, and maintaining the subordinate role of these countries in the world market. At the same time, the agricultural frontier was being expanded so that the country would never stop exporting commodities or products of low added value.

All of this went on in the middle of a military dictatorship. In 1964, with the growth of Left movements in Brazil and disputes about how our development should proceed – with some groups defending more independence in relation to international interests – the government of the United States of America supported a coup d'état led by the Armed Forces. So, while Europe was experiencing a *Wirtschaftswunder* and the welfare state was still functioning, we were being defeated in a harsh struggle against the ruling class, both Brazilian and foreign.

In the time of the welfare state, there was this dictatorship in Brazil, and when the welfare state ended in the central countries, there was a huge crisis, which peripheral countries paid for. The 1980s and 1990s were terrible years for poor people in Brazil, and so when Lula finally won an election in 2002, the country's economy was a total disaster and many existing laws made social investments and Keynesian policies very difficult. Nonetheless, the Workers' Party (*Partido dos Trabalhadores*, PT) government from 2003-2016 was successful in creating policies that attended to the poorest people in Brazil and improved the lives of the majority of the population, though clearly theirs was not a revolutionary or socialist government. Ex-president Lula and many PT members even affirmed as much, calling themselves reformists and conciliators. In fact, Lula still believes there is room for capitalists and workers to live a good life together inside the same system of exploitation, when clearly the current crisis has shown us that there is not. The ruling class cannot share and nowadays there is no Soviet Union to oblige them to do so.

Besides, the Brazilian Left doesn't play a major role currently. Everything can change of course, but even Lula's recent release from jail, which gave hope to many people, hasn't shown any effect in concrete terms. The various factions of the ruling class hold all the cards and the Left remains out of the game. Even Lula's liberation can be seen as a move made by one of the factions while the Left is still waiting to see what happens. This is perhaps the greatest problem: we on the political Left continue to wait and see, instead of acting and making our voices heard. In this sense, our Brazilian Left seems like the German SPD before WWI: waiting for the bourgeoisie to come to a peaceful agreement that never happened. As Luxemburg said about the Morocco crisis in 1911: "To expect some peaceful tendencies from this capitalist society, and to rely earnestly upon them, would be the most foolish self-deception on the part of the proletariat."[3]

Maybe over the next letters, I'll tell you more about recent events in Brazil, the coup d'état in 2016, Bolsonaro and so on. It is funny and tragic how Brazil seems to be always "*na boca do povo,*" as we say, meaning that everybody is always talking about it, learning about it, and so on, for better or worse.

Well, I would like to read about you and South Africa too.

Luxemburguian greetings!

Rosa Rosa Gomes

---

3 Luxemburg in Day and Gaido 2012: 461.

"... a violência política é apenas o veículo do processo econômico" [4]

---

4 "In reality, political violence is nothing but a vehicle for the economic process." (Luxemburg 2015: 329)

April 25, São Paulo

Dear g.

I've been thinking about your reflections on South Africa and its current context. In many ways it seems similar to Brazil. For instance, even though there were no segregationist laws here, there were some laws that forbade black culture, and social apartheid has been a constant reality throughout our history. Also, the absence of a Left opposition to the ANC government in South Africa sounds just like what we are facing here.

But first of all, I would like to clarify what I wrote about the difficulty of maintaining resistance movements in the long run. What I meant is that it seems to be impossible to keep mass movements for a long period of time. Mass struggles last for a while, sometimes months, and then if a defeat happens the backslide begins; these are critical moments for any political organization, when the struggle becomes one of surviving as an organization and keeping itself in movement as an important political actor.

When talking about possible strategies for the Left, it is essential to analyze the current political and economic situation, as Luxemburg did all her life. She never defended a tactic or strategy without analyzing it according to the political-economic moment. In this sense, I do agree that the world hasn't recovered from the crisis of 2008, which posed many questions to the Left worldwide. Yes, there was a period of rising radical, or at least progressive, movements, such as *Occupy Wall Street*, *Podemos* in Spain and the 2013 bus tariff riots in Brazil. But nowadays, in many countries, it is fascism that is arising as a strong and major political force. We can witness this here in Brazil, but also in the United States, in Germany, in India. Historically, fascism is a product of capitalist society that rises in moments of crisis when there is no Left movement to organize the workers in a revolutionary sense. It is a result of capital accumulation and its imperialistic tendency, and confronts us with the "dilemma of world history, its inevitable choice,"[5] Socialism or Barbarism.

Having said that, I do see some differences between our present-day and the era in which Luxemburg formulated the dilemma. Luxemburg posed this question when German Social Democracy had joined the war effort side-by-side with the emperor, the bourgeoisie and the aristocracy, and she affirmed that what remained were but two options: a Left that would reconstruct itself, get out of the war and fight capitalism in a revolutionary way, or another world war, i.e. Socialism or Barbarism. In our case today, I believe the period of options has passed and what lies ahead is only fascism, "a reversion [in]to barbarism. The triumph of imperialism [that] leads to the destruction of civilization."[6]

---

5 Luxemburg 2004: 321.
6 Ibid.

300

On the other hand, I ask again whether this was ever not the case for the peripheral countries or regions. When analyzing these zones' history and role in the capitalist world structure, it seems that there has always been barbarism in these territories and Luxemburg's description of capital accumulation is an accumulation through barbarism. So, maybe the question must be asked in a different way, or the task can be addressed differently. Maybe in these areas of the world the task is how to stop the police killings of people in the *favelas*, how to stop the ongoing annihilation of indigenous people, in short, *how to get out of actually existing barbarism*, how to stop it and bring back a new, different sense of humanity, in which private property will not be at the core of social formation. Once we have found this way, or ways, other problems such us environmental collapse will be easier to solve, because their roots are in social human relations, how we see and treat each other in a society based on the exploitation of humans by humans.

Of course, a lot has changed nowadays, but the essence of our social relations didn't. In the past Keynesianism was a solution to the crisis and an instrument to fight socialist revolution, today it isn't because there is no menace of social revolution and because it seems that this crisis is a far more structural one: for instance, that it is no longer possible to make the profit rate rise continuously even by reducing direct and indirect wages. If one compares this present crisis with that of the late 1920s, it seems important to stress these differences. In this scenario, what are the possibilities for Left organizations nowadays?

That is the big question, I think. And I am not optimistic about this, but I try to be realistic. I look at Brazil's situation and the things we see in the streets or among our families, and it is hard to see something good coming any time soon. For example, it is quite sobering to know how many people defend the killings in the *favelas*, the killings of so-called bandits by the police with no trial. This kind of thing makes me doubt people's capacity to simply think or have some level of basic empathy. I've been told many times that "there is no alternative for us [workers] but to resist." That is true, but "how" is the question. One thing is trying to put aside our differences and unite. And then?

In Brazil, the dissatisfaction expressed in the riots of 2013 ended up being turned against the interests of the working class. The ruling class mobilized everything in their power to persecute and block Left policies: corporate media, State agencies, the judiciary system and so on. Everything was, and still is, mobilized against us. The elections of 2014 were maybe the last breath from Left forces to influence national politics. That campaign was highly politicized, but when PT won they ended up applying the opposing program, a neoliberal one, thereby contributing greatly to the evolution of right mass movements in 2015 and 2016. Together with media and right-wing propaganda, the worst elements rose up and took control of the streets, finally bringing to the surface the trash produced by capitalist society: Bolsonaro.

The years since 2014 have not been easy. In the beginning there was a lot of tension, everything was politicized, and not in a good sense, because Fascism politicized daily life, so going to the market or the bakery became something tense. People treated each other rudely, which could initiate a fight that might end up at the police station. Then things got worse. Recently my husband and I were standing on the street waiting for a friend's Uber and some guys, ten maybe, came to us because they thought we were filming their "illegal" party. We started arguing, one of them said they would shoot us, and my husband answered, "shoot then", and started calling the police. They didn't shoot us, but we stayed there for some time, arguing with them. They called us *petistas*, a rightist swear word similar to "Communist," because I didn't want one of them to come close without a mask on. Then they ran away because the police finally came. The next few days were awkward, I was afraid to leave home to go to the market because those men worked at the bar on the corner. That is the feeling everywhere, Fascism is on the corner. Actually, it has already taken over the streets.

And as a I said, in this context of rising, open fascism, the Left isn't playing much of a role. Yes, the Left organizations persist, but what is their concrete influence in the political and economic scenario? Last year, Left parties pressured the government to give emergency aid at a minimum rate because of the pandemic. But in the end, this was passed off as Bolsonaro's policy because the Left parties were unable to make it their victory. The same with MST (*Movimento dos Trabalhadores Rurais Sem Terra*) or movements for housing in the cities, community centers and so on, they persist, but their ranks are diminished and their impact is marginal. Luxemburg emphasized many times that the mistakes of the proletariat can be very fruitful to the working class as a whole, but I feel that although we are more than 100 years apart, we haven't learned much since her time. We keep making the same old mistakes as, for example, relying exclusively on elections to change things.

Why am I referring to elections? Because in all this chaos we are living in, the talk within Leftist ranks is about the next elections, since Lula is apparently free, at least for now. But in the current scenario, are elections or the parliamentary system as it exists today a real option? Is putting all your eggs in one basket a good strategy? The recent years (and History in general) have shown that elections and parliamentary disputes don't advance in favor of the working class unless there is a political force outside the institutional politics, because the State is built to protect and favor the ruling class as it is "only the political organization of capitalist economy."[7] Needless to say, I do agree that it is important to have a presence in parliament, but as a real political force that is heard and cannot be ignored, whereas in the current situation Left organizations are being ignored or even openly threatened and persecuted with little power to overcome this status. Therefore, the most important strategy right now appears to be to find ways to keep comrades safe and to strengthen our collective ties and fight back against fascism. At the same time, it is also important to start the long-term task of engaging the minds of our people through educational or propagandist actions about what private property actually is, and the social problems it causes, as well as the urgent need to change the society we live in, as suggested by Alain Badiou in his recent text, "On the Current Conjuncture."

Luxemburg was of course doing this type of important propaganda work all her life. In a speech on March 1, 1912, she assessed the meaning of the 1912 elections when the SPD won 110 seats:

---

7 Luxemburg 1974: 59.

Until now, winning seats in the parliament has been for us not the first but the last priority of the election campaign; what matters most is still agitation – as the means to enlighten and rouse the masses.[8]

So, Left organizations should see participation in elections and parliament as a space for propaganda, stressing socialist goals and engaging workers' minds. Each day I think Luxemburg's tactics are even more appropriate in a context where the Left can't make many reforms to improve the lives of workers. And since there is no 1905-type mass strike on the horizon, it is important to do the job of agitation and propaganda. It is in this sense that the upcoming Brazilian elections must be viewed, because even if the Workers' Party really wins the next elections, it won't be able to rule with the same conciliatory politics. That moment has long passed. The current moment calls for a clear differentiation from liberal parties, taking every opportunity to talk about class struggle and the problems associated with the private appropriation of the social product.

Of course, many people in Brazil already do this work of political education and agitation, but the most popular and biggest organization of all, PT, doesn't, or it doesn't have it as a central pillar of its activities. In sum, what is necessary is a massive campaign of agitation and propaganda, showing the economic aspects of neoliberalism and how it destroys the lives of the majority of the people. Clearly, this is a task for the long run, in the sense that the results are going to appear only over time while most organizations want a result for tomorrow.

So here I am part of a small group that does this kind of work. We have courses on economic politics and Brazilian history, and we have recently founded a publishing house called *Maria Antonia Edições*. So far, we have published five books, four of them in the last six months. Our idea is to publish classic texts of Marxist thought and Marxists' works about history and sociology, etc. We are a group of historians, so we tend to stress this discipline. The main idea is to spread Left and Marxist literature.

I think this kind of political action is very important, it gathers people together, organizes them and spreads socialist ideas. The problem is that my group is too small, as are many Left groups in Brazil. Currently only the Workers' Party as a mass organization could have a large-scale impact through agitation and propaganda, but some party members seem to be more worried about winning the next elections and keeping their jobs in public offices. Ironically, in a good way, two comrades and I recently recorded an online course about fascism sponsored by the PT's Perseu Abramo Foundation, which was very good because hundreds of people across the country came to know about this course and are now watching the recorded classes. So, despite the problems I mentioned, there is still hope inside PT's internal militancy. Much like Luxemburg, I think the basic rank and file of the party are much more engaged and alive then their party leadership.

---

8 See Luxemburg 1912 (Translation: Patrick Anderson).

So, I'm out of ideas. I'll keep doing this work that I think is important. Through it I've met some amazing people, and this is also a form of expanding contacts and Leftist networks. Besides, I think I am more like a point in the crowd than a woman on the platform.

Waiting to read from you about strategies and tactics!!

Either way, a luta sempre continua !!!

Saudações !!!

Rosa Rosa Gomes

Strike (Photo: Carolina Nascimento)

June 13, São Paulo

Dear g.

I agree with most of the short World History of the 20th century you shared in your last letter. But I maintain my question when thinking about colonial countries such as ours: Have we ever lived anything other than barbarism? Our entire history is a barbaric one and the reflection on what "socialism or barbarism" means in these lands must be made. How does it apply here? Should it be addressed in a different way? Unlike you, I'm at a moment of asking questions not answering them. The current situation of fascistization in Brazil begs the question: How did we get here? What led us to this point? After answering this, new questions must be asked: How do we get out of this situation? I think that is somehow the question you propose. In my last letter, I shared some of the reasons why Brazil is in this situation, at least I told you part of the story. In your letter, you present a thesis on why and how we got here, but I must disagree entirely with you about that.

First things first. I found your concept of "vaccine apartheid" amazing. That it started from the beginning of the pandemic with central countries draining basic medical supplies – masks, syringes, respirators – to deal with the disease, the United States being the most aggressive in this case. Therefore, when the vaccines were developed, the apartheid was already outlined. This shouldn't come as any surprise to Leftists, or Marxists, since the world has been organized in this way from the beginning of capital development. Capitalism hasn't become irrational, it *is* irrational. That is what Luxemburg stresses in all her texts, that is the basis of her thought: capitalism is anarchic and irrational. It has never had the capacity to be human or humanitarian, especially in moments of catastrophe, because usually these catastrophes are generated by Capital itself, as in the Corona crisis, World War I and II, the Holocaust, Colonialism, and so on.

If during specific short moments in capitalist history, at certain geographic locations, capitalism has been a little softer, it is because the working class has forced this out of the system, such as the 8-hour working day, the right to vote, the pension system, public health and so on. These little periods and spaces of humanity in capitalist history were brought about by the workers' struggle, not because of capitalism's human face.

When analyzing the world's political economy, it is not at all strange that the developed countries have adopted a more Keynesian policy in the management of the pandemic than the peripheral ones. This has always been the case. Luxemburg wrote in her book *The Accumulation of Capital*:

> For capital, the solution was now to monopolize noncapitalist areas for its expansion, both within the old capitalist states as well as overseas, while free trade (the "open door" policy) became a specifc form of the defenselessness of noncapitalist countries in the face of international capital and its competitive equilibrium, and constituted a preliminary stage of their partial or total occupation as colonies or as spheres of interest.[9]

9 Luxemburg 2015: 328.

Since the beginning, there have been two kinds of policies: one for the central countries, to which money flows, and another for the peripheral countries, from where the money is taken. What is astonishing and a sign of Left weakness is that not much noise was heard from the popular classes to pressure their governments to apply a more humanitarian policy during the pandemic.

Entering the core of your last letter,[10] you have an entire program to be followed, a plan towards revolution. As I said, I am in a moment of analyzing our situation to seek perspectives. So, considering the application of your proposal in Brazil, I'm afraid it won't work, because it has been tried before.

In Brazil in the 1930s, there was a policy for national development promoting some basic industry branches such as metallurgy and steel. These were state industries, and the plan was that the State would invest in those branches that require larger start-up capital, encouraging the development of consumer and capital goods industries. This was organized through the *Estado Novo* dictatorship, led by Getúlio Vargas. During the same period, our labour law was consolidated and still today there is much debate as to whether this was a Vargas' concession or a victory of the working class. I advocate for the latter. Then, from 1945 until 1964, a republic was installed in Brazil. It was a period of great debates and the rise of class struggle. The Brazilian Communist Party (PCB) became an important Left-wing organization and had some influence among the workers. It elected 14 deputies for the Brazilian Constituent Assembly in 1945 despite an electoral law that excluded most of the population from the process. Two years later, the party was banned.

At that time, PCB's program was to bring about the bourgeois revolution in Brazil, defending a process of national industrialization. They thought that to get to social revolution, it was necessary to go through stages, starting with the bourgeois revolution. So, they defended an alliance with the so-called national bourgeoisie to improve Brazil's independence and position in the global market, developing productive forces within the country. In 1950, the former dictator Vargas was elected president of Brazil. In a huge national campaign called *"O petróleo é nosso"* ("The oil is ours"), Vargas nationalized our oil resources and created Petrobras, today a globally renowned company. Petrobras survived the 1990s, but it seems it won't survive the 2020s as a state company. Vargas also increased the minimum wage by 100%. So, he was a popular phenomenon, especially in this last government. This popularity made the ruling classes concerned with their profits and power. To avoid a *coup d'etat* led by the ruling class and military forces, Vargas committed suicide. In 1961, his former Work Minister, João Goulart, took over the presidency after the elected president, Jânio Quadros, renounced his position. Goulart was an adherent of "developmentalism," or *desenvolvimentismo* as we call it. It is a political economic line of thought that defends national development as a way of turning Brazil into a more economically independent country. One of the policies Goulart tried to

---

10 From this point to the end of this letter I'm debating with G. his program for revolution. He advocates that to get back on the rails of social revolution, it is necessary for mass struggles to reverse austerity policies, advance the demands of the popular classes and "challenge the social power of finance capital." This anti-austerity struggle should also impose a sovereign industrial project that wouldn't be submitted to the global market and, therefore, to unequal trade. He wrote, "This will challenge the power of foreign capital in domestic investment and will require the leading role of the state through audacious measures such as nationalization and socialization of monopolies." He called it "delinking industrialization."

implement was a tax on profits transfer. Goulart's government was a turbulent moment for Brazil, his policies were labelled as communist and there was growing polarization between his supporters and the upper classes aligned with the United States' interests. The result of these increasing social conflicts was a military coup in 1964, supported by the same so-called "national bourgeoisie."

Between 1975 and 1990, still under military rule, Brazilians lived a rebirth of popular mass movement, the redemocratization struggles. You wrote about the anti-apartheid movement as a mass struggle over a long period of time and it reminded me of this period in Brazilian history. Also, you talked about the historic bloc and its role in the struggle. Fernando Ferreira, a Brazilian historian, says that in Brazil the redemocratization movement was something similar to that, especially during the campaign for direct elections in 1984 *("Diretas Já")*. The historic bloc at the time was formed by social movements, Left parties such as PT and the Communist Party, liberals and members of a party created by former supporters of the dictatorship. This bloc was later betrayed by some deputies who changed their votes, so the direct elections weren't approved. Then, the bloc disintegrated, and some members settled on an agreement with the dictatorship in which the president and vice-president would be elected by the parliament. The result was that the first 'democratic' president was a notorious supporter of the recently defeated military rulers.

Many decades later, the Workers' Party won the elections of 2002. However, PT had changed much since its foundation. It was never a revolutionary party, but in the beginning it was definitely a more radical one. If you ask me, the Leftist governments in Latin America from the early 2000s were not a revolutionary wave, as you say, but at best a progressive one. In the case of PT, they never proposed a revolution in Brazil, though their policies made very important social improvements for the majority of the population and for the national economy as a whole. Their policies were not merely distributive, as is often claimed. Rather, theirs was what is called a *neodesenvolvimentista* project, because it followed a politics of seeking a little more independence for Brazil, trying to diversify the country's economic partners, while developing state industries and private national ones, but without confronting the neoliberal status quo. And while it is true that the PT government benefited from higher prices for commodities in the early years of their rule, thereby allowing them to finance their distributive policies, there were also changes to fixed capital industries, though these are not very well known or discussed.

In the center of those changes was Petrobras. The company became a huge industry, expanded massively and amplified its capacity to produce refined oil, thereby reducing the need for imports, the aim being greater independence in relation to this energy source. In addition, the government expanded national industry through Petrobras, because there was a rule for the exploitation of pre-salt oil which stated that the company should prefer national suppliers over foreign ones. In addition, there was the expansion of the naval industry. These basic branches that require huge amounts of money replicate themselves in other branches of industry in a long chain of effects that also affected the ordinary internal market.

One of the reasons behind the 2016 coup was this kind of policy. One of the first things the people behind this coup, such as members of the Brazilian Social

308

Democracy Party (PSDB), did was to open up Petrobras to foreign appropriation. Foreign investors hadn't been entirely out of Brazil, but now they wanted a bigger share of pre-salt oil reserves. As I am writing this, Petrobras is being destroyed, it doesn't use its entire capacity for refining oil for example, necessitating an increase in imports.

What I'm trying to explain is that, while the Brazilian situation isn't solely a result of the PT government's strategies, those policies were a major contributing factor. PT never wanted to replace capitalist society with another one, rather their project was to develop national industries and make Brazil a relevant nation on a global scale. They managed to do that until the 2008 crisis exploded. Yet even before this crisis, the Brazilian bourgeoisie was trying to remove them from power. So, the problem was not only the lack of a delinking industrialization (in some regards PT applied policies towards that). There were many other aspects of the *coup d'état* in 2016, among them: foreign capital interests in pre-salt oil reserves; the ongoing effects of the 2008 crisis, which demanded a more radical policy in response, such as increased state investment and raising taxes on the richest Brazilians; and, not to forget, class and race prejudice.

So, while your program is interesting, in the case of Brazil it has already been tried several times, by Vargas in the middle of the 20th century and by the PT at the beginning of the 21st century. You may say that they did not quite do what you propose, and I would respond that they never got there because they were stopped early on by coups (though Estado Novo is a controversial topic to discuss, since it was a dictatorship). In this short history of Brazil, I've talked about at least two dictatorships and three coups, most of them related to groups trying to hinder Brazil's economic independence in the global market. So I think Brazilian history shows that there is no possible autonomous development for former colonies (or, in my perspective, current colonies) within capitalist society.

From Rosa Luxemburg's theory of accumulation, it is possible to understand that capital survives by expanding the international division of labour and establishing different levels of development and living conditions. Hence it is impossible to seek a type of delinking industrialization in steps, or by completing a process of national liberation, as if there were a final stage of industrialization that a country could reach, because this would mean changing the international division of labour, which in turn means changing global trade relations. And that will not be peacefully tolerated by those who benefit from the current situation.

I think in some ways even Luxemburg's analysis of capitalist development in Poland has something to do with this. Luxemburg exhorted the Polish people to fight alongside the Russian proletariat to defeat Russian absolutism, forming a country that would unite many nationalities with autonomous local powers. One of her explanations was that the Polish economy was so linked to the Russian one that Poland's independence without social revolution would only mean creating a territory that would be economically subordinated to the Western countries. Following her analysis, inside the structure of capitalism and in alliance with the bourgeoisie, it is not possible to seek a different position within the global trade system. This can only be achieved through socialism.

In conclusion, I realize that it seems as if I am saying that there is nothing to be done since socialism isn't currently on the horizon. But "History is a bastard" ("*A História é mais canalha*"), as João Quartim de Moraes says. I don't believe in recipes, historically they never worked. I think the current moment is one of agitation and propaganda, as I said before. Luxemburg believed the major task of socialist organizations was to prepare the subjective component of social transformation to imbue the proletariat, women and men, with class consciousness. I believe that this is indeed the task for today and the foreseeable future, though as we know History may always accelerate its march, hopefully not in the direction of a more reactionary mode of production, as you suggested is also possible. Similarly, Lincoln Secco, in Brazil, says that historically the overcoming of capitalism has always been related to socialism for the Left, but in our time it is possible to envisage another possibility: a society worse than capitalism, in other words, Socialism or even worse Barbarism.

Thus, avoiding this worst-case scenario is our most urgent task today. It won't happen by itself. But neither will it happen by following old recipes that failed in the past. "[...] we are not lost, and we will be victorious if we have not forgotten how to learn."[11] To build the path, to make the way is something to be learned through everyday struggle, by making mistakes, changing tactics and gathering more and more people to destroy this irrational system that allows only the worst in people to come out, in favor of a society that allows us to be the best versions of ourselves.

Ngawethu ! [12]

Rosa Rosa Gomes

---

11 Luxemburg 2004: 321.
12 As, in his last letter, G. ended with "Amandla," I answered in my letter with "Ngawethu."

References

Badiou, Alain (2020), "On the Current Conjuncture." *Verso*. Accessed on 13.08, at https://www.versobooks.com/blogs/4954-on-the-current-conjuncture.

Day, Richard B and Daniel Gaido (2012), *Discovering Imperialism: Social Democracy to Word War I*. Boston and Leiden: Brill.

Luxemburg, Rosa (1912), "Unser Wahlsieg und seine Lehren." *Projekt Gutenberg*. Accessed on 13.08.2021, at https://www.projekt-gutenberg.org/luxembur/reden/chap040.html.

Luxemburg, Rosa (1974), "Die sozialistische Krise in Frankreich," in *Rosa Luxemburg: Gesammelte Werke, V. ½*. Berlin: Dietz Verlag.

Luxemburg, Rosa (2004), *The Rosa Luxemburg Reader*. Eds. Peter Hudis and Kevin B. Anderson. New York: Monthly Review Press.

Luxemburg, Rosa (2015), *The Complete Works of Rosa Luxemburg, Vol. II: Economic Writings 2*. Eds. Peter Hudis and Paul Le Blanc. London and New York: Verso Books.

"Esse 'mundo civilizado' só hoje descobriu que a mordida das feras imperialistas é mortal, que suas exa_ lações são perversas. Ele só o percebeu quando as feras enterraram as garras afiadas no seio da própria mãe, a civilização burguesa europeia." [13]

13 "This civilized world has just begun to know that the fangs of the imperialist beast are deadly, that its breath is frightfulness, that its tearing claws have sunk deeper into the breasts of its own mother, European culture." (Luxemburg 2004: 339)

Biographies

Authors' Biographies

Asma Abbas, a political theorist, reader, and educator, is Professor of Politics and Philosophy, and Director of the Annex for Transdisciplinary and Experimental Studies at Bard College at Simon's Rock. She is senior research fellow at Global Centre for Advanced Studies, associate faculty at the Brooklyn Institute for Social Research, former Fulbright-Masaryk Distinguished Chair in Social Studies in Brno, Czech Republic, and former Dean of Academics at the Indus Valley School of Art and Architecture in Karachi, Pakistan. Asma had a hand in founding and organising Hic Rosa (and its international travelling Studio in Materialist and Anticolonial Politics and Aesthetics), the Falsework School for alternative community political education, the ACCREW (art, culture, community, and radical education workers) Caucus of the Democratic Socialists of America, Some Beloved (a multi-modal production collaborative), and Common Tern (an internationalist cultural work coop). She is the author of *Liberalism and Human Suffering: Materialist Reflections on Politics, Ethics, and Aesthetics* (Palgrave Macmillan, 2010), and *Another Love: Overtures to a Politics of the Unrequited* (Rowman & Littlefield, 2018), and several essays. She co-curated and co-edited *Falsework, Smalltalk: Aesthetic Archives, Political Education, and Imagining a Future in Common.* She is currently working on an experimental political phenomenology titled *Anti-Odysseus: Fugues of the Non-Homeric,* and a series of essays on the "hatred of education" (in the key of Rancière's *Hatred of Democracy*). She lives between Richmond, Massachusetts and Karachi, Pakistan.

Jigisha Bhattacharya identifies as a researcher and writer and shares her time between Kolkata and New Delhi in India. Her research engages with politics of media and culture, the histories of progressive political movements in the global south, and the interrelation between gender and labour. She has been an active part of students' movements, gender-rights movements and community organisations. When she is not confined within her academic persuasions, she experiments with creative non-fiction and visual essays. Her article, "Tracing Rosa Luxemburg's legacy: Economic and political debates within contemporary India" was published in *Rosa Luxemburg Volume 2: Aftermath,* edited by Frank Jacob, Albert Scharenberg and Jörn Schütrumpf, Buchner Verlag 2021.

alejandra ciriza is a feisty feminist activist and human rights defender. She is the mother of Andrés, Valentín and Martina and the *abuela* of Amparo and Emiliano. She looks after plants and enjoys dancing. She is a researcher at CONICET and a professor of philosophy and feminist theories in the Faculty of Political and Social Sciences at UNCuyo in Mendoza, Argentina. Her research is situated the intersection of feminist political philosophy and the history of women and feminist ideas, based on a perspective that recognises class, racialisation and *corporalidad.* ale has written, edited and published scientific articles, book chapters and books in her realm of expertise. She currently leads the master's program in feminist studies at UNCuyo, supporting the emergence of new researchers in this field.

Sevgi Doğan gained her doctorate degree from Scuola Normale Superiore di Pisa. She is conducting research on gender balance in illiberal democracies, focusing on Turkey, in the University of Siena. She is a collaborator in the internationalisation office at the Scuola Normale Superiore as the person responsible for the SAR (Scholars at Risk Network) in Italy. Her doctoral thesis, *Marx and Hegel: On the Dialectic of the Individual and the Social*, was published by Lexington Books (2018). Her fields of research are modern and contemporary political philosophy, Marxism, Hegelianism, German and Italian idealism, Italian Marxism, Frankfurt School, Rosa Luxemburg, authoritarianism and totalitarianism, gender studies, feminism, philosophy in Turkey, social and political modernization of Turkey, and academic freedom. She has translated Gramsci's *Letters from Prison* from Italian into Turkish and submitted it to Alfa publishing house.

Haydeé García Bravo is a historian of science and an everyday Feminist. She is passionate about interdisciplinarity, understood as work undertaken collectively and collaboratively in order to generate alternatives. She has a master's in anthropology and another in history and patrimony. She is a researcher at the Centro de Investigaciones Interdisciplinarias en Ciencias y Humanidades (CEIICH) at the Universidad Nacional Autónoma de México (UNAM) and a postgraduate professor in Art & Design, Latin American Studies and Gender Studies, also at UNAM. She is currently pursuing a PhD in Philosophy of Science and has published numerous articles and book chapters. She enjoys cooking, reading literature, dancing, traveling and dreaming.

Rosa Rosa Gomes holds a bachelor's degree in History and a master's degree in Economic History, both at the University of São Paulo. As part of her master's research, she studied Luxemburg's *The Accumulation of Capital*. She is a member of GMARX, a group at the University of São Paulo coordinated by Professor Lincoln Secco, where she is the editor of the group's weekly journal, *Maria Antonia*. She also teaches courses on political economy and Brazilian history. As a conservator of paper and photography, she assists a group that manages a heritage centre, *Centro de Memória Queixadas*, for the workers of the Perus district in São Paulo.

Jane Anna Gordon is professor of Political Science, with affiliations in American Studies, El Institute, Philosophy, and Women's, Gender, and Sexuality Studies at the University of Connecticut, Storrs. She is, most recently, author of *Statelessness and Contemporary Enslavement* (Routledge, 2020) and *Creolizing Political Theory: Reading Rousseau through Fanon* (Fordham, 2013) and co-editor, with Drucilla Cornell, of *Creolizing Rosa Luxemburg* (Rowman and Littlefield, 2021). Former president of the Caribbean Philosophical Association (2014-2016), she directs its summer school and co-edits its two-book series, *Creolizing the Canon* and *Global Critical Caribbean Thought*. With Lewis Gordon, she is executive editor of the new online, open access journal *Philosophy and Global Affairs*.

Nguyen Hong Duc, an MA in Philosophy, is a researcher at The Institute of Philosophy under Vietnam Academy of Social Sciences (VASS). His research topics are Rosa Luxemburg's thought, feminism and gender equality, and democracy. He has authored many publications on Rosa Luxemburg in Vietnam from 2017 to the present. He also has an interest in phenomenology and Catholic social doctrine. Before being a researcher, he was an employee at the district party committee of Loc Ha district (Ha Tinh, Vietnam) and a lecturer at Quang Binh University. He has a particular fondness for Germany and German thinkers.

Peter Hudis is a Professor of Humanities and Philosophy at Oakton Community College and author of *Marx's Concept of the Alternative to Capitalism* (Brill, 2012) and *Frantz Fanon: Philosopher of the Barricades* (Pluto Press, 2015). He co-edited *The Power of Negativity: Selected Writings on the Dialectic in Hegel and Marx*, by *Raya Dunayevskaya* and *The Rosa Luxemburg Reader*, as well as *The Letters of Rosa Luxem*burg. He currently serves as General Editor of *The Complete Works of Lux*emburg, a forthcoming 17-volume collection; as part of this, he edited Volume I of *The Complete Works or Rosa Luxemburg: Economic Writings 1* and co-edited Volume II, *Economic Writings,* Volume III, *Political Writings 1*, and Volume IV, *Political Writings 2*.

Maureen (Mo) Kasuku is a Socialist Feminist, aspiring globe trotter and Capricorn from Nairobi, Kenya. She is a cadre with the Revolutionary Socialist League-Kenya, co-founder of Feminists in Kenya and a member of Kenyans 4 Palestine. Mo was inspired to join active political life after visiting the Ukombozi Library – a friend of the Rosa-Luxemburg-Stiftung. When she is not organizing cadres for the socialist revolution, Mo works for a lifestyle website. She enjoys spending time with her family and two cats, dancing to music by Beyoncé and TPOK Jazz and making 5-minute meals. Mo is obnoxiously opinionated on the internet but not in real life.

Julia Killet, born in 1981, studied literature and political science. She has been the director of the Rosa Luxemburg Foundation Bavaria since 2011. She completed her doctorate on "The representation of Rosa Luxemburg in biographical and literary prose" at the University of Potsdam in 2018.

Tom Kuhn teaches German at Oxford University where he is a Professor of C20 German Literature and a Fellow of St Hugh's College. He has been the principal editor of the English-language edition of Brecht since 2002. Numerous publications on Brecht and on C20 drama and exile literature include *Brecht on Theatre* and *Brecht on Art and Politics* (2015), *The Collected Poems of Bertolt Brecht* (2018) and *Brecht and the Writer's Workshop: Fatzer and Other Dramatic Projects* (2019).

Małgorzata Kulbaczewska-Figat is the deputy editor-in-chief of a leading Polish left-wing media outlet – *Strajk.eu*, a journalist at the social-democratic *Dziennik Trybuna* daily and co-host of newly launched podcast, *Cross-Border Talks*. She has written extensively about Eastern European countries, reporting, among others, from Ukraine, Belarus and the Baltic states, covering political transformations, identity questions and social movements. She is also active in the *Historia Czerwona* (Red History) association, whose aim is to commemorate the history of the revolutionary workers' movement in Poland. As a journalist, she aims to show and explain people's engagement in fighting for their rights, dreaming and building a better world – both in her native Poland and elsewhere.

Paul Le Blanc, a political activist since 1965, has been an auto worker, healthcare worker, shipyard worker, social service worker, and more. He has taught history for over 30 years, currently at Pittsburgh's La Roche University. On the editorial board of *The Complete Works of Rosa Luxemburg*, he has written *The Living Flame: The Revolutionary Passion of Rosa Luxemburg*, and co-edited with Helen C. Scott a selection of Luxemburg's writings for Pluto Press – *Socialism or Barbarism*. Other works include: *A Short History of the U.S. Working Class*; *A Freedom Budget for All Americans*; *Left Americana*; *Lenin and the Revolutionary Party*; *Leon Trotsky*; *October Song: Bolshevik Triumph, Communist Tragedy, 1917-1924*; and most recently, *Revolutionary Collective*.

Michael Löwy, born in Brazil in 1938, has lived in Paris since 1969. He is currently Emeritus Research Director at CNRS (National Center for Scientific Research), Paris. His books and articles have been translated into twenty-nine languages. Among his main publications are: *Georg Lukacs: From Romanticism to Bolshevism* (Verso, 1981); *Romanticism against the Current of Modernity* (with Robert Sayre, Duke University Press, 2001); *Fire Alarm. Reading Walter Benjamin's 'On the Concept of History'* (Verso, 2005); *The Theory of Revolution of the Young Marx* (Haymarket, 2005); and *L'étincelle incendiaire. Essais sur Rosa Luxemburg* (Temps des Cerises, 2018).

Paul Mason is a journalist, filmmaker and writer, living in London. He was born in 1960, in the coalmining and cotton town of Leigh, in northern England. He studied Music and Politics at Sheffield University, spent time as a musicologist before becoming a journalist in 1991. In 2001 he became business correspondent of the BBC flagship current affairs programme, Newsnight, and was made economics editor of the programme on the eve of the 2008 financial crash. At the BBC he covered not just the crisis but the occupation movements from Cairo to Athens and New York. He moved to Channel 4 News in 2013, covering the 2014 Gaza war from the front line. Since 2016 he has been a freelance journalist writing for The Guardian, New Statesman and Der Freitag, among others. He is the author of seven books, including the bestseller *Postcapitalism: A Guide To Our Future*, and *Rare Earth*, a satirical novel about Chinese communism and British journalism. His latest book is: *How To Stop Fascism: History, Ideology, Resistance*. His latest documentary is the three-part series R is for Rosa, commissioned by the Rosa Luxemburg Foundation in 2021.

Xiong Min is an associate professor in the School of Marxism at Zhongnan University of Economics and Law in China. Her publications include *The Logic and History of Capitalist Globalization: Research on Rosa Luxemburg's Theory of Capital Accumulation*, published by Beijing People's Publishing House, and "The Theoretical Horizons of Rosa Luxemburg's Political Philosophy" in Wuhan University Journal (Philosophy and Social Sciences).

Originally from the United Kingdom, **Helen C. Scott** is Professor of English at the University of Vermont, where she teaches contemporary global anglophone literatures and is department representative for United Academics, the faculty union. Her publications include *Caribbean Women Writers and Globalization: Fictions of Independence* (Ashgate 2006), *The Essential Rosa Luxemburg* (Haymarket 2008), *Rosa Luxemburg: Socialism or Barbarism* (with Paul Le Blanc, Pluto 2010), and *Shakespeare's Tempest and Capitalism: The Storm of History* (Routledge, 2019). She is on the board of Verso's *The Complete Works of Rosa Luxemburg* and is currently co-editing Volume 5 with Paul Le Blanc.

Rebecca Selberg grew up in a small working-class family in rural southern Sweden. She joined the Young Left at age 14. Partly as a result of the in-depth intellectual training she received in leftist activist circles, she was able to finish a PhD in Sociology at Linaeus University in 2012. Since then, she has worked as a researcher and lecturer at Lund University; her main focus is on the public sector and working conditions in care professions. Selberg is also a writer for the Swedish daily *Expressen*.

322

Editors' Biographies

Hjalmar Jorge Joffre-Eichhorn is a German-Bolivian theatre maker, compulsive reader – printed books only – and reluctant writer. In recent years, he has dedicated himself to publishing activist books and, Left despair permitting, contemplating the opening of a bookstore in the not too distant future. As a result, he has been obsessively hunting Communist memorabilia to eventually be exhibited and worshipped in the store. Given that the few original Rosa Luxemburg busts available are prohibitively expensive, he may just have to become an amateur sculptor himself. If anyone wants to teach him pro bono, please get in touch.

Patrick Anderson loves words – their sound, meaning, origins – and has been a student of language throughout his life. He is unsurprisingly an aficionado of cryptic crosswords, and spends far too much time perusing etymological databases. Patrick has lived, worked and studied in five continents. With an MA in Conflict Resolution, he devotes most of his professional life to supporting individuals, organisations and communities to navigate the world with courage, dignity and passion.

Johann Salazar is an independent researcher and photographer with a background in Sociology and Anthropology. His current interests include visual storytelling, science communication, and issues of identity and belonging.

This book has been produced in highly precarious circumstances. The editing team would hence like to express its deep appreciation to Daria Davitti, Roderick Anderson, Daevid Anderson, Jana Düring, Sonne Ince, Morgan, Kathrin, Marie and Lena Terdues, Lars Holthusen, Nieke, Mats and Janna Kunstreich, Marian Quast, Rita Pais, Petra Eichhorn-Peters, Nico Peters, Isabela Lemos, Maria Mercone, Christina Schütze, Tracy L. Hunter, Agnieszka Cwielag, Sabrina Keller, José Marques, Patricia de Menezes Cardoso, Saleem Rajabi and his family, Firoze Manji, Gunnett Kaaf, Armando Jorge Joffre-Arteaga, Ursula Zienow, Nancy Joffre, Reinaldo Imaña, Michael Brie, Holger Politt, Jörn Schütrumpf, Diana Assunção, Kate Evans, Zarina Patel, Cornelia Lindberg, Rena Seidel and Anna Minkiewicz for the various forms of patient, essential support and solidarity they extended over the course of the composition of this book.

"We must exhibit, in the pursuit of our endeavours, the same courage, determination and ruthlessness mustered by the bourgeois revolutionaries, which Danton summed up when he said that in certain situations, one needs only three words as a rallying cry: audacity, more audacity, always audacity!"[1]

— Rosa Luxemburg

---

1 Luxemburg, Rosa (1913), "Die weltpolitische Lage." *Marxist Internet Archive*. Accessed on 10.10.2021, at https://www.marxists.org/deutsch/archiv/luxemburg/1913/05/plagwitz.htm. (Translation: Patrick Anderson)

STAMP OUT
BARBARISM